THE UNITED STATES AND CHINA
SINCE 1949

For Vicki

THE UNITED STATES AND CHINA SINCE 1949

A TROUBLED AFFAIR

Robert Garson

PINTER
PUBLISHERS
LONDON

Pinter Publishers Ltd.
25 Floral Street, London WC2E 9DS,
United Kingdom

First published in 1994

British Library Cataloguing in Publication Data

A CIP catalogue record for this book is available from the British Library

ISBN 0 86187 160 X

Set in Monotype Bembo by Ewan Smith
Printed and bound in Great Britain by Biddles Ltd,
Guildford and King's Lynn

CONTENTS

LIST OF ABBREVIATIONS
AND ACRONYMS

CCP	Chinese Communist Party
Cominform	Communist Information Bureau
CPSU	Communist Party of the Soviet Union
CREEP	Committee to Re-elect the President
DRV	Democratic Republic of Vietnam
GATT	General Agreement on Tariffs and Trade
ICC	International Control Commission
KMT	Kuomintang (Guomindang)
MAAG	Military Assistance Advisory Group
MFN	most favoured nation
NATO	North Atlantic Treaty Organization
NLF	National Liberation Front (Vietcong)
NSC	National Security Council
PLA	People's Liberation Army
PRC	People's Republic of China
ROK	Republic of Korea
RVN	Republic of Vietnam
SALT	Strategic Arms Limitation Talks
SEATO	Southeast Asia Treaty Organization
SEZ	special economic zone
USIA	United States Information Agency
VC	Vietcong

PREFACE

Ignorance and inexperience have seldom inhibited people's willingness to make judgements about one another. Indeed, the reverse is often the case. Closer knowledge tends to generate doubt and uncertainty about one's own verdicts. It is probably inherent in the nature of prejudice that fear and defensiveness occur in situations and areas where the object of anxiety is scarcely known. Supporters of Senator Joseph McCarthy encountered few communist sympathizers in their daily lives; immigration scarcely touched the lives of the xenophobic Klansmen of the Midwest in the 1920s. A similar situation informed the low regard in which Americans and Chinese held one another from the late 1940s to the early 1970s. For a quarter of a century the United States and the People's Republic of China deliberately shunned each other on the assumption that non-recognition and mutual isolation served the national interest better than contact and the give and take of international life.

Both nations went their own way. To Americans China remained shrouded in obscurity. It was a revolutionary nation where blind obedience and zeal combined to produce a modern version of millenarianism. To the Chinese America was grasping, the result of an inner decay caused by material vulgarity and the exploitation of labour at home and abroad. For decades the Chinese leadership believed that a freeze on relations with the United States was an effective means of preventing the contamination of Chinese society. Each side believed what it wanted to believe; contradictory evidence was rejected either because it was inconvenient or because it was unimaginable. If the United States had understood China's nervous insecurity in 1950, it probably would not have adopted the military strategy it did in the Korean war. If Mao had known that the xenophobic Cultural Revolution that he had unleashed would retard Chinese development for years, arguably he would have tried to exercise more control over events.

It is an essential premise of this book that the state of the Sino-American relationship did not merely depend on a narrow evaluation of mutual interests and obligations. The relationship was conditioned principally by internal politics and the broad spectrum of international affairs. For example, the historic meeting between President Nixon and Chairman Mao in 1972 resulted less from fresh evaluations of the character of each nation than from a realization by both men that they could further their domestic political aims by reversing the patterns of the previous quarter-century.

This book is intended as an introduction to the troubled relationship between the United States and China since the Communist revolution. It makes no claims to superseding other more detailed studies. The book emerges from the sense that there are very few short, accessible and up-to-date accounts of this fascinating episode of contemporary history. It attempts to show, unsurprisingly, that American and Chinese policies depended not simply on a calculus about the other's intentions. They were shaped by the state of domestic developments which inevitably coloured the leaders' views of the world. China generally took bolder steps when its leadership felt secure about its own future and confident of its inner strength. In the United States, the desire to discipline China for violations of human rights usually surfaced when Americans felt that they could control events.

This study is a synthesis of available scholarship and other published materials. It attempts to draw together the strands of foreign policy and domestic development. If it stimulates students of Sino-American relations to go back to the library to investigate the matter further, it has more than served its purpose.

There are a few conventions that need noting. I have generally used the pinyin system for romanizing Chinese. I have retained the Wade–Giles system of spelling for place and personal names that are less familiar in pinyin and are still in current use. Thus Chiang Kai-shek and Taipei are used rather than Jiang Jieshi and Taibei. Despite the common use of the Portuguese name, Formosa, in the West until the 1960s, I have called the island Taiwan throughout.

This book emerges from a series of courses that I have taught over the years in the Department of American Studies at Keele and a number of related conference papers. My first debt, therefore, is to my colleagues, present and former, who have provided a convivial and challenging environment at Keele. I would particularly like to single out David Adams, Ian Bell, Martin Crawford and Richard Maidment, who always believed that tough criticism and a pat on the back do go together. I would also like to thank Keele University for its generous grants of sabbatical leave, especially through its research award scheme.

Other debts are almost too great to enumerate. However, historians specifically named in the text became mainstays of support in the course of writing. Priscilla Roberts at the University of Hong Kong became something of a patron over the years. Tao Wenzhao came up with some alternative perspectives. Robin Porter of the Keele China Business Centre bailed me out when I felt overwhelmed by my own ignorance. Jane Evans at Pinter was both painstaking and cheerful in her editorial endeavours.

I owe my greatest debts to my family. I never had the fortune to meet my maternal and paternal grandparents, Kalman and Elsa Meinbach and Sigmund and Hermione Geiduschek. They were victims of the Holocaust and disappeared without trace after their deportation from Vienna. This page is their only permanent memorial. My dear late mother and father, Selma and Gustav, escaped their parents' ordeal and offered me a secure and caring life. My son and daughter, Adrian and Sonia, taught me the value of that life. Vicki, my wife, enriched it by always making me relish today and look forward to what tomorrow brings. It is to her and in appreciation that this book is dedicated.

CHAPTER I

PRELUDE TO A TROUBLED AFFAIR: BEFORE THE REVOLUTION, 1941-49

Historians generally believe that the past possesses natural patterns and that their job is to unravel and identify them. But historical events do not always fit into the kind of logical sequence that hindsight so often suggests. It is easy, therefore, to deduce that relations between the United States and China were bound to be strained and troubled after 1949 as a result of the policies and experiences that arose in the final throes and aftermath of China's terrible civil war. But the plain fact is the American government in 1949 did not anticipate that it had embarked upon a series of policies that would result in the total marginalization of the most populous nation on earth for over a generation.

Like most things in life, the decision-making process in the case of China was carried out in a piecemeal way. Certain decisions in Washington were taken because they seemed right at the time. But they had unexpectedly durable repercussions. Some of those decisions generated reactions within Mao's China that took policy-makers in Washington by surprise. Within a short space of time, a special kind of defensiveness emerged in the United States and China. That defensiveness was exacerbated by an extraordinary lack of knowledge about the history and political traditions of the other country. The result was a chain reaction that produced one of the most drawn-out acts of mutual exclusion in this century. Each nation began to ascribe to the other characteristics that were the opposite of their own self-image. Particularly in the early years of the Sino-American confrontation, each of the two nations believed that it possessed the best hope for humankind and that the other carried the greatest danger. Each believed it had a duty to eliminate that danger. The respective contagions would have to be quarantined and somehow controlled until the other party changed its ways. It was frighteningly easy to fall into the trap of righteous certitude, as for two decades leaders of both countries deliberately avoided direct methods of gaining intelligence about each other. The United States and the Communist People's Republic of China got off to a bad start. If hostility between the two countries was not inevitable, it was not surprising that their relations remained troubled for decades to come.

One small anecdote reveals how conclusions about national character could be drawn in the face of contradictory evidence. In 1982 a group of American journalists who had worked in China during the Second World War met at Scottsdale, Arizona, to reminisce about their wartime experiences. Their conversation turned to the qualities of the contending Chinese Communist and Nationalist leaders. They remembered that when American reporters wanted the Communist slant on the civil war that racked China, they turned to Zhou Enlai, Mao's trusted deputy. Zhou, they recalled, could always charm the cosy circle of news-thirsty Americans. One journalist described Zhou as 'one of the greatest people I've ever encountered because of his charm, his skills, his mental and dramatic ability.' They were all struck by his ability to exude a sense of the cosmopolitan, when in fact he was as insular as most of his party cohorts. Quite remarkably, Zhou had the knack of pretending that he had full command of English by tripping up his interpreters now and again and saying they had selected this or that wrong word in their translation. In fact, Zhou's grasp of the language was not as good as he claimed, but it did not stop him from his corrective strictures. By contrast, the wife of the Guomindang Party leader, Madame Chiang Kai-shek, spoke English fluently. She was a good conversationalist who could engage Americans on all subjects. But her arrogance and pretensions destroyed the advantage she should have enjoyed by virtue of her fluency. On one occasion in 1941 she was chatting to Annalee Jacoby Fadiman in a restaurant in Chungking, the seat of the Nationalist government. The restaurant was adorned with signs asking diners not to smoke as it was harmful to the war effort. The use of arable land to grow tobacco when food was in such short supply was deemed wanton. Madame Chiang ignored the signs and offered Fadiman an inviting and rather scarce Camel cigarette. Fadiman was tempted but refused. After two hours of further tantalization, Fadiman recalled saying: 'Madame Chiang, I do smoke. I thought it would offend you. I've seen all the signs in the restaurants.' She smiled beautifully and said, 'Oh, that's for the people.'[1]

This small incident encapsulates the delicacy of the relationship between the leaders of the United States and China. Throughout China's bitter civil war the United States had more contact with the Nationalists than with their Communist rivals. But those contacts were often counterproductive for the Nationalists. Several Nationalist leaders spoke English. They were urbane and seemed to hold out a promise for the eventual development of a government that broadly reflected the liberalism so cherished by the United States. Yet the majority of Americans – journalists, soldiers, State Department officials, businessmen and Christian missionaries – who met members of the ruling Guomindang Party consistently expressed their disquiet over the haughtiness, corruption and venality of President Chiang Kai-shek and his entourage. They often warned against America's growing involvement with China's rulers. How then did the United States come to support a leader and a regime that most informed opinion believed to be corrupt and unworthy of support?

As with most stories, the beginning starts somewhere before the beginning. The mould already began to set with America's entry into the Second World War. The attack on Pearl Harbor on 7 December 1941 by Japanese aircraft was something of a godsend to the Nationalist government in China. Since 1931 it had endured alone the humiliations and cruelty inflicted by the conquering Kwantung Army of Japan. Although most Americans were sensitive to China's plight in the 1930s, they were not prepared to fight Japan in order to defend either China's sovereignty or the principle of equality of economic opportunity. The United States did want world stability. It believed that Japan's war against China undermined that stability, but it never believed that it had sufficient interests in China to challenge Japan openly. Both countries were relatively self-sufficient and few resources derived from foreign trade. Americans were less concerned about the fate of China than they were about international lawlessness in general. Their sympathies lay with China, but they were not willing to risk the peace to defend a country half-way round the world that seemed isolated from international life and that had shown little aptitude for defending itself. Most Americans wanted to keep out of the conflict altogether. Failing that, they sought to apply selective sanctions against Japan in order to maintain a system of collective security. In short, helping China was a low priority.[2]

So when the United States declared war on Japan in December 1941, China believed its moment had come. It seemed that the nightmare of the previous ten years was about to end. China was now an ally of the United States, the wealthiest nation on earth. China's leader, Chiang

Kai-shek, was jubilant. His ill-trained army had been no match against Japan's highly disciplined war machine. Chiang had watched China's territory shrink in the face of the advance of the Kwantung Army. He had been forced to withdraw his government to Chungking in the interior, well away from the Japanese onslaught. He had surrendered his own political authority in other areas to warlords who seemed better equipped to carry on the fight against Japan. China's ability to resist had crumbled before the Japanese advance. Its status as a viable national entity was in doubt: outside aid was its only chance. American involvement in the Sino-Japanese war offered Chiang the prospect of regaining control over the country and of becoming a major broker in the new order that would emerge after the war. He was confident that the United States would now supply his beleaguered armies with money and military hardware. He presumed that Japan would meet its end in mainland China. It would either be defeated directly there, or his country would serve as the base for the final assault on the Japanese homeland.[3]

The United States did not have a master plan for the defeat of Japan. Japan's lightning conquests in the Dutch East Indies, Malaya, Hong Kong and Singapore had come as a shock. By early 1942 Tokyo's military arc stretched further and wider than had been imaginable. America's military options in the Far East boiled down to two strategic alternatives. It could try and squeeze Japan's new empire by selective attacks on its outposts. Such a plan would enable America to exercise a degree of control over its military engagements and to coordinate its Pacific strategy with the European campaign. The gradual occupation of selected island outposts in the Pacific would permit the Americans to establish air bases from which their combat aircraft could take off for bombing missions to Japan's home islands in preparation for the final invasion. The alternative strategy was to revive China's flagging military capability, so that it could directly engage the Japanese forces that occupied China. If China's fighting capacity could be revitalized, it could act as the launch for an invasion of Japan. That would have two attractions: it would revive China's role as a major player in Asian affairs, and would reduce the number of American troops that would need to be deployed in the final battle against Japan.[4]

But if Chinese troops were to be used with any effect, there would have to be active involvement by the United States. The Nationalist army had been no match against the Japanese. However, increased participation by American forces raised the potential for a serious conflict of interests between the US and China. The establishment of a full American military command in China could be easily interpreted as yet another bid by foreigners for influence in Chinese affairs. Washington would have to convince China that a more direct American involvement in China's war effort would not in any way compromise the country's sovereignty. President Franklin Roosevelt always knew that he would have to tread carefully. After all, Japan had justified its blitzkrieg by arguing that Asia had been exploited by the West for over a century. Under Japanese auspices, Asia was to be developed for Asians. Chiang himself had risen to power by denouncing Western interference in the affairs of China. It was by no means clear that interference was a thing of the past. The British Prime Minister, Winston Churchill, had said publicly that he would not fight a war in Asia just to watch the British empire disintegrate before him. The President knew that if the Chinese and other Asian peoples were to have confidence in the allied war effort they would have to be persuaded that the old order would not return. Roosevelt's solution was fairly simple. China and its leaders would have to be treated as equal allies. Chiang himself would be dignified as a great war leader. He would also be assured that China would have a formative say in the shaping of the world order that would emerge from the ashes of war. It would be accorded the status of a great power. Thus throughout the first two years of the war Roosevelt, at least in the words he used, treated Chiang as a world leader, who would receive the same treatment as the other leaders in the Grand Alliance.[5]

Roosevelt's inclination to place Chiang on an equal footing with Churchill and Stalin bewildered the other leaders. The President's faith in creating personal bonds and obligations also set the mould of Sino-American relations for years to come. Churchill told Roosevelt that he 'must not expect me to adopt what I felt was a wholly unreal standard of values.'[6] The British did not want to see China play a major post-war role in Asian affairs, as they hoped to see the restoration of imperial rule in Southeast Asia. They believed that a strong Sino-American presence in Asia would damage the brittle structure of the Asian order. At the Cairo conference held in November 1943, they reiterated the importance they attached to the concentration of forces in the European theatre. Britain successfully deflected American plans for landings in the Andaman islands and parallel land advances along the coast of Burma on the grounds that such enterprises would change the balance in Asia and deflect attention from the major aim of rescuing western Europe from German control. Some of Roosevelt's advisers were equally baffled by the President's vacillating ambitions in East Asia and his obsessive wish to give China a greater role by granting it great power status. General John Magruder, who headed the American military mission in China at the beginning of the Pacific war, warned of China's 'penchant for alluring fiction.' He feared that 'People in other countries swallow such glib untruths without realizing that they are being deceived.'[7]

If Roosevelt wanted to include China in a great power consortium at the end of the war he had to treat Chiang as the leader of a great power. In his view there was no other leader capable of rallying the Chinese against Japan. He believed that Chiang was the only leader who could maintain unity in China. However, the President's policies did not match his sentiments. He confided that China was 'still in the state of the eighteenth century' and, much to Chiang's indignation, excluded China from meetings of the Combined Chiefs of Staff.[8] Most of his closest military advisers agreed that China's presence at planning sessions was unwarranted. They saw no evidence to indicate that Chiang had the control and power, even within those areas not occupied by the Japanese army, to fight and organize.

The most consistent and arguably the most vehement critic of the Chinese leader was the American general, Joseph W. Stilwell. Stilwell had spent a large part of his professional military career in China and could speak Chinese. He was appointed to serve as Chiang's chief of staff and Commander-in-Chief US Armed Forces, China-Burma-India. Stilwell was a professional soldier who could not abide inefficiency, physical weakness and the snobbery of leaders. He held Chiang in utter contempt. He considered him corrupt and self-serving. He dubbed him 'Peanut', reflecting the utter lack of regard in which he held him. Stilwell's mission was to reform the Chinese armies and instil in them a fighting spirit. Stilwell tried to impress upon Washington the horrors of life in the Chinese army and the contrasting living conditions of the ruling Guomindang. The leaders indulged in luxury quite openly, while Chinese troops and the people they purported to serve could scarcely scrape an existence. Stilwell despaired of the Nationalists' ability for leadership in the resistance against Japan. He advised against granting Chiang aid unconditionally under the Lend-Lease programme. He maintained that the 'Peanut' squandered most of the aid in building up his party following. Some of it even went to the warlords on whom

Chiang relied. Most of the money just disappeared. Where it was spent on weapons and training it was done with a view to fighting the Communists, rather than the Japanese. Stilwell believed that Chiang should only receive American aid if he could deliver. 'Logic and reason, or personal influence,' he maintained, 'will not produce satisfactory results. Pressure and bargaining are the means that must be relied on.'[9]

Stilwell was convinced that Chiang was prepared to sit back, wait for American forces to do all the fighting and then reap the reward at the peacemaking. By contrast the Communist forces in the north, under the dynamic leadership of Mao Zedong, were inflicting serious damage and were gaining strength. Stilwell admired their fighting spirit. At the beginning of the war he had instructed his staff not to make contact with Mao's forces, but only because he did not want to embarrass the US administration. He soon began to send out more beckoning signals. Stilwell believed that if he was given direct command of all Chinese forces they might join ranks under a unified command. The Communists would not accept orders from the Nationalists, but they might do so from the United States. 'Outside of this one shot I see no chance to save the situation,' he wrote to General George Marshall, the American chief of staff. 'Somehow we must get arms to those who will fight.'[10]

Stilwell was not alone in his willingness to consider the active participation of Mao's forces. Most Americans who served in China in a military or diplomatic capacity came to believe that the Communists were the more dynamic power in the Chinese cauldron. They respected the Communists' fighting spirit and their concern for the lot of China's poor. Although they did not relish the prospect of a hostile ideology challenging the United States at the end of the war, they were convinced that the Communists would be a permanent force in Chinese politics and that only they were effective in keeping Japanese troops tied down in mainland China. American observers, many of whom spoke Chinese and had lived in China for a large part of their lives, believed that the only way China could emerge as a strong democratic nation at the end of the war was if all the competing forces united under the military command of a disinterested outsider. They thought that a unified command structure would serve as a rehearsal for political unification at the end of the war.

Roosevelt began to be swayed. In February 1944 he asked Chiang to permit a team of military observers to go to Yenan, where Mao Zedong had his headquarters. To head the mission Stilwell picked Colonel David

Barrett, who was said to be the only American who could tell jokes in Chinese. The mission, under the codename DIXIE, was sent to appraise the Communists' military potential and to assess the possibility of channelling aid through them. Barrett and John Stewart Service, who represented the State Department, met Mao, Zhou Enlai and other leaders at the end of July. Mao and his circle exuded camaraderie. They aimed to impress their American visitors and they succeeded. The Americans were struck by the Communists' high spirits, the good physical health of their followers and the vibrancy of their lives. They spoke enthusiastically about their good clothing, their level of learning and their diet. John Stewart Service was particularly impressed by the Communists' sense of purpose and by their ability to sustain morale. They commanded the respect of the local populace and through that respect they were able to enlist it to the cause.[11]

Favourable reports about the Communists persuaded the President that more effort should be put into pursuing Chinese unity. He sent Patrick Hurley, a temperamental and mercurial troubleshooter, to Chungking to try his hand at bringing the warring factions together. He was the wrong man: he knew little about communism, and even less about China. Although he was instructed to get the two sides to come to an agreement he assumed that his primary objective was to support the Guomindang. Chiang did not see any point in budging. The United States had recognized and supported his Nationalist regime through its most trying times. Hurley reinforced his conviction that the United States would not drop its ally because it had run into difficulties. The war, after all, had been fought to allow nations to determine their own futures. The United States had decried foreign intervention in China and would hopefully practise what it preached. Hurley made it clear that Washington might cajole but would not use its full power to usurp Chiang's authority. It believed that it could secure peaceful reunification by peaceful means. Chiang would have to be persuaded to adopt reform. If Chiang changed, the Communists would then realize that they shared common aspirations. Few Americans understood that trading and bargaining were alien to China's political tradition. Mao and Chiang regarded each other as deadly enemies; political compromise was not regarded as a viable solution by either faction. Neither would risk vesting real power in his adversary.[12]

The United States believed that it was the only nation capable of using its power to avert civil war in China, and that its special role in the war against Japan had qualified it to act as a broker between the warring sides. Roosevelt anointed himself as China's champion. Even when it had become clear that China would not serve as a major theatre of war in the defeat of Japan, he seemed intent on bolstering Chiang. He gave in to Chiang's sense of wounded pride by recalling Stilwell. His chose Patrick Hurley as his special envoy, later naming him ambassador, because Hurley was untainted by the prejudices of those more experienced in Chinese affairs.

The Chinese Communists watched the drift of American policy with growing concern and disdain. They were aware of the support they had attracted from Americans who had lived and served in China for long periods of time, but they realized that these 'China hands' had limited influence. It became increasingly apparent that the United States government was unwilling to break new ground and tip the balance against Chiang any further. The death of Franklin Roosevelt on 12 April 1945 and the succession of Harry S. Truman to the White House generated a new sense of uncertainty. It was unlikely that the new President would repudiate Ambassador Hurley, particularly when the United States faced so many problems with the Soviet Union over Eastern Europe. The Chinese Communists had no reason to believe that the new administration would review policy. The fragile wartime coalition was on the verge of collapse, and all powers appeared to be jostling for political advantage and territory in order to reinforce their positions in the peacemaking process.

The Communists did not intend to be left out of the tussle. As the Soviet Union entered the Pacific war on 8 August 1945, a new and ferocious fight for the control of northern China began. When Japan surrendered the Communists claimed the right to liberate territory that had been held by the Japanese and ignored orders from Chiang to reserve surrender for the Nationalists. They realized that the form and procedure of surrender would decide the structure of post-war China, and were determined to fight to enjoy the fruits that military victory would bring. The scramble to accept the surrender brought the Communists into direct military conflict with the United States. The Americans had ordered the Japanese forces to surrender only to Chiang's Nationalist forces, but as the Nationalists were not in a position to take the surrender, General Wedemeyer was instructed to rush United States Marines to key points in northern China in order to hold them until Chiang's forces were in a position to take over. Extra transportation facilities were also provided to enable Nationalist forces to beat the Communists to the various surrender points.[13]

The assistance given by the United States to the Nationalists in accepting the surrender and disarming the Japanese served to discourage Chiang from negotiating with the Communists. It was a case of each man for himself. John Carter Vincent, a liberal China hand who had just taken over as head of the Office of Far Eastern Affairs in the State Department, realized at once that America's cooperation with the Nationalists constituted a major setback for the policy of securing a unified and independent China. Puppet troops and those who had collaborated with the Japanese had been allowed to stay in their positions for the sole purpose of preventing the Communists from taking their place. The assistance provided by Wedemeyer's forces played straight into the hands of the CCP. While Zhou Enlai was in Chungking trying to negotiate a basis for collaboration between the two sides, Chiang launched a fierce attack on the Communists in Manchuria. Zhou left Chungking and went back to his headquarters at Yenan. He and Mao realized that the Communists could not depend on any outside support, and that they would have to fend for themselves. They could not even trust the Russians. Mao suspected that Stalin's intervention in the war in China had been undertaken to increase Soviet influence in Manchuria, and perhaps to detach Xinjiang province. Stalin had warned Mao that civil war would bring complete ruin to China and advised Mao to negotiate with the Nationalists. Stalin went through the motions of throwing his support behind the Nationalists. Under the terms of the Sino-Soviet agreement, which was signed on 14 August, Stalin recognized Chiang, acknowledged Chinese sovereignty in Manchuria and undertook to hand back territory to Nationalist forces.[14]

It soon became clear that Stalin was hedging his bets by assisting both sides in the civil war. Soviet forces disregarded their commitments to the Nationalists and were handing over Japanese arms to the Communists instead. Washington believed its hand was being forced by an inescapable dilemma. If it did not help move Nationalist troops into areas being occupied by the Russians, it could be held responsible for permitting a key part of East Asia to fall under the dominion of the Soviet Union. If it did intervene, its pretensions of non-involvement in China's feud would prove vacuous. Any hope of securing a reconciliation between the warring parties would recede further. Ambassador Hurley paid lip-service to negotiations between the Nationalists and Communists, although he accepted that any final deal would have to involve the CCP's acceptance of Chiang's leadership. He believed the Soviets could play a constructive role in reconciling the factions, and would make sure that Mao's Communists did not emerge in the negotiated outcome with any distinct advantage. Although Hurley met Chinese leaders personally, they had no confidence in his public proclamations of impartiality. American policy was clearly weighted in favour of the Guomindang. The armed forces of the United States were transporting Chiang's forces by sea and air to disarm the Japanese. In addition, the United States had advanced fresh credits to the Nationalist government and had promised further military equipment at knock-down prices. Thus the American mediation effort was perceived by the Communists to be a hollow exercise.

The Communists were given no incentive to exercise restraint. In their race to beat the Nationalists for the control of China they came up against the US Marines, who had been sent to facilitate the hand-over of arms. General Wedemeyer realized that the situation was volatile. He had been instructed to avoid a confrontation. However, if the Marines remained inactive or even withdrew, the ultimate beneficiaries would be the Soviets. As it was America's stated policy not to get involved in clashes between the two factions, Wedemeyer informed Chiang that he would not interfere in internecine fighting. American policy-makers realized that Wedemeyer's hand could be forced un-willingly. Secretary of State James Byrnes did not want Chiang to think that America's support could always be guaranteed. He suggested that the USA should try to force the two rivals to negotiate by threatening to cut off aid from Chiang if he did not cooperate. Hurley sensed that the State Department was wavering in its commitment. On 27 November he announced in a fury that he would resign his post. He said that his hands had been tied by foreign service officers with misplaced and misguided loyalties to the cause and blamed the breakdown of his efforts to get reunification in China on career officials in the State Department who, he claimed, sided with the CCP.[15]

Hurley's dramatic resignation served to highlight the fact that the Truman administration was boxing itself in. It also sowed the seeds of the bitter partisan divisions on China policy that would divide Washington in the years to come. Many Americans, principally in the Republican Party, believed that Roosevelt's advisers had given away too much and that their advice was at odds with America's general toughening in its attitude towards the Soviet Communists. Supporters of Chiang in Washington, the so-called China Lobby, rallied around Hurley and insisted that the desire to show an even hand in China ran contrary to America's evolving national policy towards the communist world as a whole. It made no sense, they claimed, to resist the Soviets while trying to accommodate both sides in China's civil war. The controversy that followed on Hurley's resignation placed China firmly on the political agenda. The prospect for quiet and discreet diplomacy was fast disappearing. President Truman was put on the spot. His China policy would receive careful scrutiny from his Republican critics. Truman understood the position. He had decided by the beginning of 1946 to get tougher with the Soviets, and did not want his China policy to go against the grain by appearing contradictory.

However, Truman did not give up on the idea of a mediated settlement. He believed that conciliation was still possible and consequently dispatched General George Marshall, the well-regarded former Chief of Staff, to China as Hurley's successor. Marshall's mission was to persuade Mao and Chiang to call a truce and establish a coalition government. But Marshall was aware that if his efforts failed the United States would need to have a back-up policy to which it could resort. He obtained a directive confirming that, if his endeavours collapsed, the US would still back Chiang and the Nationalists. Marshall still hoped the Chinese could be persuaded to give up the use of force and adopt American practices of parliamentary procedures, ballots and political compromise. If they did not, the US would throw its weight behind the Guomindang. Marshall was told that the United States would continue to support Nationalist positions in north China, and was authorized to offer more aid to Chiang as an inducement to negotiate. Shortly after his arrival in China, Marshall persuaded the warring parties to accept a ceasefire and attend a Political Consultative Conference. It was just a respite; by April 1946 the truce had fallen apart. Each side began to jostle to improve its position. Chiang repudiated the resolutions of the Political Consultative Conference and ordered his army to occupy positions in Manchuria that had been evacuated by the Red Army. The Communists tried to beat the Nationalists to it, and the civil war was back in full swing. Marshall tried to get the two sides to stall, but Chiang was determined to push his temporary advantage. Marshall's efforts backfired: they tainted him in the eyes of the Communists. He had tried to be even-handed in a situation where sometimes decisive strictures had to be made. The Communists thought him personally cool. Above all, they could not take his purported neutrality seriously when American troops were used to guard the supply and trans-portational points in Manchuria.[16]

Marshall continued to try to get a semblance of unification, but both sides dug in their heels. Chiang overestimated his ability to defeat the Communists, and was reinforced in his confidence by American policy. At the end of June the House Foreign Affairs Committee recommended a military assistance bill for the Nationalist government and Under-Secretary of State Dean Acheson announced new arrange-ments for the provision of military equipment. Chiang was convinced that the United States would not abandon him and, portentously for the future, the Communists shared that conviction.

When Chiang prepared to drive the Communists out of Manchuria and north China, the Communists gave up on trying to accommodate American sensitivities and embarked on a new programme of militancy. They reorganized their forces as the People's Liberation Army, con-fiscated land, and meted out violent punishments to their enemies. The war knew no boundaries of cruelty. Communist and Guomindang forces indulged in almost indescribable brutality in their attempts to demoralize one another. Heads of household were randomly murdered, peasant leaders were buried alive and landlords branded with hot irons. The Communists intensified their campaign against the United States by organizing anti-American riots, and kidnapping and attacking American servicemen. In one ambush four Marines in a village between Tianjin and Beijing were killed and a dozen injured. Mao had come to the conclusion that the United States would never abandon the Guomin-dang, and decided that there was nothing to be gained in making the American position any easier. In August the official news agency dismissed Marshall's efforts at conciliation as a deceptive exercise. Reasonably enough, it claimed that mediation and support for Chiang were incompatible. When an agreement for the sale of surplus property was signed at the end of August, the Communists cut the frayed cord. They denounced the United States and assured their followers that they would not be daunted by American power.[17]

Marshall's mediation efforts were in shreds. The Communists refused to participate in the National Assembly convened by the Nationalist government on 15 November 1946. When Marshall asked the Com-munists whether they wanted him to continue with the conciliation exercise and no reply was forthcoming, he realized that there was little point in carrying on. Mediation is only ever possible if the parties to a dispute believe they can gain more by compromise than by continuing with force. Neither faction believed this to be the case. On 6 January 1947 Marshall was recalled by Truman to succeed James Byrnes as the new Secretary of State. In a formal statement marking the end of his mission, Marshall blamed the 'reactionary group' in the Guomindang and the CCP's 'unwillingness to make a fair compromise' for the breakdown of his attempt to secure a peaceful settlement.[18]

The Communists, increasingly confident of ultimate victory, were dismissive of Marshall's analysis. Only full American support would have changed their attitude. Such support was inconceivable. The Americans still believed that there existed in China a corpus of liberals who could be organized around Chiang's leadership. Some of the most influential decision makers, such as Secretary of the Navy James V. Forrestal and Secretary of War Robert P. Patterson, believed that Mao served the interests of the Soviet Union. The only way to keep the Soviets out of China, they argued, was to prevent a Communist victory in the civil war. Marshall's mission was doomed to fail because the Communists thought they would win and because the Americans were tainted by their continued support for the national government. Battle, not words, would resolve matters.

The belief of the Truman administration that it could go through the motions of even-handedness in the Chinese civil war was brought to a severe test by the enunciation of the Truman Doctrine on 12 March 1947. The administration believed that America's anti-communist policy had to be put onto a surer footing. It feared that if Greece went communist a bandwagon effect would be created. It wanted to send an indication to the Soviet Union that American policy was rooted firmly in coherent principles. Congress and public opinion had looked forward to a period of retrenchment after the war and did not want to see public spending rise, especially for new foreign policy initiatives. So Truman had to dramatize the communist danger and give it a sense of moral urgency in order to carry the new programmmes through Congress. Truman calculated that the use of ideological language would mobilize public opinion for a crusade against communism and instil a new sense of national identity. He believed that by grafting liberal principles on to foreign policy he would overcome entrenched attitudes on overseas commitments.[19]

Although administration officials had insisted in the Congressional hearings that the Truman Doctrine applied only to Greece and Turkey, they knew it had global implications. Nevertheless, priorities had to be established. The Joint Chiefs of Staff ranked areas of the world in order of importance. Britain, France and Germany were at the top of their list, while China and Korea were at the bottom. In their view China paled before Western Europe, the Middle East and Japan in strategic and economic significance. Relativities aside, Secretary of State Marshall and John Carter Vincent, Director of the State Department's Office of Far Eastern affairs, were disillusioned with Chiang and believed that the provision of large quantities of aid to the Nationalist regime was wasteful. Such resources could be put to better effect elsewhere. Marshall realized that China's political fabric was in the process of disintegration and that China did not offer the kind of network, such as existed in western Europe, through which the United States could operate.

Notwithstanding his own sense of disillusion, Marshall still hoped to avoid a Communist victory in China. In his view such a victory would have granted the Soviets a considerable aggregation of power. As conditions in China worsened during the spring of 1947, with galloping inflation and new and successful offensives in Manchuria, Marshall reluctantly concluded that limited asssistance to the Chinese should be resumed. Defence officials and the Chinese government had been urging him to assist the beleaguered Nationalists. They realized that the enunciation of the Truman Doctrine had added a new vigour to their case. Although Marshall turned down the requests for large-scale assistance from the Chinese, he authorized the American Marines, who were in the process of leaving northern China, to hand over their ammunition to the Nationalists and sold off other war supluses at bargain prices. At the same time, largely on the advice of Republican supporters of Chiang, he sent General Wedemeyer on a fact-finding mission to China. The choice of Wedemeyer, who in the past had actively assisted the Nationalists, was another indication that the administration was still prepared to throw its weight behind the Guomindang cause.

Wedemeyer arrived in China at the end of July 1947 and stayed a month. He reported back in September, and informed Marshall that matters had deteriorated further since he had last been there. He was appalled by the corruption and ineptitude of Chiang's supporters and warned the administration to resign itself to a defeat in Manchuria. Nevertheless he still proposed a large-scale assistance programme to the

Chinese Nationalists to the south, on the grounds that the alternative was worse. He believed that domination of all China would tilt the balance of power dramatically. In his report he proposed the dispatch of some 10,000 US military advisers, together with the implementation of a five-year assistance programme. Marshall had Wedemeyer's report suppressed. The proposals for large-scale assistance stretched America's resources too thinly. and the report as a whole was too scathing of Chiang. Its publication would have raised obvious questions about the compatibility of even a limited aid programme, given Wedemeyer's negative assessment of Chiang.[20]

Although there was a degree of spontaneous improvisation in American policy, Truman had not reversed the fundamental aim of the Roosevelt administration. He understood that a united China, revolving around Chiang, would have enhanced the chance of creating a *pax Americana* in Asia. However, the United States recognized that its ability to determine China's destiny was almost beyond its control. While its foreign policy was directed to the resistance of communism and the maintenance of pro-Western governments in key areas of the world, it appreciated that it had to tailor its ambitions to its resources.

China was, quite simply, low on the list of priorities. However, Truman did not want to be branded with the stigma of having forsaken China. Although much of Eastern Europe had come under the dominion of the Soviet Union, the United States had not assumed any direct responsibility for sustaining particular political groupings there. In contrast, the US had embraced Chaing as an ally, had supported him throughout the war and had prepared the American public for the emergence of a strong, united China. Moreover, through the rhetoric of the Truman Doctrine and the European Recovery Plan it had stimulated the view that a failure to assist anti-communist movements constituted an abdication of responsibility. Thus through 1947 and 1948 the administration sought to combine a policy of disengagement with a policy of gesturing. It did not wish to be identified as the government that had abandoned China to communism. It was acutely aware that it needed Republican support for its European reconstruction policies. Many Republicans insisted that it made no sense to combat communism in Europe and the Near East and then ignore the threat in Asia, where the United States had carried the brunt of the fighting in the Second World War. Congressman Walter Judd, a former missionary doctor in China, believed that the recovery of Europe could not be disentangled from the recovery of Asia. He thought that America's major economic interests lay in Asia and agreed with General Douglas MacArthur, who had said that the Asian continent would determine the course of history for the next century. He and other conservative Republican Congressmen who formed the so-called China bloc on Capitol Hill believed that Truman had betrayed China by applying pressure on Chiang to strike a deal with the Communists. The administration had seen that the tide was turning against the Guomindang. It made limited concessions to the pro-Chiang lobby in order to gesture that there was an inner consistency in its anti-communist policies and to persuade it to vote for the measures on European reconstruction.[21]

Secretary Marshall was sensitive to the criticism that US China policy did not conform to the general thrust of America's containment policy. He proposed a programme of limited aid to China in order to assuage his critics. He had no illusions about the impact of the aid programme on the course of the civil war, and did not want to furnish military aid. It would be ineffective in tipping the balance, and arms might well end up in the Communists' hands. It would also blatantly reverse the policy of trying to secure peaceful unification. Marshall did not consider that the tide could be turned. He did believe that economic assistance, ostensibly granted for non-military purposes, would soothe the Republicans and would provide some relief from the dreadful hardships experienced in China. He also hoped it would encourage the Guomindang to undertake some eleventh-hour measures of reform. Accordingly the administration accepted the China Aid Act of April 1948, which provided for an appropriation of $400 million, including a special fund of $125 million which could be used to buy military equipment in order to improve the morale and the 'administrative integrity' of China.[22]

The China Aid Act was largely symbolic. It was passed to demonstrate that Europe would not have a monopoly on American economic assistance and to mitigate the worries of the administration's Republican critics. The Act may have promoted American foreign policy within the United States, but it did little to promote its cause in China. Chiang deemed the Act totally inadequate, while the Chinese Communists condemned it for prolonging the agony of the civil war. Anti-American demonstrations swept through China. The China Aid Act became the focal point of criticism of Chinese Communists. It made no difference anyway – it could not stave off Communist victories in the field. Only a small proportion of arms shipments made it to China during the rest of the year. Nationalist forces were often better equipped than the Communists, but their morale was low. Rampant inflation resulted in the virtual collapse of the price system and the necessities of life either were not produced or were hoarded. The Guomindang's fighting units were inefficient and confused; they deserted in droves. The Communists repeatedly outmanoeuvred the Nationalist troops, even though they were more poorly equipped. In Xuzhou, to the north of Nanjing, 600,000 Nationalists were overcome by the Communists, despite their complete superiority in the air. In January 1949 Lin Biao captured Tianjin, turned west and forced the Nationalist commander of Beijing to surrender. On 31 January 1949 troops entered the old imperial capital, some ten days after Chiang had resigned as President. The civil war was virtually at an end. Chiang fled to Taiwan to join the 300,000 loyal troops (and the crates of treasure taken from the imperial palace) which had been sent ahead in anticipation of the defeat.

Last-minute pleas from the Guomindang for American military intervention were ignored. Marshall realized that to be effective the United States would have to take over the Nationalists' war effort. It was neither logistically feasible nor politically desirable. The Nationalists may have hoped for a change of policy under a Republican administration, but Truman won the 1948 election in a victory that took nearly everyone by surprise. Truman had confounded the pundits and was returned to the White House. Chiang's cause was hopeless.

The United States had backed the losing side in the civil war. Its client had been discredited. But Chiang had survived by fleeing to the island of Taiwan, from where he held out the hope for an eventual return. Washington now had to decide whether to continue to back the losers, now ensconced on Taiwan, or whether to reach an accommodation with the Communists.

The decision was not, of course, entirely in the hands of the United States. If the Americans had to make adjustments to their previous commitments and to memory, so did Mao and the Communists. They realized that they had endured and come through their trial despite the active intervention of the world's greatest military power. Mao's struggle against overwhelming odds became deeply embedded in his evolving attitude towards the United States. The Communist victory in China also posed a new conundrum for the United States. It could attempt to come to terms with Mao and endeavour to entice him to pursue an independent course, and so foster an Asian version of Titoism. After all,

Mao's victory owed little to the Soviets. Or it could continue to support the beleaguered Chiang and wait for the day when the Communist regime would fall apart. Memory and grudge are hard to eradicate, and commitments are difficult to reverse. Nothing is preordained. Accommodation is only possible when the parties to a dispute believe that new beginnings are within their grasp. Neither Washington nor Beijing was convinced that the day had come.

NOTES

1. Quoted in Stephen R. MacKinnon and Oris Friesen, *China Reporting: An Oral History of American Journalism in the 1930s and 1940s* (Berkeley and London, 1987), pp. 91–2.

2. Among the best works on America's Far Eastern policy before 1941 are: Herbert Feis, *The Road to Pearl Harbor: The Coming of the War between the United States and Japan* (Princeton NJ, 1950); Dorothy Borg, *The United States and the Far Eastern Crisis* (Cambridge, MA, 1964); Stephen Pelz, *The Road to Pearl Harbor* (Cambridge, MA, 1974); Gordon Prange, *Pearl Harbor: The Verdict of History* (New York, 1985); Akira Iriye, *The Origins of the Second World War in Asia and the Pacific* (London and New York, 1987).

3. Herbert Feis, *The China Tangle: the American Effort in China from Pearl Harbor to the Marshall Mission* (Princeton NJ, 1953), pp. 3–13; Michael Schaller, *The U.S. Crusade in China, 1938–1945* (New York, 1979), pp. 39–63, 87–100; Paul Varg, *The Closing of the Door: Sino-American Relations, 1936–1946* (East Lansing, 1973), pp. 18–35; U.S. Senate, Committee on the Judiciary, *Morgenthau Diary (China)*, I (Washington DC, 1965), pp. 534–5, 547–8.

4. On military strategy in Asia see Charles Romanus and Riley Sunderland, *The China-Burma-India Theater* (3 vols, Washington, DC, 1953–9); Maurice Matloff and Edwin Snell, *Strategic Planning for Coalition Warfare, 1941–42* (Washington, DC, 1953); S. Woodburn Kirby, *The War Against Japan* (5 vols, London, 1958–69); A. Russell Buchanan, *The United States and World War II* (2 vols, New York, 1964); Ienaga Saburo, *The Pacific War: World War II and the Japanese, 1931–1945* (New York, 1978); Milton E. Miles, *A Different Kind of War* (Garden City, New York, 1967); Barbara W. Tuchman, *Stilwell and the American Experience in China, 1911–45* (New York, 1972 edn).

5. Akira Iriye, *Power and Culture: The Japanese-American War, 1941–1945* (Cambridge, MA, 1981); William Roger Louis, *Imperialism at Bay: The United States and the Decolonization of the British Empire, 1941–1945* (New York, 1978); Feis, *The China Tangle*.

6. Winston Churchill, *The Second World War, IV: The Hinge of Fate* (London, 1951), p. 119; also, Chiang Kai-shek to Chinese Minister for Foreign Affairs, 19 April 1942 in U.S. Department of State, *Foreign Relations of the United States: China, 1942* (Washington, DC, 1956) pp. 33–4. (hereafter cited as *FRUS*, relevant volume).

7. Plenary meeting, Combined Chiefs of Staff minutes, 23 November 1943;

meeting of Combined Chiefs of Staff, 23 November 1943 in *FRUS: The Conferences at Cairo and Tehran, 1943* (Washington, DC, 1961), pp. 311–15, 316–22; Military Mission to War Department, 10 February 1942; also, Hornbeck to Undersecretary of State, 16 February 1942 in *FRUS: China, 1942*, pp. 14, 20–22; Christopher Thorne, *Allies of a Kind: The United States, Britain and the War Against Japan, 1941–1945* (London, 1978), pp. 306–20.

8. Elliott Roosevelt and James Brough, *A Rendezvous with Destiny: The Roosevelt of the White House* (New York, 1975), p. 345; Sumner Welles, *Seven Decisions that Shaped History* (New York, 1951), p. 151.

9. Stilwell to Marshall, 30 July 1942 in Charles F. Romanus and Riley Sunderland, *Stilwell's Mission to China* (Washington, DC, 1953), p. 179.

10. Tuchman, *Stilwell and the American Experience in China*, pp. 596–604.

11. Tuchman, *Stilwell and the American Experience in China*, pp. 591–3, 609–11; Kenneth Shewmaker, *Americans and Chinese Communists, 1927–1945: A Persuasive Encounter* (New York, 1971), pp. 175–9; Varg, *The Closing of the Door*, pp. 120–29; David D. Barrett, *Dixie Mission: The United States Army Group in Yenan, 1944* (Berkeley, 1970); report No. 2, John S. Service to Commanding General, U.S. Armed Services, China-Burma-India Theatre, 28 July 1944 in U.S. Senate, Committee on the Judiciary, *The Amerasia Papers: A Clue to the Catastrophe of China* (Washington, DC, 1970), pp. 684–85.

12. Russell D. Buhite, *Patrick J. Hurley and American Foreign Policy* (Ithaca, NY, 1973).

13. Marc S. Gallicchio, *The Cold War begins in Asia: American East Asian Policy and the Fall of the Japanese Empire* (New York, 1988), pp. 96–102; Feis, *The China Tangle*, pp. 355–67.

14. Gary May, *China Scapegoat: The Diplomatic Ordeal of John Carter Vincent* (Prospect Heights, IL, 1982), p. 131; Robert Messer, *The End of an Alliance: James F. Byrnes, Roosevelt, Truman, and the Origins of the Cold War* (Chapel Hill, 1982), pp. 118–19; Steven I. Levine, *Anvil of Victory: The Communist Revolution in Manchuria, 1945–1948* (New York, 1987), pp. 32–43.

15. Buhite, *Patrick J. Hurley and American Foreign Policy*, pp. 190–202, 268–74; James Reardon-Anderson, *Yenan and the Great Powers: the Origins of Chinese Communist Foreign Policy, 1944–1946* (New York, 1980), pp. 116–31; Schaller, *The U.S. Crusade in China*, pp. 278–87; Lisle Rose, *Roots of Tragedy: The United States and the Struggle for Asia, 1945–1953* (Westport, 1976).

16. Memorandum by Gen. Marshall, 14 December 1945 in U.S. Department of State, *Foreign Relations of the United States: 1945, China* (Washington, DC, 1969), p. 770.

17. U.S. Department of State, *United States Relations with China: With Special Reference to the Period 1944–1949* (Washington, DC, 1949), pp. 172, 187; Tang Tsou, *America's Failure in China, 1941–50* (Chicago and London, 1963), pp. 430–31.

18. Statement by Marshall, January 7, 1947, *United States Relations with China*, pp. 686–9.

19. The following is just a small sample of the work on the background to the Truman Doctrine. See Richard M. Freeland, *The Truman Doctrine and the Origins of McCarthyism: Foreign Policy, Domestic Politics and Internal Security, 1946–1948* (New

York, 1972); John Lewis Gaddis, *The United States and the Origins of the Cold War, 1941–1947* (New York, 1972); Joseph M. Jones, *The Fifteen Weeks* (New York, 1955); Bruce R. Kuniholm, *The Origins of the Cold War in the Near East: Great Power Conflict and Diplomacy in Iran, Turkey, and Greece* (Princeton, NJ, 1980); Deborah Welch Larson, *Origins of Containment: A Psychological Explanation* (Princeton, NJ, 1985); Melvyn P. Leffler, *A Preponderance of Power: National Security, the Truman Administration, and the Cold War* (Stanford, CA, 1992); Thomas G. Paterson, *Soviet–American Confrontation: Postwar Reconstruction and the Origins of the Cold War* (Baltimore, MD, 1973); Robert A. Pollard, *Economic Security and the Origins of the Cold War, 1945–1950* (New York, 1985); Daniel Yergin, *Shattered Peace: The Origins of the Cold War and the National Security State* (Boston, MA, 1977).

20. Report to President Truman by Wedemeyer, 19 September 1947, *United States Relations with China*, pp. 766–74; also William Stueck, *The Wedemeyer Mission: American Politics and Foreign Policy during the Cold War* (Athens, GA, 1984).

21. Stanley D. Bachrack, *The Committee of One Million: 'China Lobby Politics, 1953–1971'* (New York, 1976), pp. 31–2; Varg, *The Closing of the Door*, pp. 232–4.

22. Statement by Marshall, 20 February 1948; Economic Aid Agreement between the United States and the Republic of China, 3 July 1948 in *United States Relations with China*, pp. 983–5, 994–1001.

CHAPTER 2

FROM REVOLUTION TO WAR IN KOREA, 1949-53

The Communist revolution in China and the rapidity with which it occurred posed critical questions for China's new leaders. Its primary task was national reconstruction. But there were some crucial issues relating to the new regime's international role that had to be confronted. Mao Zedong, who had formally announced the founding of the People's Republic of China at a ceremony on 1 October 1949, was particularly concerned. While he was impatient to consolidate the political revolution, he also wanted to create a fresh identity for the new nation. Political consolidation, he realized, would be eased by assistance from other nations and by formal recognition. Such normalization would not only give the new regime legitimacy, but would also result in much-needed commerce and economic aid. But the Chinese leadership would not compromise its national honour in the quest for international approval. One of the principal rallying cries of the Communist forces had been protest against foreign exploitation. This would not be permitted to happen again. Non-interference was to be a minimum condition for normal diplomatic relations and friendship. In the case of the United States this was especially testing, given its previous support for the Communists' bitter enemy, the Nationalists.[1]

The American government had a parallel dilemma in its consideration of future relations with the new regime. Mao had succeeded in ousting Nationalist opposition on the mainland but had failed to prevent the flight of Chiang Kai-shek to the island of Taiwan. Although the United States had endeavoured to bring the two sides together during the civil war and had exerted pressure on Chiang to negotiate their differences, in the final resort the Truman administration had come down on the side of the Nationalists. It had continued to funnel aid through them. The China Aid Act had authorized some $463 million for military and economic aid to the Nationalist government of China, but not all the

22

money had been spent. The question now arose as to whether the USA should continue to assist Chiang in his exile in Taiwan and so enhance his chance of survival. Chiang contended that his government was still the legitimate government of China. He posed an immediate problem for the United States. If it cut off the remaining aid available to the Nationalists, it would have significantly reinforced the position of the Chinese Communists. It would also open itself to charges that its opposition to communism worldwide was hollow. At home the China Lobby, inspired by the charges of former US ambassador Patrick Hurley, had accused the State Department of sabotaging national policy on support for the Nationalists. It did not want to provide its critics with further ammunition.

There was also the larger issue of the national security and the role of East Asia in the Cold War to consider. The new Secretary of State, Dean Acheson, was an Atlanticist by upbringing and by inclination. He thought the United States should invest its resources in the European Recovery Plan and in collective defence, through the North Atlantic Treaty Organization. He was disinclined to throw more money at a cause he saw as doomed. He also believed, as will be seen, that a *modus vivendi* could be attained with Mao. He thought the Soviets posed a greater danger to international peace. An understanding with Communist China would strengthen the United States in its policy of containment of the Soviet Union. However, the Defense Department and most military leaders disagreed. They believed that Mao and Stalin were natural allies and that communist power stretching across Europe to the Pacific posed a direct strategic threat to the United States. It was essential, in their view, to try to stem the apparent tide of the communist advance, irrespective of its source. Even some of Dean Acheson's closest advisers in the State Department were troubled by the Secretary of State's inclination to let matters ride in East Asia. For example, W. Walton Butterworth, director of the Office of Far Eastern Affairs, had been critical of Chiang's political acumen, but believed that Taiwan should not be allowed to fall to the Communists from mainland China. Dean Rusk, Deputy Under-Secretary of State for Political Affairs who succeeded Butterworth in March 1950 at the Far Eastern desk, wanted the United States to use its muscle to combat communism in Asia. He feared that mainland China now possessed the potential to spread communism to other parts of Asia. He advised Acheson that the United States should employ its power to deny key parts of the continent to the Communists. In his view it was particularly vital to keep the Chinese Communists out of Taiwan. This could only be accomplished through military and economic aid to the island. Such assistance could only be funnelled if the USA continued to declare that the government on Taiwan was the government of all China.[2]

The new regime in Beijing also deliberated on its relations with other nations. Mao himself had grave doubts about the prospect of an accommodation with the United States. He saw the United States through the prism of revolutionary Marxism. However, he was not impervious to suasion. His closest advisers on foreign affairs, particularly Zhou Enlai, Zhang Hanfu and Qiao Guanhua, had more open minds. They had attended modern schools, could speak English and generally had a cosmopolitan outlook on life.[3] Certain steps were taken to explore the possibilities of links with the United States but the immediate past caught up rather quickly. Old prejudices do not disappear, particularly in a nation that feels itself to be in a state of siege. Mao's middle-ranking cadres had been reared on the idea that the West and the United States in particular had suppressed progress in China, and had witnessed the active involvement by US Marines in the hand-over of Japanese arms. Years of fighting had bred hostility and magnified it. If counter-revolution was to be prevented, American influence had to be eliminated from China. The ending of all foreign privilege and dependence was an article of faith for the zealous cadres as they sought to crush the final vestiges of resistance. As far as the Beijing government was concerned, it was up to the United States to show that it would abandon earlier designs so that old animosities could be buried.

The Chinese could immediately identify three crucial sources of resentment. First, the China Aid Act had, in their view, prolonged the civil war. Without military assistance the Nationalist forces would have surrendered earlier and bloodshed and hunger been avoided. Second, American policy throughout Asia seemed to threaten the very stability of the new regime. In Japan General Douglas MacArthur, as Supreme Commander for the Allied Powers, had instituted policies to restore Japan's pre-war economic might. He advocated an early peace treaty with the retention of naval and air bases for American use. In South Korea the last American troops had withdrawn in 1949, but that withdrawal had been replaced by a deepening commitment to Syngman Rhee's government through increased military and economic assistance. Finally, and to China most important, the United States did not appear to be in a position to draw a line through the immediate past. There was no sign that it would accommodate Mao's China in its international stratagem.

Leading Republicans were demanding that the United States protect Chiang Kai-shek's last stronghold on Taiwan. Former President Herbert Hoover suggested, in a well-publicized letter of 31 December 1949, that the United States should give the Nationalist government naval protection on its outposts in Taiwan, the Pescadores and Hainan. Influential Republican Senators, such as Robert Taft of Ohio and William R. Knowland of California, joined Hoover's call for military protection. As far as the Chinese Communists were concerned some of the most powerful political figures in the United States were still clamouring for American intervention in the civil war. It seemed that the Truman administration would continue to recognize the renegade regime on Taiwan as the true government of China. The Chinese leadership was not privy to what was going on behind closed doors. It is important to bear in mind that reservations about continued aid to the Nationalists were expressed in confidential memoranda. Members of Congress who were interested in Chinese affairs publicy advocated the provision of aid to Chiang on Taiwan. Thus the Chinese Communists saw little evidence of any weighing of considerations. They only knew what they were told. As far as they were concerned, the decision-making process in Washington was stacked against them.

By October 1949 there were only a few pockets of resistance to Communist rule in mainland China. If the Truman administration had entertained serious hopes of hindering the progress of the Maoists' consolidation, there was little prospect of achieving a counter-revolution. Dean Acheson and the State Department still had something of an open mind on the issue of recognition. The status of Taiwan posed the greatest complication, but even then Acheson had few illusions about the Nationalists. There was even something to be said for letting the island fall into Communist hands. Quite apart from the legal position— the United States had accepted at Cairo in 1943 that Taiwan was an integral part of China – the demise of the Nationalists as rival claimants to China's seat of government would free the administration to deal with China on its own terms and without encumbrance. The overthrow of the last vestiges of Nationalism would also have removed the mainstay and focus of the China bloc. The final deposition of Chiang would have caused a shockwave, but in the long term it would have removed an akward political canker. The State Department recommended in October that Chiang should be warned that the United States would not commit its armed forces to the defence of Taiwan and that further economic aid would be dependent on reform on the island.

Louis Johnson, the new and outspoken Secretary of Defense, disagreed with the State Department's tendency to distance itself from the Nationalists. He believed that a general policy of containment for the Far East as a whole should be developed, and he was determined to loosen Dean Acheson's grip on Asian policy. He advocated a more precise plan of national defence which would include a guarantee for Chiang's position on Taiwan. The Joint Chiefs of Staff opposed an American occupation of Taiwan, but counselled assistance in the form of military advisers and material. Louis Johnson's most influential ally was General Douglas MacArthur. MacArthur warned that if the Chinese Communists took Taiwan America's whole defensive position in the Far East would definitely be lost. MacArthur believed if Chinese or Soviet planes operated from Taiwan they would be able to dominate East and Southeast Asia. His view was something of an exaggeration. The Chinese had adequate air provision on airstrips along the whole of its east coast. The addition of Taiwan would have made little strategic difference. The security needs of the United States were more than adequately served by its Pacific bases.[4]

Secretary Johnson initiated a proposal to get the National Security Council to develop a comprehensive strategy for the Far East. The proposed study was designated NSC-48 and became the focus of deliberations within the administration for policy towards China. His staff within the Defense Department worked hard to secure a tough approach. They warned of the dangers of a Sino-Soviet hegemony in Asia and called for firm countermeasures. In particular they proposed a defensive buildup on Taiwan, the arming of anticommunist forces in Southeast Asia, and the isolation of mainland China through an economic blockade. The need for guidelines assumed a new urgency after the administration had proposed in July a Mutual Defense Assistance Program which was designed to fund defence production in Europe and Asia. When the bill was finally passed it contained a provision for the expenditure of $75 million for covert operations to contain communism 'in the general area of China.' Johnson and the China bloc saw an opportunity to use the money for helping the Nationalists on Taiwan to destabilize the regime on the mainland. The Bureau of Far Eastern Affairs in the State Department did not trust the military, and was concerned that further intervention in China's civil war would fuel conflict in the Far East, alienate the Chinese Communists once and for all, and aggravate the British, who were worried about the safety of Hong Kong. The State Department mobilized to defuse its critics and undermine the advocates of confrontation with the Chinese Communists.[5]

The administration hoped to placate its domestic critics through the publication on 5 August 1949 of a White Paper on China. The White Paper, titled *United States Relations with China with Special Reference to the Period 1944–1949*, consisted of a long account of America's role in Chinese affairs until the Communist victory and supporting documents. It attributed the victory of the Communists to Chiang's own weakness. According to Dean Acheson's Letter of Transmittal, there was nothing the United States could have done to alter the course of events. Acheson and the State Department had hoped that the release of the White Paper would dampen the criticisms of the administration and also serve notice to the Joint Chiefs of Staff that limited intervention was unproductive. It made no attempt to demonstrate that Mao's victory could threaten Soviet power in East Asia. It produced the opposite of the intended effect, and played into the hands of the administration's critics. The China Lobby regarded the White Paper as proof of the fact that China had been 'lost' through poor judgement in Washington. And in China itself the White Paper confirmed the prejudices of the Communist leadership. Mao said it showed that America's professions of impartiality in its mediation attempts after the war were hollow. He castigated the United States for interfering in the domestic affairs of China, and remonstrated that the documents demonstrated America's imperialist designs. And he was close to the mark when he said that the administration had released the White Paper 'in order to argue with opponents in their own camp as to which kind of counter-revolutionary tactics is the more clever.'[6]

Mao's reaction to the White Paper was consistent with the direction of the revolutionary process in China. His immediate objective was the elimination of the final vestiges of the *ancien régime*. The old officialdom was to be purged; the educational system was to be overhauled; the dominion of foreign capital ended. The termination of Western authority would be achieved by reducing or destroying the influence of foreign businessmen, educators and missionaries. It also meant that the representatives of other governments would have to recognize the legitimacy of the new regime and cut off all ties with the Nationalists. The revolution had triumphed as a result of the zeal and the discipline of the Communist Party. In the flush of victory, the Communist leadership wanted to assert itself. It did not wish to compromise the ideas that had sustained it through years of bitter fighting. China needed international help, but if that help meant that the patterns of the old order were to be continued then the new China would do without. As one historian has commented: 'For accommodation to have been reached in the late 1940s, the Chinese Communist movement would have had to behave as something other than it was.' It had no intention of doing that.[7]

Although foreign policy was not the major preoccupation of China's leaders, it was crucial to the establishment of the direction of the new People's Republic of China. The victors of the civil war were sombre realists. They were mindful of the fact that in the past many revolutions had fallen apart as a result of foreign intervention or compromise. If this revolution were to succeed it had to eliminate all sources of possible opposition and corruption. The West still dominated parts of the economy, and China's new leaders feared that it could stifle the revolution. Foreign firms accounted for about one-third of the output of manufacturing industry. In 1948 the United States had accounted for 48 per cent of China's imports and 20 per cent of its exports. The newly victorious troops and cadres that took control could not avoid their encounters with the Western presence, particularly in the cities. They had been told to distinguish between governments and peoples, but they were in no mood to make such distinctions. In Shanghai, for example, the foreign presence was almost inescapable. Nearly three-fourths of American trade passed through Shanghai; the British had four-fifths of their Chinese investments in the city. Its wide avenues, tennis courts, private clubs and European buildings were physical reminders of the depth of foreign influence.[8]

China's new government set about the task of overhauling the country's administrative structure, its investment policy, the curbing of inflation and the reform of the education system. The state moved quickly towards central control of the economy and industry. Inevitably, the new policies were set on a collision course with the sizeable contingent of Western missionaries, educators and businessmen. The Communists' early experience and encounters with the American presence in China were shaped by their desire to assert national independence, and to transform Chinese society. Calculations about foreign policy were only part of the equation. By and large they wanted to eradicate the remnants of Western predominance; they did not necessarily wish to end all links with the West. The Chinese authorities seemed prepared to treat with the United States, but only on the condition that it did not threaten the stability and unity of the new political order. A cautious *pas de deux* took place. In the spring of 1949 a Communist intermediary indicated that Zhou Enlai wanted the American ambassador, J. Leighton Stuart, then in Nanjing, to travel to Beijing to hold talks on common difficulties.[9] (The idea was thwarted in Washington, as it implied recognition.) The Chinese leadership wanted Washington to do the running. It was also aware that its zealous supporters and cadres had not forgotten the role played by the United States in upholding the power of the Nationalists. If the American residents were to remain in China they had to alter their lifestyles, reject their old allegiances and embrace the new order.

However, the Chinese were not prepared to wait for change, and developments in Washington did not encourage patience. American residents in China soon experienced harassment, or, at the very least, ostracism. Foreigners were required to register and were often portrayed in the press in an unfavourable light. Special and high taxes were levied on Western businesses. Missionary schools, colleges and universities came under the scrutiny of the state and were soon subject to pressure, particularly if they had a record of antipathy to the Communists. Diplomatic and consular personnel fared worst – they bore the brunt of the antagonisms that arose over conflict in foreign policy. The new authorities wanted nothing to do with representatives who were still also accredited to the Guomindang. Heads of mission were told they would be given no diplomatic privileges, and embassies were deprived of confidential mail services. Personal harassment also occurred. In Shanghai Vice-Consul William Olive was beaten up and held in custody for three days in July 1949, though arguably he may have provoked that harsh treatment. Angus Ward, the elderly Consul-General in Mukden, was earlier put under virtual house arrest and held incommunicado for over six months when he refused to hand over the consulate's radio transmitter.[10]

The Chinese authorities believed that the humbling of the United States was crucial to the attainment of revolution. In all probability they believed that once the humbling process was complete, scope would exist for normalization. For then it would be a normalization between equals. There had to be some kind of penitence for the West's exploitation of China in the past. In addition, the United States would have to demonstrate its acceptance of the regime by cutting off support from Taiwan and the Guomindang. They were in no hurry. The revolutionary process would come first. If they were to develop closer relations with another power, then they would turn towards the Soviet Union. In a celebrated speech of 30 June 1949, Mao proclaimed that there was only one great imperialistic power left and that was the United States. Accordingly, he told his audience, 'we must lean to one side' – the side of the Soviet Union. The speech, 'On the People's Democratic Dictatorship,' did not represent a new policy. It gave indirect sanction to the current spate of anti-Americanism and prepared the ground for Mao's approaches to Stalin for economic aid. It identified him firmly with the radicals who called for international socialist solidarity and was the first of many claims making China the centre of revolutionary socialism. He indicated that he would not be an Asian Tito. He confirmed this when he went to Moscow in December 1949 where, after lengthy negotiations, he secured $300 million in credits and a security treaty.[11]

In the United States the Sino-Soviet agreements were interpreted in different ways. Officials in the State Department were aware that a $300 million loan from the Soviets would hardly help China's chaotic economy. Also the granting of the right of the Soviet Union to post troops in Xinjiang and the Northeastern provinces was not a good omen for a Sino-Soviet entente. The administration still believed that its most effective policy towards China was to try to drive a wedge between the Soviet and Chinese Communist Parties. Thus although it delayed recognition it did not wish to close the door. It hoped that it could disentangle the confused ties with the Nationalists, and that the perceived cosmopolitanism of Zhou Enlai and his circle would prevail. Truman and Acheson still believed that if Taiwan were unable to defend itself and fell to the Communists, the consequence would have little impact on the strategic balance. They believed that the defence of America's Pacific interests could be best served by a vigorous stand against the Soviet Union. If a Sino-Soviet split could be encouraged, then American interests would be served. Acheson told the Senate Foreign Relations Committee in March 1950 that the Chinese would inevitably come into conflict with the Soviets 'because the very basic objectives of Moscow are hostile to the very basic objectives of China.'

He believed that the recent Sino-Soviet accords hung by a thread. He was aware that as long as the administration supported Chiang Kaishek's claims, there would be little hope of wresting Mao towards America. But he admitted to the Senate that it was domestic pressure rather than inclination that restricted the administration in its China policy.[12]

The influence of the domestic lobby that supported the Chinese Nationalists was out of all proportion to its numbers. Various groups and individuals coalesced to form the 'China Lobby.' The two most important groups were a private citizens' group, the American China Policy Association, and a loosely organized body in Congress, the so-called China bloc. The American China Policy Association was led by Alfred Kohlberg, a textile importer who had worked in China until the Japanese occupation. He had continued to trade with China after the war. He had concurred with Patrick Hurley that the Far East bureau of the State Department was run by men sympathetic to communists. In 1946 he founded the magazine *Plain Talk*, in which he published vitriolic articles about the pro-communist bias of the State Department. *Plain Talk* conducted a consistent guerilla campaign against the 'China Hands' and contributed to the witch-hunt that would destroy the careers of such foreign service officers as John Carter Vincent and John Stewart Service.[13]

Kohlberg and his associates drummed up the support of a group of Congressmen and Senators, who lobbied with persistent energy for support of the Nationalists and an unequivocal rejection of the Maoists. Some of the congressional China bloc had first-hand personal connections with Nationalist China. Republican Congressman Walter Judd, for example, had been a missionary doctor in China before the war. Other vocal members of the China bloc were Senators William Knowland of California, H. Alexander Smith of New Jersey and Styles Bridges of New Hampshire. They did not form a single, coherent group; their specific interests, motives and styles varied. But they did keep in close touch with one another and maintained regular contacts with the overseas representatives of the Nationalist government on Taiwan, particularly the ambassador, Wellington Koo. They were open in their admiration for Douglas MacArthur, who argued that the key to the future of the world lay in the Far East and not in Europe. The China bloc believed that it made no sense to support the political and economic structure of Western Europe without a parallel policy in Asia.

They held that it was inconsistent and short-sighted to incur heavy expenditure in Europe while keeping aid to China and non-communist East Asia at a minimum. Such a contradiction in policy, they argued, was the result of poor judgement by foreign service officers, to say nothing of a deliberate attempt on their part to swing China into the hands of the Communist Party. Overwhelmingly Republican, they also realized that the 'loss' of China and the administration's wavering over its relations with the Chinese Communists provided useful ammunition for a partisan campaign against the Truman administration.

These friends of Nationalist China fought on two fronts. First, they were determined to bring the 'China Hands' in the State Department to book for permitting America's immediate post-war advantage to be frittered away. Kohlberg, Smith, Bridges and their supporters elaborated on and repeated the charges of betrayal first levelled by Ambassador Patrick Hurley in November 1945.[14] As early as 1946 the State Department had responded to such charges by initiating a series of loyalty investigations, and had dismissed a number of employees as potential security risks. But it was the Communist victory in China, the publication of the White Paper, the struggle within the administration over recognition policy, and the continuance of aid to Taiwan that catalyzed the China bloc. They accused the 'China Hands' of disloyalty in their favourable judgements of the Chinese Communist Party. The second and related crusade of the China bloc was for foreign aid to Asia. They believed that military and economic assistance to areas still outside communist control would ensure that they remained outside that control. In the case of China this would mean continued support for the Nationalists' campaign to return to the mainland, and guarantees for the security of Taiwan. One way of increasing the level of commitment was to play on the guilt of past mistakes. The attacks on foreign service officers who had been responsible for China policy during the civil war served to keep China policy in the limelight. Sensational accusations of disloyalty and even treason also helped to keep their own names in the news headlines. Their vendetta against one such foreign sevice officer, John Carter Vincent, illustrates the point.

John Carter Vincent first went out to China in 1924 and served in the consular office in Changsha in Hunan province. He had subsequent postings in Beijing, Jinan, Mukden and Dalian. In 1941 he was transferred to the embassy in Chungking, where he was first secretary, and then counsellor. As a result of his long service in China he spoke good Chinese and he was knowledgeable about its history. His dispatches from Chungking were highly critical of Chiang. He condemned the use of torture and the venality of the Nationalists and their warlord allies. But he had few illusions about the Communists. He recommended that the United States should make aid to Chiang conditional, and that it should seek out alternative liberal groupings within China. His analyses caught the eye of Acheson, then Under-Secretary of State, who appointed Vincent Director of Far Eastern Affairs. As Director he advised the administration to be rigorous in its demands on Chiang. This was grist to the mill for Alfred Kohlberg and his supporters in Congress. They tried to block Vincent's further promotion by accusing him of betraying the interests of the United States. At first they failed, but when Senator Joseph McCarthy began his campaigns in 1950 the old allegations were revived and relentlessly pursued. Vincent was accused of espousing the Chinese Communists' position and of working to further the interests of the Soviet Union in China. He was subjected to a gruelling ordeal by the Senate Internal Security Subcommittee. He then underwent an inquisition from the State Department's Loyalty-Security Board and afterwards the Civil Service Loyalty Review Board. That Board ruled that Vincent had violated the declared policies of the United States in his alleged sympathy for Mao and ruled that there was 'reasonable doubt' about his loyalty. It recommended that his services be terminated. John Foster Dulles, the new Secretary of State, accepted the recommendation and forced him into retirement.[15]

John Carter Vincent was only one of several victims of the legislative and administrative inquisitions that received the backing of the China lobby. John Service, John Paton Davies, and O. Edmund Clubb suffered similar fates. Although men and women connected with China were only a small fraction of those who experienced the purging process in the late 1940s and early 1950s, they did provide an easy first target as their written advices, many of which were reproduced in the White Paper, were readily available for scrutiny and easily distorted. Joseph McCarthy hinged his charges against the State Department on the opinions given by the Far Eastern Bureau. The campaigns against the foreign service officers showed that Congress was not prepared to defer to the judgements of an unelected policy-making establishment. Bipartisan support was not to be taken for granted; if the administration wanted support for NATO, European recovery or the foreign assistance programme, it would have to accede on the China question.

The inquisitions of the early 1950s also showed that Americans believed that in times of national crisis – and the nation's mobilization in the face of the perceived Soviet threat was just such a crisis – there had to be a closing of the ranks. While naked ambition did indeed drive some of the inquisitors, many of the administration's critics genuinely believed that there had been a baffling tolerance and acceptance of counsel that seemed inconsistent with the policy of containment. Unsurprisingly, the authorities in Beijing came to the same conclusion. If the United States was committed to the containment of communism it was hardly likely to make an exception of the new revolutionary regime in China. As far as they were concerned, even if Acheson did want to keep the door ajar to Communist China, the political system did not permit such discretion. Thus any attempt to lean to the other side, the side of the United States, would not serve China's interests.

In early 1950 the Truman administration was still adopting a policy of letting the dust settle in China. It believed that the initial flush of hostility to the United States might subside. It still hoped to save Taiwan, although it was that hope that fuelled the hostility of the Communists. However, the future of Taiwan was secondary to the wish to halt communism in Asia by ending the American occupation of Japan and strengthening China's neighbours in Southeast Asia. Defence chiefs and General MacArthur disagreed strongly with Truman's priorities. They believed Taiwan should be strengthened for the use of stationing troops and as a base for air and naval operations. They also realized that preserving a non-Communist Taiwan would delay international recognition of the government in Beijing. Truman and Acheson were still determined not to close off their options. On 5 January 1950 in a statement to the press Truman proclaimed that there would be no further involvement in the Chinese civil war and that no military aid or advice would be given to Taiwan. A week later, in a public speech to the National Press Club, Acheson reiterated that the Guomindang had only their own ineptitude to blame and that the Chinese Communists owed their victory to the tide of revolutionary nationalism that was sweeping Asia. He then went on to describe a Pacific defence perimeter for the security of the United States. That line ran from the Aleutians through Japan to the Ryukyus and the Philippines. He did not refer specifically to Taiwan or South Korea, although he singled out the latter for financial aid.

Acheson's speech conveyed the impression that the United States was unlikely to spring to the defence of South Korea or Taiwan. Since then critics have singled out the speech as a specific encouragement for the subsequent North Korean attack on South Korea. However, these critics ignore the context of the speech. In the same speech Acheson warned of the Soviets' territorial ambitions in inner Mongolia and Manchuria. The Chinese, he suggested, had turned against the wrong foe. The administration still believed that recognition of China would eventually come and public statements about national security were directed at the Soviets, rather than the Chinese. While the China lobby was a force to be reckoned with, the overwhelming majority of legislators and opinion makers were concerned with European issues. Acheson and Truman were making a bid for flexibility in the Far East. Mao was still negotiating in Moscow; the administration had no desire to rock the boat further.[16]

Nevertheless, it was becoming increasingly difficult to keep to a moderate course. McCarthy's charges, the harassment of American officials and the publication in February 1950 of the Sino-Soviet accords did not give the administration the flexibility it would have liked. It was also being pressed by the military establishment. Secretary of Defense Louis Johnson, an ambitious and abrasive man who believed that his political future lay in an alliance with the right, believed that the Communist regime could still be destabilized by providing aid to Chiang and the Nationalists. He authorized limited arms deliveries to Taiwan and encouraged private organizations to forge links with Chiang. MacArthur engaged in similar tactics; some verged on private policy-making. He was aware that Syngman Rhee of South Korea and Chiang had been involved in negotiations over a Pacific pact, and may well have intimated that the United States would underwrite such a pact. On 20 May 1950 he introduced a metaphor into the strategic vocabulary of the United States that would stick. He compared Taiwan to an 'unsinkable aircraft carrier' that served to defend America's Pacific interests. If the carrier were to sink and fall into Communist hands the shipping lanes from Malaya to Japan would be cut off and Japan would be isolated. In that event the United States would have to beat a major retreat.[17] The threat to Taiwan seemed to mover ever closer. At the end of April Hainan fell, according to Robert Strong, the American chargé d'affaires in Taipei, 'like a house of cards in a windstorm' to Mao's forces. On 16 May the Nationalists ordered the evacuation of the Chusan islands. The State Department was advised to prepare itself for the evacuation of Taiwan. Even John Foster Dulles told Hollington Tong, a key member of the central advisory committee of the Guomindang, that expectations of Chiang's ability to defend Taiwan were low. Americans wanted to protect Taiwan from the Communists, but they realized that Chiang would not be an effective leader in such a resistance. One of the main incentives for keeping Taiwan out of the hands of the Communists was that this would, it was hoped, pin down Chinese forces along the east coast and deflect them from any possible move into South East Asia.[18]

In the event the administration's equivocation about its China policy was resolved by fate as much as by design. On the night of 24 June Washington learned of the outbreak of hostilities between North and South Korea. The precise immediate origins of the war are still somewhat murky. Each side accused the other of starting the war. Syngman Rhee, President of the Republic of Korea (ROK) in the South, had called for unification by force on many occasions and there had been forays by ROK forces north of the 38th parallel. On the other hand Kim Il Sung, President of North Korea, or the Democratic People's Republic of Korea, had amassed his forces at key points along the border and had even occupied salient points to the south. Kim Il Sung wanted to unite North and South Korea not only to fulfil a national dream but also to end his dependence on the Soviet Union and China. There is no evidence that China actively encouraged the attack or wished to get involved in the war. It was preoccupied with national reconstruction. If it was going to get involved in any military campaign it would do so to unite itself with Taiwan. Mao did give his blessing to Kim's plans for the use of force in the quest for reunification. But it is unlikely that he foresaw that China would be drawn into the war. Indeed, China had begun a partial military demobilization as it realized that an invasion of Taiwan was an expensive project. The unification of Korea was not on its agenda. Although a large proportion of North Korean officers had fought with the PLA in China, they had not been sent back to Korea to fight a vicarious war. The Korean war began as a local war; it was not conceived by China or any other power as a ground for national expansion.[19]

However, as far as Washington was concerned there had been an unprovoked attack on the regime in the South. In its view the Soviets had connived in the plan. The administration regarded this attack as a test of America's resolve; it also enabled Washington to deal with a series of dilemmas in one swoop. By intervening in Korea it would lend assurances to Western Europe that America's participation in the the new security arrangements under NATO would have teeth. The strategy would also enable the administration to forge ahead with a major rearmament programme in accordance with the recommendations of the National Security Council in a detailed document, coded NSC-68. Yet there was one ironical outcome. President Truman did not intervene in the Korean war to put pressure on China – China was not originally part of the equation. Yet by intervening in the war he in effect reversed the policy of waiting on events to solve the vexed issue of the recognition of China. He had now committed his administration – and administrations for the next twenty years – to sustaining the Guomindang on Taiwan and to the deliberate isolation of the People's Republic of China from the world community.

The first step to a more active role in Chinese affairs came two days after hostilites broke out. On 27 June Truman ordered the Seventh Fleet to 'neutralize' the Taiwan Strait, a deed that had been contemplated for some weeks. The intercession of the fleet between China and Taiwan was designed to prevent one side from attacking the other. The immediate purpose of the order was to buy time and to prevent complications arising from hostilities across the Strait. It sought to use America's muscle in the Chinese civil war to prevent a confrontation between the Nationalists and the Communists. Overturning previous policy the President proclaimed that 'the occupation of Formosa by Communist forces would be a direct threat to the security of the Pacific area.' The neutralization policy was designed to yield a domestic dividend too. Truman hoped it would win Republican support for his Far East policy, and for the intervention in Korea in particular. After months of resisting pressure to increase aid to Taiwan, the administration had finally committed itself to the protection of the island.[20]

The neutralization of the Taiwan Strait may have served to freeze the balance in the area; it did little to promote good relations with either the Nationalists or the Chinese Communists. Chiang and his principal American advocate, Douglas MacArthur, were frustrated with the restrictions imposed. Nationalist raids on airfields and ports on the mainland were stopped. The removal of the threat of harassment from the island freed Communist forces deployed along the Strait to move north and to continue the pacification programme. Beijing's hostility to and distrust of Washington was magnified. Because Taiwan was viewed as an integral part of China the intercession of the fleet was regarded as a direct intervention and as a violation of Chinese territory. Beijing posed as the protector of all Asia. Mao declared 'the affairs of Asia should be administered by the peoples of Asia themselves.' Zhou Enlai called on people throughout China to unite against the 'premeditated move by the United States, designed to create a pretext for the United States to invade Taiwan, Korea, Vietnam and the Philippines.'[21] Thus while Truman sought to get his allies to view America's intervention in the Korean peninsula and the Taiwan Strait as a limited action, the regime in Beijing regarded it as a bid for hegemony in the Far East. And as the war unfolded, nothing occurred to persuade the Chinese to change their minds. The Korean war would shape the Sino-American agenda for the next quarter-century.

The neutralization of the Taiwan Strait and the UN action in Korea energized the diplomatic activity of the Nationalists. Their interests were pushed in Washington not only by an invigorated China Lobby but also by Louis Johnson's Defense Department, the Joint Chiefs of Staff, and MacArthur's Far Eastern command. The Joint Chiefs began to press for a rush programme of military aid to Taiwan. They urged that the ban on military forays from Taiwan be lifted so that the island could defend itself against the threat posed by the concentration of forces along the coast of the mainland. The administration would have none of it, but it was forced into a defensive position by the public campaigning of General MacArthur. He travelled to Taiwan at the end of July and gave the Nationalists full encouragement. In Tokyo the following month he asked Averell Harriman, on a personal mission from Truman, to tell the President to remove Chiang's fetters. He also planned to go public. In a message that was scheduled to be sent to the Veterans of Foreign Wars convention in Chicago he reiterated his view that Taiwan was like an 'unsinkable aircraft carrier'; whoever controlled it controlled the Pacific. He accused official Washington of not understanding 'the pattern of Oriental psychology,' which respected 'aggressive, resolute and dynamic leadership.' Truman was furious. MacArthur's message was out of turn; it could be construed as an insult to other Asian peoples; and it practically invited Taipei to determine US policy. He ordered MacArthur to withdraw the message. But the damage was done: MacArthur complied, but only after it had appeared in the press. Relations between the White House and MacArthur were bruised and went downhill from that point on.[22]

The attempts to silence MacArthur did nothing to reassure Beijing.

The Chinese moved closer to war with the United States. They felt
threatened from many fronts. Their troops faced American ships in the
Taiwan Strait. American soldiers had amassed in the Korean peninsula
under the auspices of a United Nations resolution that had been taken
without either the Chinese or the Russians present at the decisive
meeting. There was no safeguard against the deployment of forces against
China. The troops were under the supreme command of MacArthur,
who was outspoken in his support for the Nationalists and in his wish
to use the opportunity of war to unite Korea, even at the risk of war
with China. At first the Chinese stayed out of the Korean conflict,
particularly as UN forces suffered some serious reverses when they were
pushed south and cornered in the Pusan perimeter in the extreme
southeast of the peninsula. As long as North Korea and its own frontier
were not threatened, China would play a watching game. The United
States was aware of China's tentativeness. It hesitated about expanding
the war north of the 38th parallel. However, on 15 September 1950
UN forces launched a surprise and brilliant assault at Inchon, just twenty
miles from Seoul and close to the parallel. They simultaneously broke
out of the trap at Pusan and forced the Noth Korean forces to beat a
hasty retreat.

The dramatic changes in the fortunes of war had an intoxicating
effect on the Truman administration, and previous caution was thrown
to the winds. There seemed to be no point in negotiating. The China
Lobby was clamouring to push home the initiative. Most of Truman's
close advisers urged that the military momentum be used to achieve
unification. Unification, they argued, would eliminate at least one
trouble spot. It would also strengthen America's position in the non-
communist world, and might even silence the China Lobby. Two weeks
after the Inchon landings MacArthur was authorized to move into
North Korea on condition that there were no signs of Soviet or Chinese
intervention and that only South Korean troops were used near the
frontiers of Siberia and China. George Marshall, who had replaced
Johnson as Secretary of Defense, authorized MacArthur to feel 'un-
hampered strategically and tactically.'[23]

The Chinese waiting game now changed. Zhou Enlai warned
publicly that China would not remain supine. He told the Indian
Ambassador, K.M. Panikkar, that China would intervene if MacArthur's
thrust north was not stopped. China's leaders believed that the United
States was trying to reverse their revolution. The advance towards its

borders, the reinforcement of Taiwan, and the extension of aid to France in Southeast Asia confirmed their sense of encirclement. But the administration believed the Chinese were bluffing. Economic reconstruction and military weakness would combine, it thought, to restrain them. It completely misread Chinese intentions. As US troops captured Pyongyang, the North Korean capital, on 19 October and pushed northward to the Chinese border along the Yalu River, China's leaders decided that they could not wait on developments. On balance the risks of staying out of the fighting were greater than the risks of intervening. Mao did not take the decision lightly. He decided that it was better to fight on foreign soil than on home territory. Accordingly, units of the Chinese People's Volunteers were ordered to advance by night across the Yalu River, which divides Manchuria from North Korea. As MacArthur's forces marched towards the Yalu, 300,000 Chinese troops were waiting. At first UN forces only encountered limited numbers of Chinese soldiers, who seemed to fade away. They presumed the Chinese were bluffing, but on 25 November they faced a massive Chinese attack and were forced to retreat. The administration had made a huge error of judgement. MacArthur wanted to meet force with force and escalate the war. He advocated bombing attacks on Manchuria and the use of Nationalist troops, and even suggested dropping atomic weapons. Washington wanted to avoid a general war with China and determined to limit the fighting by holding a defensive line at some point in Korea. Policy-makers did not want to risk global war and tie down American forces in an unknown part of the world. The US had embarked on the war to check communism in Asia. It did not want to stay in Korea and so expose itself to possible challenges from the Kremlin in Europe. It was this more limited objective that led to the confronatation with General MacArthur and his dramatic dismissal.[24]

The events that led to MacArthur's recall in April 1951 are well known. After the Chinese had entered the war, combat settled into repeated patterns of advance and retreat. Accordingly, the administration decided that it would not seek the forcible reunification of Korea. It would settle for an armistice that saved American lives and the independence of South Korea. MacArthur had different ideas and went public with them. He wanted to push for reunification and to humiliate China by taking the war over the border into Manchuria. In this way he hoped to destroy its war-making capacity and to employ Nationalist forces in the process. He wanted to manipulate the administration into a showdown with China. The last straw for the administration came when the Minority Leader of the House of Representatives released a letter from MacArthur which criticized the Truman administration for tying his hands on the battlefield. 'We must win,' he wrote. 'There is no substitute for victory.' Truman had had enough: he did not want the war to escalate further. On 10 April MacArthur was fired and command was handed over to Matthew Ridgway.[25]

The recall of MacArthur did nothing to improve Sino-American relations, nor did it do anything to enhance the People's Republic's own sense of security. The Chinese government launched a 'Resist America and Aid Korea' campaign. The assets of foreign businesses were frozen, organizations with overseas links were shut down and the few remaining missionaries were imprisoned or deported. In the summer of 1951 the Chinese Communist Party began a campaign against domestic subversion. The focus of the new campaign was alleged sympathizers with the Guomindang party. Rallies were held and committees were formed to investigate past affiliations. Accusation sessions were set up to get 'bandits' and other pro-Guomindang suspects to recant. There was worse to come. The authorities made mass arrests and held public executions in this new reign of terror. In 1952, as the Korean war settled into military stalemate, a new campaign, the so-called Five Anti campaign, was launched. That drive was directed at the bourgeoisie of China and in particular the rural landlords. It sought to expunge bribery, tax evasion, and cheating on contracts. This repressive and brutal campaign to establish full administrative control and to dampen even the slightest prospect of counter-revolution was prompted largely by the war in Korea. The Chinese leadership felt threatened. MacArthur had called for an invasion of Chinese soil; the United States was trying to get the UN to impose an international trade embargo; the reinforcement of Taiwan kept the prospect of a new civil war alive. Hit-and-run commando raids were still being conducted from Taiwan despite the neutralization of the Strait. Taipei radio was calling for more such raids. Mao's decree of February 1951, 'Regulations Regarding the Punishment of Counter-revolutionaries,' sanctioned a reign of terror. Even according to official statistics some 135,000 executions took place in the first six months of 1951. According to Maurice Meisner about 2,000,000 were people were executed in the first three years of the PRC's existence, the majority of them in the campaigns of 1951 and 1952.[26]

The administration in Washington was aware of the drive against dissenters. It drew two conclusions from the events within China. First, it perceived a certain fragility in the Beijing regime which, it claimed, lacked confidence. It could only summon the collective will to carry on fighting in Korea if it had the full backing of Moscow. It was therefore beholden to the Soviets and could not act with any degree of autonomy. On the other hand, it still believed that the interests of Mao and Stalin were fundamentally divergent and that China could eventually be weaned away. Several reports to the Secretary of State argued that the campaigns in China confirmed the existence of an opposition to the Communist government. An alternative force in China still seemed possible. Chiang Kai-shek hardly fitted the bill. However, if the United States continued to encourage an opposition and turned a blind eye to the raids from Taiwan on the Chinese coast, it might encourage the emergence of such a 'third force.' Secret meetings were set up in Hong Kong with men thought to have access to the Chinese Communists to try to get the Chinese to believe that it was not in their interests to align with Moscow. A National Intelligence Estimate of July 1951 stated that the war was fomenting dissent within China and was creating severe economic shortages. Its best troops were pinned down in Korea and Manchuria, thus leaving the country badly exposed. If the economy of Taiwan could be put on a steady course and the political corruption ended, it could become a model for China's leaders to emulate. Taiwan could, according to the officer in charge of Chinese Economic Affairs, 'offer a hope and an inspiration to the Chinese suffering Communist tyranny.'[27]

It became clear by the middle of 1951 that the war in Korea had reached a stalemate. The dramatic advances and retreats that had characterized the fighting had ceased. The Americans halted their northward advance just north of the 38th parallel and began to dig in. It seemed that China and the United States were content to hold the line. The belligerents concluded that armistice negotiations would yield the same results as fighting. Talks opened in Kaesong, just below the parallel, between the UN side, represented by American officers with one ROK delegate in attendance, and a joint North Korean–Chinese delegation. These talks, later transferrred to Panmunjom, turned out to be a long drawn out affair. The greatest obstacle to the conclusion of an armistice was the issue of the repatriation of prisoners of war. The Americans insisted that repatriation should be voluntary. The Chinese and North Koreans argued that the Geneva Convention prescribed immediate repatriation, irrespective of whether prisoners wanted to return home or not. In addition they argued that Communist prisoners in UN custody could not choose freely, because of threats and violence in the POW camps. The talks degenerated into sessions of accusation and counter-accusation about treatment in the camps. The two sides were concerned about the welfare of the prisoners, but beyond this they were trying to inflict a propaganda defeat on one another. The Americans were trying to show that, given a free choice, Chinese prisoners would not choose to live under a Communist regime. A poll of 106,000 Communist prisoners on Koje-Do island revealed that a large majority did not want to be exchanged and had asked to be sent to Taiwan.[28]

So the talks dragged on. Neither side seemed willing to give way on substance. Fighting continued, sometimes sporadically, sometimes with intensive violence. The United States launched a massive bombing campaign in July 1952 over the North Korean capital, Pyongyang, in the hope of squeezing concessions from the negotiators. But it was not to be. It took the death of Stalin and the election of a Republican president in the United States to get peace.

The Korean war had a profound effect on both the United States and the People's Republic of China – to say nothing of the sufferings of the Korean people. It is estimated that China suffered nearly one million fatalities, including one of Mao's sons. Those who survived would remember the killings, the frostbite, the inadequate food and clothing. Economic reconstruction had to be sacrificed in order to pay for the war. The level of assistance from the Soviet Union had been modest, and was often in the form of obsolete military equipment. Yet China had to pay back its debt to the Soviets. Its resentment would grow. The war also stopped China from taking Taiwan and reunifying the nation, and destroyed the prospect of international recognition and participation in the United Nations. But there were gains for China too. Its very ability to stand up to the United States reversed the sense of humiliation China had felt since the middle of the nineteenth century. There was no longer any danger of an American military presence along the Yalu River. America's superior economic and military power had failed to ruffle the regime. The United States would not miscalculate and underestimate the People's Republic of China again. A new mystique of Chinese endurance emerged from the ashes of war, a mystique that was elaborated in plays, films and political polemics. If anything, the war enhanced the internal support for the new regime.[29]

The war had far-reaching results in the United States too. Although American casualties were low in comparison with those of China or the two Koreas – over 54,000 American troops lost their lives – Americans did not rejoice at the outcome. The war was unpopular with both troops and the general public. People felt it was being fought in the wrong place; and there was not even the satisfaction of a victory over communism to compensate. There was nothing to celebrate. The restraints imposed on its military commanders did not make sense. MacArthur's dismissal diminished the stature of President Truman, and confirmed the worst suspicions of the China Lobby. The war had no decisive outcome – Washington now seemed committed to containing communism in peripheral areas of the world. The war also permitted McCarthy and the anti-Communist witch-hunters to prosper. It had strained relations with inportant allies, such as India and Great Britain. Unlike the Chinese, Americans did not emerge from the Korean conflict feeling good about themselves.

Britain and the United States would patch up their differences. China and the United States moved further apart. The Chinese saw American involvement in Korea as a first step towards the attempted domination of Asia: not only had it poured money and men into Korea, it had also moved to prop up crumbling colonial regimes in Southeast Asia. Above all, whatever wavering the Americans had exhibited about the Nationalists before Korea, it had now gone. Not only was Taiwan now protected by the Seventh Fleet, it was being shored up with military and economic aid. In the right circumstances, armistice talks and negotiations can create bridges of their own. Nothing of the kind happened at Panmunjom. The talks revealed just how great the chasm was. Americans still talked about the possibility of internal division in the communist world, but they did nothing to foster the potential for division. Washington's continued embargoes against China, its support for the Nationalists and its related refusal to recognize the Beijing government as the only government of China, inevitably reinforced the People's Republic of China's own sense of isolation. There seemed no alternative to an alliance with the Soviet Union. The Korean war did not resolve differences between the United States and China. It underscored them and served, if anything, to harden attitudes. The troubled affair was only just beginning.

NOTES

1. For general information on the Communist takeover see: Suzanne Pepper, *Civil War in China: The Political Struggle, 1945–1949* (Berkeley, CA, 1978); Donald Gillin and Ramon Myers, eds, *Last Chance in China: The Diary of Chang Kia-ngau* (Stanford, CA, 1989); A. Doak Barnett, *China on the Eve of Communist Takeover* (New York, 1963).

2. E.J. Kahn Jr., *The China Hands: America's Foreign Service Officers and What Befell Them* (New York, 1975), p. 23. See also: Warren I. Cohen 'Acheson, His Advisers, and China, 1949–1950' in Dorothy Borg and Waldo Heinrichs, *Uncertain Years: Chinese–American Relations, 1947–1950* (New York, 1980), pp. 13–32; William Adam Brown and Redvers Opie, *American Foreign Assistance* (Washington, DC, 1953); Tang Tsou, *America's Failure in China, 1941–1950* (Chicago, 1963), pp. 464–86.

3. Michael H. Hunt, 'Mao Tse-tung and the Issue of Accommodation with the United States, 1948–1950' in Borg and Heinrichs, *Uncertain Years*, pp. 198–209.

4. Quoted in Michael Schaller, *Douglas MacArthur: The Far Eastern General* (New York, 1989), p. 169.

5. An excellent account of the battle over NSC-48 can be found in Robert M. Blum, *Drawing the Line: The Origin of the American Containment Policy in East Asia* (New York, 1982), pp. 125–77; also Schaller, *Douglas MacArthur*, pp. 158–80.

6. Mao Tse-tung, *Selected Works, IV* (Peking, 1961), p. 430; U.S. Department of State, *United States Relations with China* (Washington DC, 1949); Melvyn P. Leffler, *A Preponderance of Power: National Security, the Truman Administration, and the Cold War* (Stanford, CA, 1992), pp. 293–6.

7. Steven M. Goldstein, 'Sino-American Relations, 1948–1950: Last Chance or No Chance' in Harry Harding and Yuan Ming, *Sino-American Relations, 1945–1955: A Joint Reassessment of a Critical Decade* (Wilmington, DE, 1989), p. 138; David Allan Mayers, *Cracking the Monolith: US Policy Against the Sino-Soviet Alliance, 1949–1955* (Baton Rouge, LA, and London, 1986), pp. 51–2. See also A. Doak Barnett, *Communist China: The Early Years, 1949–1955* (New York, 1955); Kenneth Lieberthal, *Revolution and Tradition in Tientsin, 1949–1952* (Stanford, CA, 1980).

8. Beverley Hooper, *China Stands Up: Ending the Western Presence, 1948–1950* (Sydney, 1986), pp. 9, 20–22; Theodore Shabad, *China's Changing Map: National and Regional Development, 1949–1971* (New York, 1972).

9. Kenneth W. Rea and John C. Brewer, eds, *The Forgotten Ambassador: The Reports of John Leighton Stuart, 1946–1949* (Boulder, 1981), pp. 324–8; Philip Fugh, ed., *John Leighton Stuart's Diary (Mainly of the Critical Year 1949)* (Palo Alto, 1980), p. 36; Yu-ming Shaw, 'John Leighton Stuart and U.S. Rapprochement in 1949: Was There Another "Lost chance in China"?' *China Quarterly* 89 (March 1982), pp. 74–96.

10. Hooper, *China Stands Up*, pp. 71–95, 160–71; Nancy Bernkopf Tucker, *Patterns in the Dust: Chinese–American Relations and the Recognition Controversy, 1949–1950* (New York, 1983), pp. 27–51; Goldstein, 'Sino-American Relations, 1948–1950', pp. 119–21.

11. Mao Tse-tung, *Selected Works IV*, pp. 411–24; Tsou, *America's Failure in China*, pp. 504–7; Steven M. Goldstein, 'Chinese Communist Policy Toward the United

States: Opportunities and Constraints, 1944–1950'; Hunt, 'Mao Tse-tung and the Issue of Accommodation', both in Borg and Heinrichs, *The Uncertain Years*, pp. 210–18, 253–4; Mayers, *Cracking the Monolith*, pp. 46–8.

12. U.S. Senate, Committee on Foreign Relations, *Reviews of the World Situation: 1949–1950*, Hearings Held in Executive Session, 81 Cong. 1 and 2 Sess. (Washington, DC, 1974), pp. 273–5; memorandum of conversation by Secretary of State, January 5, 1950, U.S. Department of State, *Foreign Relations of the United States, 1950: VI, East Asia and the Pacific* (Washington, DC, 1976), p. 262 (hereafter cited as *FRUS*, relevant volume); Mayers, *Cracking the Monolith*, pp. 67–72; also Robert Blum, *The United States and China in World Affairs* (New York and London, 1966), pp. 9–11.

13. Further discussion of the China lobby can be found in Ross Y. Koen, *The China Lobby in American Politics* (New York, 1975); Joseph C. Keeley, *The China Lobby Man: The Story of Alfred Kohlberg* (New York, 1969); Stanley Bachrack, *The Committee of One Million: The China Lobby in American Politics, 1953–1971* (New York, 1976).

14. Tucker, *Patterns in the Dust*, p. 167; for general background see Russell Buhite, *Patrick J. Hurley and American Foreign Policy* (Ithaca, NY, 1973); Lewis Purifoy, *Harry Truman's China Policy: McCarthyism and the Diplomacy of Hysteria, 1947–1951* (New York, 1976).

15. Gary May, *China Scapegoat: The Diplomatic Ordeal of John Carter Vincent* (Prospect Heights, IL, 1979); Ernest R. May, 'The China Hands in Perspective: Ethics, Diplomacy, and Statecraft,' in Paul Gordon Lauren, *The China Hands' Legacy: Ethics and Diplomacy* (Boulder and London, 1987), pp. 97–123; Kahn, *The China Hands*, pp. 191–2, 232–7.

16. Consul General at Shanghai to Sec. of State, 26 January 1950 in *FRUS, 1950, VI*, p. 217; Dean Acheson, *Present at the Creation: My Years in the State Department* (London, 1970), pp. 350–7; U.S. Senate, *Reviews of the World Situation*, pp. 113–17, 154–70; Glenn D. Paige, *The Korean Decision [June 24–30, 1950]* (New York and London, 1968), pp. 66–68; Gaddis Smith, *Dean Acheson* (New York, 1972), pp. 175–6.

17. William Whitney Stueck, *The Road to Confrontation: American Policy toward China and Korea, 1947–1950* (Chapel Hill, 1981), pp. 138–40; Peter Lowe, *The Origins of the Korean War* (London, 1986), pp. 150–52; Schaller, *Douglas MacArthur*, pp. 174–7.

18. Chargé in China to Sec. of State, 27 April 1950; Chargé in China to Sec. of State, 17 May 1950; memorandum of conversation by J.F. Dulles to Sec. of State, 25 May 1950 in *FRUS, 1950, VI*, pp. 335–9, 340–44.

19. Allen Whiting, *China Crosses the Yalu: The Decision to Enter the Korean War* (New York, 1960), pp. 18–21; Karunker Gupta, 'How did the Korean War Begin?' *China Quarterly*, 66 (October–December 1972), pp. 699–716; Kathryn Weathersby, 'New Findings on the Korean War,' *Cold War International History Project Bulletin* (Fall 1993), No. 3, pp. 1, 14–18; Kathryn Weathersby, 'Soviet Aims in Korea and the Origins of the Korean War, 1945–1950: New Evidence from Russian Archives,' Working Paper 8, *Cold War International History Project* (November 1993); Li Xiaobing, Wang Xi, and Chen Jian, 'Mao's Dispatch of Chinese Troops to Korea: Forty-Six Telegrams, July–October 1950,' *Chinese Historians*, 5 (Spring 1992), pp. 67–8; Maurice Meisner, *Mao's China and After: A History of the People's Republic* (rev. edn. New York and London, 1986), pp. 73–9. See also James Matray, *The Reluctant Crusade: American Foreign Policy in Korea, 1941–1950* (Honolulu, 1985). An excellent popular account of

the Korean conflict based on the television series is Jon Halliday and Bruce Cumings, *Korea: The Unknown War* (London, 1988).

20. See Bruce Cumings, *The Origins of the Korean War, II: The Roaring of the Cataract, 1947–1950* (Princeton, 1990), pp. 508–44. This is the definitive work on the prelude to the Korean War.

21. Both quoted in Tsou, *America's Failure in China*, p. 562.

22. Memorandum by JCS to Sec. of Defense, 27 July 1950; Sec. of Defense to Sec. of State, 29 July 1950; Sec. of State to Sec. of Defense, 31 July 1950; extracts of a memorandum of conversations, Harriman with MacArthur, 6 and 8 August 1950; Sec. of State to Certain Diplomatic Officers, 26 August 1950, all in *FRUS, 1950, VI*, pp. 391–3, 401–2, 427–9, 451–3; Harry S. Truman, *Memoirs, II: Years of Trial and Hope, 1946–52* (Garden City, NY, 1956), pp. 406–8.

23. Joint Chiefs of Staff to MacArthur, 27 September 1950, *FRUS, 1950, VII*, pp. 781–2, 792–3; Cumings, *The Origins of the Korean War: II*, pp. 662–5; Russell D. Buhite, *Soviet–American Relations in Asia, 1945–1954* (Norman, OK, 1981), pp. 233–4; Acheson, *Present at the Creation*, p. 445; Callum A. MacDonald, *Korea: The War before Vietnam* (London, 1986), pp. 48–50; Schaller, *Douglas MacArthur*, pp. 200–1.

24. MacDonald, *Korea*, pp. 68–78; Jonathan D. Pollack, 'The Korean War and Sino-American Relations' in Harding and Yuan, *Sino-American Relations, 1945–1955*, pp. 217–22; James E. Schnabel and Robert J. Watson, *The History of the Joint Chiefs of Staff: The Joint Chiefs and National Policy, 1945–1953, III: The Korean War, part I* (Wilmington, DE, 1979), pp. 260–346; Robert J. Donovan, *Tumultuous Years: The Presidency of Harry S. Truman, 1949–1953* (New York, 1982), pp. 353–8; Rosemary Foot, *The Wrong War: American Policy and the Dimensions of the Korean Conflict, 1950–53* (Ithaca, NY, 1985).

25. John W. Spanier, *The Truman–MacArthur Controversy and the Korean War* (New York, 1965).

26. Memo, Richard Johnson to Director, Office of Chinese Affairs, 4 June 1951, *FRUS, 1951: VII, Korea and China* (Washington, DC, 1983), pp. 1698–1700; Meisner, *Mao's China and After*, pp. 80–82.

27. National Intelligence Estimate, 10 July 1951; memo, Barnett to Rusk, 3 October 1951; memorandum of conversation, 9 May 1951; Rankin to Secretary of State, 19 April 1951, in *FRUS, 1951: VII*, pp. 1737–43, 1816–27, 1638–9.

28. Richard Whelan, *Drawing the Line: The Korean War, 1950–1953* (London, 1990), pp. 322–38; David Rees, *Korea: The Limited War* (London and New York, 1964), pp. 289–363; Joseph C. Goulden, *Korea: The Untold Story of the War* (New York, 1982), pp. 548–623; William H. Vatcher, *Panmunjom: The Story of the Korean Military Armistice Negotiations* (New York, 1958).

29. Pollack, 'The Korean War and Sino-American Relations,' pp. 231–2; for an imaginative account of the Chinese experience of fighting see Russell Spurr, *Enter the Dragon: China's Undeclared War against the U.S. in Korea, 1950–51* (New York, 1988).

CHAPTER 3

TOWARDS THE BRINK,
1953–1961

A new incumbent in the White House is often thought to provide the possibility for a fresh start. Although he brings inherited policies and political debts with him, in the flush of novelty there are opportunities, albeit limited ones, to float new ideas. On 20 January 1953, the new President, Dwight D. Eisenhower, was inaugurated in Washington. He had reason to be confident, not only of himself but also of his scope for new initiative. In voting for him, the American people had indicated that it was time for a change and that they trusted him, despite his lack of experience in political office. He was an optimist in his view of political society. He believed that differences between individuals could be ironed out by good sense and good will. In the same vein, he felt that there was no reason why nations could not live in harmony. The possibilities for peace seemed brighter in the first few months of 1953 than they had been for years. On 5 March Joseph Stalin, the Soviet leader whom Americans had held responsible for the Cold War, died. Now both the United States and the Soviet Union would have a new leader, and perhaps together they could begin a process of *rapprochement*. In China, the other great Communist power, there was no change of government. However, the nation did reveal a new sense of confidence. The Chinese had demonstrated that they were major players on the world stage. They had held down American positions in Korea. They had succeeded in combining mobilization for war with consolidation of the revolution. Industrial and agricultural production had increased despite the ravages of war. There were signs that both the United States and China wanted to terminate their open hostility. Despite continued deadlock in the Korean peace negotiations, it became clear that neither side wanted to see the war go on. The odd hill or field gained in battle provided neither influence nor satisfaction.

Yet in both the United States and the People's Republic of China, there were too many deep-seated resentments and inextricable commitments. While Eisenhower privately held a guarded hope for improved relations with Moscow, there were no equivalent prospects with China. In his election campaign Eisenhower had pledged to bring the war in Korea to a conclusion. If this entailed a tougher approach, then he was prepared to stake his reputation. He had no intention of surrendering on the issue of the repatriation of prisoners of war, and began his presidency by intensifying the level of hostilities. He even indicated that in certain circumstances he was prepared to use atomic weapons. He considered that the taboo against their use was counterproductive and announced on 6 May that it was time for the USA 'to consider the atomic bomb as simply another weapon in our arsenal.' The Joint Chiefs applauded the sentiment. They argued that an escalation of the aerial war in Korea would reduce China's capabilities throughout the Far East.[1] Ike did not want matters to drag on any further. In order to secure an armistice speedily he was prepared to raise the stakes of confrontation even further than his predecessor. Like any new president, Eisenhower had to establish his credentials with critics and supporters at home and with other world leaders. He was aware that he depended on the support of conservative Republicans, who would not tolerate any softening of policy towards East Asia and in particular towards China. Senator Joseph McCarthy was at the height of his power, and Eisenhower was not prepared to cross swords with him. Expectations were high that the United States would adopt a resolute policy on Taiwan and the revolutionary war in Indo-China. His principal voice was his Secretary of State, John Foster Dulles. Dulles combined his skill as a corporation lawyer with his extensive knowledge of international affairs. Like all good lawyers, he liked a good fight. He did not hesitate to move into the fray head-on. When it came to it, he did not believe there was much the new President could do that had not been done by the Truman administration. But he did believe the new administration could speak more forcefully. Fighting words would show the nation's adversaries and the right wing of the Republican Party that Eisenhower would resist communism on all fronts. There would be no doubt that the new team meant business.[2]

Both Eisenhower and Dulles were primarily concerned with European affairs. They would defend Western interests wherever they could, but they could not fight everywhere. They believed that the United States could not afford to police every corner of the globe. Equally, they could not ignore communist advances. If threats did arise in places where a conventional response was either too risky or too expensive, it would use the nuclear threat. East Asia was especially suitable for this defence strategy. The administration wanted to establish a record for toughness from the beginning. It threatened nuclear options in Korea, and made sure that appointments in the State Department went to people who had a clear reputation for being sympathetic to the Chinese Nationalists. Dulles did not want to see a repeat of the attacks that Dean Acheson had endured. The Assistant Secretary for Far Eastern Affairs, Walter S. Robertson, and the Director of the Office of Chinese Affairs, Walter P. McConaughy, were avidly pro-Nationalist. They liaised with the China lobby and always gave Chiang's emissaries a warm welcome. Chiang held Dulles in high regard, but the assessment was not mutual. The Secretary of State occasionally expressed grave reservations about Chiang. He found him unduly meddlesome and sometimes complained that he hindered the United States' management of its rivalry with Communist China. Both Dulles and the President believed they could develop an effective defence strategy against China in the Far East. They would reinforce the island chain, particularly Japan, the Philippines and Taiwan, and employ the threat of military intervention in the defence of the Pacific region. They believed that China, rather than the forces of revolutionary nationalism then enveloping colonial and post-colonial Asia, was the principal threat to Pacific stability. They maintained that if it were not for the support, material and inspirational, of the Chinese, communism in Asia would exhaust itself. China, in their view, was intent on expansion. Only the threat of military intervention would restrain it. A vigorous and energetic defence of Western interests in Asia would halt the advance of communism and would serve to free the United States to concentrate on Europe.[3]

The Chinese, for their part, did not give priority to improving relations with the United States. Their military intervention in Korea had enhanced their national self-esteem and had demonstrated that they could resist the United States in a conventional and limited war. They exhibited an outward confidence, and the evidence indicates that they were not cowed by nuclear threats. Chinese strategic thinking had always been based on the assumption that China was impervious to defeat through aerial bombing, as its population was scattered throughout the countryside. They believed that the atomic bomb was essentially a device for threatening the adversary; it was not useful in warfare.[4] The high human and material costs of the Korean war confirmed China's insistence on distinguishing between a defence against aggression and assistance in wars of national liberation. China had intervened in Korea not to defend socialist brotherhood but to fight against its perceived encirclement. It was for this reason that China's assistance to the Vietminh in Indo-China was limited to arms supply and a trickle of military advisers. The bulk of its resources was kept back for the task of economic reconstruction at home under the first Five Year Plan, inaugurated in 1953. The Plan provided for a restructuring of the economy, with output targets established for each specific industry. In the countryside the peasantry was regrouped into cooperative units of thirty to fifty households. Procurement quotas were established for each cooperative, and grain prices were set at an artificially low price in order to guarantee food supplies in the cities. Reform pervaded the army too. A large reorganization was undertaken. Professional training in conventional fighting replaced guerilla tactics. The size of the PLA was cut down. Weapons were modernized and a new professional army began to emerge. It was tasks such as these that absorbed the Chinese leadership as the fighting in Korea waned.[5]

China's efforts at restructuring also involved a visible change in its foreign policy. The period immediately after the end of the Korean war was the era of closest collaboration between the People's Republic and the Soviet Union. Thousands of Soviet advisers came to China to help with planning and construction of factories and transport networks. Chinese leaders sought to enhance their international standing by subordinating ideology to the wider task of economic reform. Zhou Enlai, Premier of the State Council and Foreign Minister, attended Stalin's funeral in Moscow and stood with the new Soviet leaders at the ceremony. At the funeral Georgi Malenkov, the new Soviet Premier, stated publicy that all disputed issues could be resolved peacefully. Zhou sought to identify China as the peacemaker and leader of the communist movement in the underdeveloped world. Afterwards Zhou went on to sign cultural and economic agreements with the Mongolian People's Republic and North Korea and forged closer ties with the Vietminh. He also took steps to establish China as a potential leader of the emerging non-aligned states. He was disinclined to embark on costly ventures involving confrontation with the United States. However, there were weeping sores that would not go away. The Chinese leadership insisted that reform without sovereignty over all Chinese territory would compromise the revolutionary process. The United States was still thought to be the greatest obstruction to sovereignty. The policies of the new Eisenhower administration did not permit the outstanding matter of the Chinese civil war, the status of Taiwan, to go away.

One of Eisenhower's earliest measures as President was the announce-ment, in his first State of the Union message, that the Seventh Fleet was to be ordered out of the Taiwan Strait and that it would no longer serve as a shield between Taiwan and the People's Republic of China. Eisenhower's primary purpose was to put pressure on the Chinese to end the log-jam in the Korean armistice negotiations. But there was also a political premium. In the past the interposition of the navy had been criticized by the friends of Chiang because it provided a defensive shield for the Chinese Communists against a possible invasion from the island. The removal of naval cover and the 'unleashing' of Chiang appeared to be a victory for the hardline supporters of the Nationalists.

The withdrawal of the fleet was certainly welcomed by Chiang. On the day of Eisenhower's announcement, Taiwan's ambassador in Washing-ton, Wellington Koo, called on John Allison, Assistant Secretary of State, to welcome the news. Koo interpreted the order as a strengthening of the commitment to Taiwan. Koo said that as a result of the rescinding of the order the Nationalists would increase the number of raids on the mainland. He assumed that such raids would provoke a retaliatory response from the Communists. This would, it was hoped, draw the United States into the conflict. Koo's views were shared by some American military advisers. The chief of the Miltary Assistance Advisory Group (MAAG) on Taiwan, General William Chase, was exhilarated by the decision. He envisaged that assistance to Taiwan would be stepped up and made specific proposals for an American involvement in the planning of raids on the mainland. The apparent removal of constraints enabled MAAG to enlarge its role in military planning and training exercises on the island. The Commander-in-Chief, Pacific, Admiral Arthur Radford, was instructed by the Joint Chiefs of Staff to conduct aerial reconnaisance, to maintain security on military bases and to train Nationalist forces. However, the Nationalists and their supporters were premature in their ambitions. The administration did not intend to help Taiwan reoccupy the mainland. Eisenhower wanted to maintain the island's nuisance value. Although American diplomats in Taipei, and especially the ambassador, Karl Rankin, egged the Nationalists on, the administration aimed to fortify the island for defensive reasons. The reunification of China was regarded as a remote prospect.[6]

The Eisenhower administration aimed to sustain the Nationalists on Taiwan without raising their hopes for an early recovery of the mainland. Dulles was convinced that in the short term at least the Soviet Union and China shared common goals and that there were no major differences in their foreign policies. He believed that there was no point in expending energy on trying to drive a wedge between them. In his view, the United States should not bank on the possibility that Mao might become another Tito figure. If there was ever going to be a serious rift, that rift would only come about by China's resentment of its dependence on Moscow. Beijing had not changed its policies towards the United States, despite changes in the Soviet leadership and the ending of the Korean war. But not everybody in Washington agreed with Dulles. The Cabinet was divided. Those responsible for the management of the nation's economic affairs did not want to see money spent unproductively. They were determined to fulfil their pledges of balanced budgets through reductions in defence spending. The Secretary of Commerce, Sinclair Weeks, and the Secretary of the Treasury, George M. Humphrey, warned that American businessmen would become disenchanted with embargoes, especially when America's allies were not applying them with the same rigour. In an NSC meeting in February 1954 Humphrey argued that America's commitment to Taiwan was wasteful and stated that he simply did not understand the nature of US objectives in the Far East. Secretary of Defense, Charles E. Wilson, agreed. He thought Chiang was 'very much like the Pretenders to various thrones in Europe and no more likely than these to recover his lost power and position in China.' He urged the President to adopt a more realistic policy towards China and feared that money was being 'poured down a rathole.'[7]

The National Security Council adopted a new policy document on China, NSC 166/1 as it became known in its final form, on 6 November 1953. That new policy reflected in part the reservations expressed by Weeks and Humphrey. It acknowledged that the Chinese Communists had established effective political control on the mainland and were confronting its economic problems. It categorically repudiated the idea that the United States could overthrow the regime by armed force, either on its own or in collusion with the Nationalists. The principal instrument for eroding Chinese power would be a policy of gradual isolation. American policy should aim to develop the military and economic resources of non-communist Asian countries and to stifle the

PRC's economic growth. The NSC recommended that the United States should continue to recognize the Guomindang government on Taiwan as the government of all China and the sole representative of China in the United Nations and other international bodies. The NSC believed that the security of Taiwan was an essential element of the US's Far East defence policy. In addition it held that the limited use of Nationalist armed forces in military operations on the mainland would serve American interests, as it would pin down the PLA along the east coast of China. Such operations, however, were not to be treated as the vanguards of a returning army. It recommended that the USA should 'effectively incorporate Formosa and the Pescadores within U.S. Far East defense positions' and that the US should make it clear that it would risk war to prevent the island's fall to the PRC. It urged logistical support to anti-Communist guerillas on the mainland and an extended programme of military assistance to enable the Nationalists to develop an army of 350,000 men, capable of offensive action. It also wished to make Taiwan the focus for Chinese living in other parts of Asia as a symbol of economic success and continued resistance against the Communists. Taiwan had to be supported, as the US could not rely on non-Chinese counterforce. If Chinese communism were to be replaced, the alternative force would have to stem from the Chinese themselves and not through American military intervention. 'Ultimately the roots of Chinese Communist political power must be attacked by the Chinese themselves,' the NSC pointed out. 'It is essential to foster and support non-Communist Chinese political movements.' But that support was not to be given unconditionally. The United States would not underwrite Chiang's government, nor would it 'guarantee its return to power on the mainland.'[8]

Chiang's government on Taiwan campaigned hard to try to lock the United States into the destiny of the island. It was aware that Japan, Britain, and its major European allies were critical of the extent of America's support of Taiwan. The Nationalists were also afraid that they might be abandoned by the United States in the negotiations at Geneva on the future of Indo-China. A security treaty would serve to anchor the United States to Taiwan's future. They argued that a mutual security treaty would simply place Taiwan on an equal footing with Japan, South Korea, the Philippines and other Asian countries which already enjoyed the protection of security treaties.

Dulles and Eisenhower were reluctant at first to follow this course.

They knew that any contention that the proposed treaty was defensive would be treated with scepticism. The recurring operations launched by the Nationalists were offensive, not defensive. The administration wanted to maintain some flexibility in its options in East Asia and did not relish the prospect of being drawn into a conflict by a blindly ambitious Chiang. But it was mindful of the power of the China lobby and remembered Dean Acheson's fate. Chiang's supporters in the Far East section of the State Department pushed persistently for a treaty, but the administration was only finally persuaded in September 1954 when the Communists, as will be seen below, began shelling the offshore islands of Quemoy (Jinmen) and Matsu (Mazu). The Chinese had initiated the bombardment in order to warn the United States of the consequences of signing a security treaty with Taiwan. Paradoxically the hostilities produced the very result the Chinese Communists were trying to prevent: the mutual security treaty. Yet as Nancy Tucker has persuasively argued, Eisenhower and Dulles acquiesced by convincing themselves that the treaty would serve to harness Chiang and remove his irritating proclivity to embark on sudden military raids on the mainland. The mutual defence treaty could be used to eliminate the destabilizing effect of such escapades.[9]

That the United States was less than enthusiastic about its Nationalist ally on Taiwan was of little interest to Mao's government. As far as the Chinese were concerned, a commitment by Washington to defend Taiwan made their dream of ultimate repossession more difficult to realize. They regarded Taiwan as the last obstacle to security and full national sovereignty. By the middle of 1954 the People's Republic seemed secure along all its borders. Relations with the Soviet Union were good. Beijing was consolidating its dominion over Sinkiang, Tibet and Manchuria. The only major threat, in its view, came from Taiwan.

As the reality of a mutual security treaty drew nearer, Beijing warned that it would try to forestall it. The existence of similar mutual security treaties with other Pacific nations made the Beijing government feel it was being encircled. In its view it had shown flexibility at the Geneva summit, where it had prevailed on the communist Vietminh to trim their territorial claims. It did not want the United States to take its conciliatory stance as a sign of weakness. On no account would it compromise on the issue of national unification. China's leaders believed that the security treaty would permanently separate Taiwan from the mainland and would create the kind of entrenched division that had developed in Korea and Vietnam. They made a determined effort to resist. They probably did not know that Eisenhower had grave reservations about the treaty, and that his administration was divided about the value of continued support of the Nationalists altogether. The Chinese leadership decided to place the status of Taiwan on the international agenda, and a new press campaign was undertaken to agitate the issue. Zhou Enlai lodged a complaint with the United Nations protesting America's intervention in China's domestic affairs. A Joint Declaration of All Democratic Parties and People's Organizations of the People's Republic of China Concerning the Liberation of Taiwan stated: 'We solemnly proclaim to the whole world: Taiwan is China's territory. The Chinese people are determined to liberate Taiwan.' However, words alone would not convince the rest of the world that the Chinese meant business. They wanted to give the new campaign teeth. So they embarked on the first phase of the military campaign, the bombardment of the offshore island of Quemoy, in order to focus attention on the issue and to gain some kind of initiative.[10]

The island groups of Quemoy and Matsu lie just a few miles off the coast of China's Fujian province. They had always been part of China. But when Chiang fled in 1949 the Nationalists retained their hold over the islands. They were heavily garrisoned and were used for the various raids that were made on the mainland from time to time. They were not only an affront to Communist China's national pride, they were also a source of instability. So when the shelling of the islands began in September 1954, the aim was to demonstrate that the irritation would not be accepted without challenge and to serve notice that the mutual defence treaty would not be tolerated.

It is now known that the Chinese leadership did not regard the bombardment of the islands as a prelude to the invasion of Quemoy, let alone Taiwan. Mao ordered the shelling in order to make a political point. He had initiated a 'Liberate Taiwan' campaign and wanted a mechanism for mobilizing the Chinese people. He did not want a military confrontation with the United States. He even had to restrain his local commanders, who wanted to escalate the operation. Mao and Zhou believed that if they did not show some kind of initiative early on, militant cold warriors in Washington would be less restrained in an advocacy of all-out war at a later date. By initiating a bombardment the Chinese Communists would demonstrate their ability to upset the peace in the area. It would be within their power to escalate or calm the confrontation. Above all, they recognized that the Nationalist regime based its legitimacy on the claim that it would eventually recover the mainland. The proximity of the small offshore islands to the coast of the mainland was a stepping-stone for this destiny. In particular, the Tachens, the northernmost of the KMT-occupied islands, were the weakest point in the Nationalists' defence line. A bombardment of Quemoy could serve as a feint for the occupation of the first of the stepping-stones on the Tachens. Beijing calculated that its siege of the islands delivered two blows at once: one to Washington's cold warriors, the other to the fragile nerve centre of Chiang's Nationalist Republic. To Beijing the status of the offshore islands and that of Taiwan was indivisible. Their insistence on that indivisibility prompted Washington to hurry in drawing a defensive line around Taiwan to forestall the projected invasion. The Chinese made it quite clear that they would try to take one island at a time in order to achieve a breakthrough to Taiwan; this seemed to leave President Eisenhower no choice but to take a stand on Beijing's terms. If the matter was indivisible then Washington would have to respond in the same vein and treat China as an indivisible issue.[11]

Eisenhower instinctively knew that he should be firm, although he was not clear as to where and how he should take a stand. He did not want to risk plunging the United States into war with China over the tiny and militarily insignificant offshore islands. China kept up the pressure by escalating its bombing campaign against other small islands and continuing to build up its military forces opposite Quemoy and Matsu. The President believed that China was preparing for an invasion of the islands, but there were warnings from his advisers and allies. The British government warned that it could not support the United States in a war over tiny islands that possessed a geographical link to the People's Republic, even if they were outside its political jurisdiction. In February 1955 Winston Churchill advised that the islands were rightly part of mainland China. In Washington the service chiefs were divided. Army Chief of Staff Matthew Ridgway insisted that the islands lacked strategic importance. Secretary of Defense Wilson dismissed the 'doggoned little islands' as an irrelevance and a handicap to the defence effort of the United States in the Far East. He argued forcefully that since the United States had decided against a confrontation with Communist China over Indo-China, it would be absurd to seek such a conflict over the less important offshore islands. He advised Eisenhower to establish his priorities. 'The real thing we ought to do,' he said, 'is to clean up the past of World War II and make a new and fresh start with Asia.' The offshore islands were a 'part of China ... We are in danger of making a great mistake about this.' Admiral Radford, on the other hand, took serious issue with his defence colleagues. He was 'firmly convinced' that unequivocal support by the United States of the Nationalist positions would serve US interests, 'enhance the position of the free world and will lead to a deterioration of that of the Communists.' A National Intelligence Estimate counselled caution; it argued that the bombardment of the offshore islands was not a prelude to a full-scale invasion of Taiwan. The Communists had a policy of gradualism, and would not risk a general war with the United States. John Foster Dulles too tended to believe that the Communists would take only one step at a time. He contended that public opinion would not support a war over the offshore islands.[12]

The President agreed. He did not want to risk war over the islands. It was better to accept some loss of face in the world than go to war with China in the defence of these small outposts. So when the Chinese Communist air force raided the Nationalist-held Tachen islands some two hundred miles from Taiwan, Eisenhower decided that 'the time had come to draw the line.'[13] He did not want to leave the Chinese in any doubt that the Americans were prepared to defend Taiwan and the Pescadores. At the same time, he would not defend every rock and every island off the China coast just for the sake of Chiang's pride. He arrived at a formula that would, he hoped, give something to everybody. He decided to let the Tachens go. The status of Quemoy and Matsu was to be kept open. He wanted no misunderstanding over Taiwan, and made it quite clear that the US's commitment to Taiwan itself was uncompromisable. He also made sure that Congress felt involved in the decisions by keeping its leaders fully informed. Accordingly, he advised Chiang to evacuate the Tachen islands and ordered the American navy and air force to provide cover for the retreat of the 40,000 Nationalists garrisoned on the Tachens.[14]

Eisenhower did not want the Chinese to misinterpet his accession to a withdrawal from the Tachens. On 24 January 1955 he asked Congress for a resolution that would permit him as commander-in-chief to employ forces for the defence of Taiwan, the Pescadores and 'closely related localities.' In the Senate an attempt was made to exclude Quemoy and Matsu from the resolution, but Eisenhower resisted the move. He did not want to encourage the Chinese Communists. In drawing Congress into the crisis the President could demonstrate to China that American policy had full backing. After three days of debate in the Senate the Formosa Doctrine, as Eisenhower came to call it, was passed by eighty-three votes to three. Congress had given the President authority to engage in a war if he saw fit and in the circumstances of his own choosing.

In fact Eisenhower had no intention of employing American forces to defend Quemoy and Matsu. He would only contemplate the use of force if it appeared that the mainland was preparing for an invasion of Taiwan. America's allies were worried that it was overextending itself. Winston Churchill was afraid that the United States would become embroiled in a war 'for no strategic or political purpose' over islands of insignificance. He was concerned that the Formosa Doctrine would embolden Chiang to begin hostilities and so destabilize the area further. 'Chiang deserves the protection of your shield,' he wrote to Eisenhower, 'but not the use of your sword.' Eisenhower justified his position in a letter to General Alfred Gruenther, Supreme Allied Commander, Europe. He explained that he faced pressure along all fronts on China policy. He could not give *carte blanche* protection to the islands. They were, he said, 'almost within wading distance of the mainland.' The United States should not be seen to be goading the Chinese Communists into a fight, especially where it was likely that Americans would 'get badly tied down.' It was important, Eisenhower claimed, to preserve the morale of the Chinese Nationalists. If they lost that morale they would not be able to defend Taiwan itself. Eisenhower elaborated on the point to Churchill. Now that the French had gone from Indo-China, Chiang's Nationalist regime was one of the last strongly pro-Western governments in East Asia. The United States could not afford to estrange him further. If America abandoned all the offshore islands, it would encourage desertions from Taiwan to the mainland. America would stick by its friends, Ike said pointedly. Britain would expect the same if the Chinese suddenly put pressure on Hong Kong.[15]

Eisenhower was determined to show that he meant business. He sent Dulles on a tour of Asia to drum up support. When he returned the Secretary of State informed the National Security Council that a Communist attack on Taiwan was likely, and that the United States should prepare itself for war. He warned that the US did not have sufficient conventional forces to fend off an attack from the mainland. He had been advised by the military that atomic weapons were 'the only effective weapons which the United States could use against a variety of mainland targets.' He told his colleagues that it was 'of vital importance, therefore, that we urgently educate our own and world opinion as to the necessity for the tactical use of atomic weapons.' A few days later Dulles began his undertaking to prepare Americans for the possibility that atomic weapons might be used. He stated publicly that the United States was prepared to use such weapons in the Taiwan Strait. On 16 March Eisenhower appeared to back his Secretary of State when he told reporters that nuclear weapons were a legitimate instrument: 'In any combat where these things can be used on strictly military targets and for strict military purposes, I see no reason why they shouldn't be used just exactly as you would use a bullet or anything else.' These comments created war fever, and there were leaks from military leaders about the imminence of war. Eisenhower was afraid that trigger-happy comments would allow the situation to get out of hand. He did not want a war: the offshore islands were simply not important enough. Like his predecessor, he was afraid that US policy was being manipulated by Taipei and its friends in Washington. On 20 April he sent Radford and Assistant Secretary Walter Robertson to Taiwan to get Chiang to tone down his threats and to reduce the size of the garrisons on the islands. He wanted them to be seen as defensive outposts rather than launching points for an invasion of the mainland. They did not get much joy from Chiang, but the crisis passed, largely at the initiative of the Chinese. At the end of April Zhou Enlai told delegates at the Bandung conference that the Chinese did not want a war with the United States and offered to negotiate. The Chinese leader probably balked at the prospect of a general war, and realized that Moscow was not providing support. The shelling eased off and by the middle of May it had stopped altogether.[16]

The first offshore island crisis ended in a stand-off, but both China and the United States believed they had gained something. The Chinese had illustrated that the situation in the Strait was not settled, and that they possessed the power to open up the question of the status of Taiwan and the offshore islands at any time. As in Korea, they had demonstrated their ability to challenge American influence in East Asia. They had secured an American withdrawal from the Tachens and had highlighted the existence of significant conflicts of interest between Washington and Taipei. They also drew a lesson from Eisenhower's nuclear threats, and appreciated that their own lack of nuclear weapons weakened them. In January 1955 Mao Zedong began discussions on the development of a Chinese nuclear industry. As for Eisenhower, he had strengthened his position by persuading Congress to pass the Formosa Resolution and had fended off the Chinese occupation of Quemoy and Matsu. His deliberate ambiguity and deception kept everyone in Beijing and in Taipei guessing. He had managed to keep the Chinese out of Quemoy and Matsu without having to specify whether he was committed to the defence of those islands. The United States and China also developed what Kalicki has called 'the Sino-American crisis system,' based on understanding through coercion and conflict. Both Beijing and Washington learned that through an appropriate reading of each other's signals conflict could be contained. Each side escalated and de-escalated the crisis with care and gave the other party room for manoeuvre. The mistakes of Korea were avoided, and no miscalculation occurred. Each side had made its point, and each side realized that mechanisms should be created to insure against future miscalculation. As a result of the crisis a new channel was opened up between the two countries. Ambassadorial talks commenced in August in Geneva. The two sides were finally in face-to-face discussions.[17]

Although the Taiwan question was probably the most serious foreign policy issue for the government of the People's Republic of China, it was only one piece in the mosaic of America's quest for security in Asia. The United States faced a more lasting problem in the crumbling colonial possessions of France in Indo-China. France's authority in the region hung by a thread: Indo-China was almost like a prize waiting to be claimed. It was a novel and indeterminate factor in the struggle against communism. There were no personal commitments or ties to an individual or a party; there was no equivalent to Chiang, who had managed to entwine his fate in the party politics of the United States. Although Eisenhower's fellow Republicans were intent on preserving a non-communist Asia, their commitment to the area was looser than it was to Taiwan. The administration had inherited a policy, drawn up by the National Security Council and approved by Truman in 1952, of preparing for war in the event of a Chinese intervention in Southeast Asia. That was clear enough. But what would happen if there was no overt military intervention from China? This perplexing problem came to haunt policy-makers as they drew Southeast Asia into America's national security orbit.[18]

The Eisenhower administration's stress on liberation and the commitment to reduce the strength of communist parties enabled the President to overcome the difficulty. He had claimed in his 1952 election campaign that containment had failed and that a more energetic and ambitious stance towards the communist world was necessary. He advocated a defence policy that would serve to deter nations from aggression and to instil within the United States a sense of confidence in the ability to force communism to retreat. In the case of Indo-China, the President believed that France's colonial policies had tarnished its claims of legitimacy. However, French authority was still preferable to an independent communist government. In his view it was the lesser of two evils. American support of the French effort could be justified, as it would stem the power of the Vietnamese communists and would act as a stepping stone in the transition from colonialism to independence within a pro-Western orbit. A stand had to be taken, as the future and vitality of communism in Asia was at stake. Eisenhower believed, as did John Foster Dulles, that monolithic communism, rather than national aspiration, was the driving force in Indo-China and was responsible for the turmoil throughout the Far East. The adoption of a firm policy of liberation would serve to deter potential aggression and also establish identifiable goalposts for the foreign policy of the Republican administration. The situation in Indo-China was to become one of the major tests of the administration's strength of will.

A civil war had been raging in Indo-China since the end of the Second World War. The Vietminh insurgents, led by the avowedly communist Ho Chi Minh, had sought to oust the French from the Associated States of Vietnam, Laos and Cambodia. After the outbreak of the Korean war, the Truman administration had committed itself to aiding the French. By the time Eisenhower had become President, the United States was bearing about three-quarters of the costs of the war effort. The French, encouraged by the anti-communist rhetoric of the Republicans and by fresh infusions of money in 1953, developed a plan to overcome the Vietminh. The level of French troops was increased, as was the number of Vietnamese forces. The best units were concentrated in the fortress around Dien Bien Phu, which was surrounded by high ground held by the Vietminh. In early 1954 Dien Bien Phu became the site of a showdown between the French and the Vietminh. Soon the French position deteriorated and French military chiefs turned to Washington for military aid to avert a disaster. The administration was put on the spot. If it intervened and sustained its repeated pledge to resist communism, it risked military disaster or a repeat of the stalemate that characterized the last two years of fighting in Korea. If it declined to bail out the French the credibility of its assertive determination would be called into question and an important strategic area of Asia would have been conceded to the communists.[19]

The pressure on Eisenhower to come to the aid of France began to build up. The French warned that they would have to retreat. The United States was eager to exhibit its dependability. It hoped that France would participate in the new European Defence Community; aid for the war in Vietnam could serve as an inducement. Eisenhower felt compelled to show his concern, but he knew that in the event of a military disaster at Dien Bien Phu it would not be possible to commit American troops. He laid down conditions for an American intervention, conditions that he knew could not be met. But pressure was building up. The Chairman of the Joint Chiefs, Arthur Radford, had on his own initiative made a tentative proposal to the French for an American air strike. Eisenhower was not ready to move so fast. He believed Southeast Asia was vital to the security of the United States, but attached conditions to any aid. Assistance would only be forthcoming if the French agreed to grant eventual independence, if the British participated, and if Congress gave clear and prior approval. He was probably on safe ground. Recent scholarship has demonstrated that Eisenhower never believed these conditions would be met and that they were something of a ruse in order to demonstrate the administration's concern.[20]

One issue that was never confronted with any precision was who, exactly, was the enemy in Indo-China? Was it the revolutionary Vietminh, was it Asian nationalism in general, or was it the People's Republic of China? In some ways it did not matter, as Dulles and Eisenhower deliberately blended these forces together in their public statements for the purposes of policy formulation. However, clarification would have been crucial if the United States had decided on intervention. If American action was designed to deter the Chinese, it made sense to attack China directly with air and naval forces, the main props of the 'New Look' defence policy. But this would have brought about another direct conflict, possibly involving the Soviet Union. Furthermore, a war with China would not necessarily have stopped the communists in Southeast Asia. The Vietminh would have carried on fighting, and the United States would still have responded by sending armoured divisions into Vietnam. A victory, in short, would have been as difficult to define as it would have been to achieve.

The administration wanted to stave off a defeat for France, but it did not want to commit American troops to the field and to repeat the Korean nightmare all over again. If the 'enemy' was nothing more than a group of zealous nationalists, the United States did not want to see China fill the void. But it was by no means clear that this was happening or that it would happen. The role of China was largely an unstated issue, though there were times when its presumed involvement was raised. For example, on 29 March 1954 Dulles, in a speech to the Overseas Press Club, ostensibly defined the region's strategic importance for the United States. He pointed out that the area was rich in food resources and described it as the 'best developed sea and air route between the Pacific and South Asia.' But he also claimed that the Vietminh's activities would not be possible without 'Chinese agitators,' Chinese 'military instructors' and the 'nearly two thousand Communist Chinese [who] had infiltrated Vietnam to support, train, and even direct Vietminh troops.' On 5 April Dulles warned the House Foreign Affairs Committee that China was 'coming awfully close' to the kind of aggression that might result in American retaliation. He accused the Chinese of providing General Giap with technical advisers, installing and maintaining enemy communications systems and supplying weapons to the Vietminh. This was the only public evidence the administration offered of the PRC's intervention. Even this official account revealed only a slight degree of Chinese support for the Vietminh's military effort. In any event, the extent of China's assistance was insignificant in comparison to the level of American support for the French and Associated States.[21]

The Beijing government must have been rather bemused by the allegations of Dulles. It rejected them outright, and accused the Americans of fabricating in order to justify intervention and to sabotage the conference in Geneva, which had been convened to try to settle the issue. They remembered that it was the Republicans who had condemned Truman for negotiating the Korean armistice prematurely. The earlier controversy over General MacArthur also confirmed their suspicion of a rift between Washington and the field. They were able to take the high ground, and with some confidence. They expressed the hope that the Geneva conference would create a better climate for the resolution of conflict in Asia. The New China News Agency declared that peace was difficult when the United States had 'not only not abandoned their activities for building a military crescent for aggression but rather intensified them.' Washington did nothing to diminish China's fears of encirclement. Two aircraft carriers were dispatched to the South China Sea off the waters of China and Indo-China. This gunboat diplomacy did not deter the Vietminh. Nor did Beijing rise to the bait. The *People's Daily* dismissed the tactics by saying that 'the American adventurist intrigues have reached highly boisterous proportions.' [22]

The Chinese knew that short of intervention on a massive scale, the United States could do nothing to change the outcome of events in Vietnam. They would not gain from further instability and uncertainty. They agreed to come to the four-power conference at Geneva, which had been convened to mitigate the tensions in Asia and Indo-China in particular. Although military success in the field obviated the urgency for bargaining, the Chinese, in particular Zhou Enlai, realized that there were benefits to be had by taking a more moderate line. At this stage in China's political and economic development prestige was more important than territory, particularly when territorial enlargement for Vietnam could pose a potential problem for China in the future. The Chinese delegation hoped to exploit the differences between the United States and its allies and to impress the non-aligned states of the world by its moderation. Its task was eased by the well-publicized recalcitrance of the United States at Geneva. Dulles even refused to shake Zhou Enlai's hand. The impact of that rebuff would linger for years. China itself was tough on its communist proxies. It urged the Vietminh to withdraw from gains they had made on the battlefield, even though more gains were a certain prospect. They withheld further support from the Cambodian communists and agreed to recognize the royal governments of Cambodia and Laos. The Vietminh were persuaded to accept a temporary demarcation line at the 17th parallel with political control to the north of the line. The Vietminh could not resist Chinese pressure – indeed, they came to resent it. Fifteen years after the signing of the Geneva agreements Ho Chi Minh accused the Chinese of betrayal. He claimed that they had prevented the Vietminh from gaining a total victory over all Vietnam, to say nothing of Laos and Cambodia. [23]

The Geneva Accords – which were not actually signed by the United States – crystallized the strategic relationship between the United States and China. Both nations accepted a *modus vivendi*. The negotiations showed that, notwithstanding America's consideration of air attacks on

Vietminh positions, both sides recognized the limits of their own power and that they were prepared to make concessions to preserve that balance. They revealed that Britain, with its own interests in Asia, was not prepared to risk what could be an open-ended conflict. Britain had also come to believe that Chinese power could be accommodated by integrating it into the international system. It could be used to sustain regional stability in Asia. The United States, on the other hand, still held that China was a force for disruption. However, it was not prepared to police the world on its own. Instead, collective action would be the principal mainstay of America's Asia policy. Even Dulles was not prepared to harm relations with Europe in the interest of Asia. China recognized that it was not in its interest to have a strong southern neighbour which could become a rival claimant for the leadership of communist movements elsewhere in Asia. Although the Geneva agreements were viewed as temporary arrangements, they marked the beginning of muted communication between Beijing and Washington. A year later, ambassadorial talks between the two commenced in the same city. The miscalculation that had arisen during the Korean conflict had been averted.

The acknowledgement of the Eisenhower administration that it was limited in its ability to influence developments in the People's Republic of China extended also to trade policy. Ike had inherited a tight trade embargo from the Truman administration. The United States had persuaded its allies to impose export controls on all communist countries, but the list of proscribed items was far greater in the case of China than it was for the Soviet Union – the so-called 'China differential.' But by 1958 the curbs on trade with China had been eased; Ike was convinced that the trade controls had been harmful to America's allies. Japan, in particular, suffered from the restrictions. The President acknowledged that a relaxation of controls would strengthen the Western economies and drive a wedge between China and the Soviet Union. He believed the controls were ineffective anyway – China could obtain goods from the Soviet Union and Eastern Europe. Indeed, some goods from the West probably still reached China. They were first exported to the Soviet Union, and then made their way over Siberia to China. However, Dulles and the Office of Chinese Affairs did not want to encourage trade and strongly opposed Eisenhower's inclination to ease the restrictions. They believed that the embargoes hindered China's industrialization programme and that isolation from the trading community gave China a sense of inferiority which hindered its diplomatic effectiveness. Above all, they wanted to give as much encouragement as possible to those in the front line of opposition to China, in particular Chiang and Rhee. There was no reason, they argued, to make life more comfortable for China by decreasing its isolation.

However, pressures grew on the administration to review its embargo policies. Most pressure came from Britain and Japan. For the Japanese an expansion of trade would assist them in becoming more self-sufficient. British businessmen were also eager to gain access to the China market. There was the added worry about Hong Kong, which relied on China for its food. Britain echoed the views taken earlier in the crises in Indo-China and the offshore islands: stability in the Far East was essential, and could be best achieved through limited rapprochement with the PRC. The British government went ahead with its own revision of the list and in May 1957 announced that the differential controls on strategic exports were to be abolished. British policy spurred the United States on. Despite the opposition of Chiang's supporters, talks about trade were begun between the United States and Britain. In June 1958 the strategic list was revised and the number of items still embargoed was reduced. The allies eliminated the China differential. Eisenhower's policy of easing gradually the pressure on China had prevailed.[24]

It was one thing to secure a relaxation of controls on the allies' trade with China; it was quite another thing to get America itself to end its own total embargo. Few policy-makers in Washington thought China had anything to offer the United States through trade. One report estimated that if controls were removed the level of trade would be $70 million per year at the most, so the economic incentives for relaxing controls were negligible. The State Department believed that an easing of trade restrictions would not have much effect on either the Chinese economy or on its domestic policies. The only feasible reason for lifting the embargo was to change the international climate. However, the State Department believed that China was impervious to suasion through diplomacy or contacts. Eisenhower found that the cards were stacked against change. The Republican Right would not have agreed, and any push for the liberalization of trade with China would have jeopardized legisalation in other spheres. The political constraints frustrated the President. He told an NSC meeting in December 1955 that American trade policy was a 'patchwork puzzle.' 'The history of the world down to this time,' he said, 'proved that if you try to dam up international trade, the dam ultimately bursts and the flood overwhelms you.' But the administration had gone as far as it could. The ban on trade remained.[25]

American liberals have always held that trade, communications and travel would serve to advance the interests of the United States through the creation of an interdependent international order. Yet it became an axiom of policy in the 1950s that there should be no economic or social intercourse between the United States and China. In a speech delivered by Dulles in San Francisco on 28 June 1957 and broadcast live on television, the Secretary of State attempted to spell out publicly the rationale of America's policy. He explained that the United States' refusal to extend diplomatic recognition, to trade, and to sanction cultural exchanges stemmed from the belief that China did not comply with fundamental standards of international law. Contrary to its repeated avowals of peaceful intent, China advocated armed force to take Taiwan, it held American nationals in its prisons without just cause and it provided military support to the forces of revolution. Dulles justified the exclusion of China from the United Nations on the grounds that it could not join an organization whose primary purpose was to renounce force, when the Chinese had employed force as a principal instrument of policy. He defended America's trade policy by arguing that trade would only buttress China's military establishment. He acknowledged that China met the main criterion for recognition: namely that its regime governed effectively. Dulles insisted that the ability to govern was 'not a controlling factor.' Recognition was an instrument of national policy, designed to serve enlightened self-interest. He was convinced that 'under present conditions, neither recognition, trade, nor cultural relations, nor all three, would favorably influence the evolution of affairs in China.' He asserted his strong belief that the Chinese people did not want communism and that Mao's regime was 'a passing and not a perpetual phase.' A more lenient policy, he claimed, would not promote the acceleration of that passing.[26]

Such speeches, coupled with America's policies on trade and travel, convinced the Chinese that the United States was not interested in closer relations. Its support of Chiang, its failure to observe the Geneva agreements in the refusal to hold elections in Vietnam in 1956, the formation of the Southeast Asia Treaty Organization (SEATO), and such personal slights as Dulles' refusal to shake Zhou's hand reinforced China's negative image of the United States. The Chinese were keen to present themselves in a positive light. At the Bandung conference of non-aligned nations, held in 1955, Zhou Enlai spearheaded a move to create a neutralist caucus of nations. He castigated the United States for being the principal source of international instability. The Chinese associated themselves with the struggles of the Third World. The 'Five Principles of Peaceful Coexistence', which were to become the benchmark of China's foreign policy, were enunciated. These Five Principles, or pre-conditions for any international agreement, were respect for each nation's territorial integrity, non-aggression, non-interference in other nations' domestic affairs, equality among states, and peaceful coexistence. Zhou cultivated and reinforced his image as a flexible, open-minded and humane negotiator. Beijing no longer overtly called for subversion and revolution in the newly emerging Afro-Asian nations. It relied on closer links through trade and cultural exchanges. Trade agreements were signed with Indonesia, Pakistan, and several Arab countries. In the year following the Bandung conference, the volume of China's trade increased by 28 per cent. The size of the army was cut back and a modern professional army emerged. In 1953 over one-quarter of budgetary expenditure had been allotted to military items. By the end of the decade the proportion had fallen to just over 8 per cent.[27]

China had become a more confident nation. Organized opposition to the regime on the mainland had been stamped out. The production of food and consumables had increased. Party membership was growing, even in the recalcitrant regions of Tibet and the border areas. Under-developed nations looked to China as a possible role model. Its refusal to cower to American power in Korea, Indo-China and Taiwan won admiration from many quarters. The main sign of this new confidence was the decision by Mao and senior members of the Politburo to relax controls over the intellectuals, even allowing them to criticize the party leadership. Mao had come to believe that the ruling elite in the party had become distanced from society. He and his colleagues were strengthened in their decision to allow freer rein for ideas by Khrushchev's denunciation of Stalin in 1956. In the spring of the same year Mao urged party leaders to tolerate more criticism and to learn more about the rest of the world, including the West. Mao looked forward to 'letting a hundred flowers bloom' in cultural matters and to seeing 'a hundred schools of thought' contend in science. Mao threw himself into the Hundred Flowers campaign. He called for people to speak their thoughts and for an end to the oppressive restrictions on schools, foreign literature and the agendas of party meetings. The intellectuals responded with more enthusiasm and frankness than Mao had counted on, and he soon realized that the tide of criticism was undermining the authority of the party. By the end of 1957 the experiment was over. Critics of the party were branded as rightists and many intellectuals were imprisoned, sent to the countryside or even shot. However, the Hundred Flowers campaign did project a sense of greater certitude. China demonstrated that economic growth and a broadening of cultural horizons were not dependent on closer contact with the West and with the USA in particular.[28]

The Chinese leadership's profession of wider horizons was paralleled by a cautious attempt to resolve outstanding issues between the United States and China. The Hundred Flowers campaign provided the framework for a *démarche*. The immediate trigger, however, was the crisis in the Taiwan Strait and the lingering issue of American prisoners held in China and the repatriation of Chinese citizens living in the United States. Both sides realized the need for some kind of structure in the tenuous pattern of communication. As a result talks at ambassadorial level were held in Geneva from August 1955 until December 1957. The Chinese assumed that the talks would result in closer dialogue with the United States and greater participation of China in world affairs. They hoped that the talks might even prepare the way for a direct meeting between Zhou and Dulles. The United States was less enthusiastic about the enterprise, and participated somewhat reluctantly. It balked at the legitimacy that such talks conferred on the Chinese and accordingly refused to elevate the negotiations to foreign minister level.

The United States was aware, however, that it could not be seen as a saboteur of the peacemaking process. Dulles instructed U. Alexis Johnson, head of the American delegation, to ensure that the talks kept going and to avoid provoking the Chinese to walk out. Eisenhower wanted to establish his credentials for 'waging peace.' However, his first objective was to safeguard American nationals and he therefore instructed Johnson to concentrate on securing the release of Americans still held in China. When this issue was resolved neither party was prepared to discuss means of overcoming their other difficulties in small stages. The Geneva talks had only limited success. The principal sticking point was Taiwan. Ambassador Johnson sought to get the Chinese to renounce force as an instrument in its claims over Taiwan. The Chinese refused, arguing that the American position was an unwarranted interference in China's internal affairs. A spokesman of the Ministry of Foreign Affairs stated in January 1956 that 'the root of the tension is the United States' armed occupation of Chinese territory.' One Chinese commentator asked: ' Since Taiwan is the territory of China, what right has the United States to claim for the right of self-defense there?'[29] Ambassador Wang Bingnan took the opportunity to denounce repeatedly the United States' continuing military support of the Nationalists. The Chinese believed that the Americans aimed to sustain a separate regime on the island for so long that eventually there would be international recognition of two Chinas. The problem was intractable. After more than two years of sterile negotiations between the two sides at Geneva the exercise was called off. Even though the talks produced only one concrete agreement – for the repatriation of nationals – they did provide a forum that enabled the two nations to gauge the other. They also served to deflect conflict from the military arena to the diplomatic. The two ambassadors got on with one another. They even invited each other to concerts, although they sat apart in order to avoid comment. Each side calculated that as long as it continued to talk there would be no clash of arms.[30]

Eventually the negotiations folded, after seventy-three tedious and frustrating meetings. In August 1958, a few months after the collapse of the talks, Mao authorized another series of bombardments against the offshore islands of Quemoy and Matsu. The crisis was in most respects a rerun of the first. There was little to restrain Mao. Negotiations with the United States were not getting anywhere, and Mao wished to show resistance against the growing level of American support for the Nationalists. The United States had placed Matador surface-to-air missiles on Taiwan and had constructed an airport with runways for B-52 bombers. There was no outward sign that the United States would reconsider its position on Chinese membership in the United Nations or on diplomatic recognition.

At the same time, with the abandonment of the Hundred Flowers campaign, a searching debate took place within China over future growth strategy. Mao advocated that increased production could be most effectively achieved through moral exhortation and mass mobilization. Private interest was to be subordinated to the attainment of full socialism. Continuing revolution was necessary, but it could only be achieved if there was higher output. If Chinese workers could produce rapid growth, their revolutionary spirit would be strengthened. Mao did not believe that political vitality and sluggish growth were compatible. The Chinese needed to be both 'red and expert,' to be able to combine revolutionary commitment with technical skill. New organizational forms had to be found that would not in any way result in the dilution of mass commitment. A new social organization was imposed, at first in the countryside, later in the cities. Seven hundred and fifty thousand cooperatives were merged into 24,000 people's communes. Private plots were outlawed. Higher productivity was enforced by imposing longer working hours. Production, households and child-rearing were all pooled to allow for a greater degree of planning, use of resources and the attainment of production targets. This Great Leap Forward, as it came to be called, was a disaster. Production figures were inflated by commune officials in order to meet the targets, and as a result of these exaggerations planners assumed that vast surpluses had accrued which were to be made available for export, particularly to the Soviet Union. Investment was given priority over consumption, which, because of the invented figures, was presumed to be adequate for basic subsistence. The result was famine on a large scale. It is estimated that the famine claimed 20 million lives. The median age of dying in 1963 was 9.7 years. That means half of those dying in China were under ten years of age.[31]

The confrontation with the United States over the offshore islands came at the height of the Great Leap Forward. There is no evidence to show that Chinese leaders manufactured a foreign policy crisis in order to deflect people from the hardships of the Great Leap. However, Mao was single-minded in his determination to make the Great Leap succeed. He believed that Taiwan, armed with American missiles, was a threat to the nation's security. That threat, which could erupt at any time, had to be removed in order to protect the momentum of the transition to people's communes. Thus the renewed bombardment of the offshore islands was undertaken as a warning to the Americans. Their policy of strengthening Chiang's regime and encouraging continuing resistance to the mainland would be resisted. It may also have been a warning to the Soviets. The Chinese showed increasing displeasure at the Soviets' pronouncements on peaceful coexistence and the projected test ban treaty. They did not want the communist world to associate the Kremlin's peace overtures with Beijing. Internal developments made the Chinese particularly determined. The revival of the people's militia, the arming of the peasantry and the campaign of politicization in the ranks of the army made it easier to open up old wounds. According to party doctrine, struggle for new modes of organization was linked to struggle against national enemies. After the shelling had commenced again the *Red Flag* commented: 'If an external enemy should dare to attack us, all people can be mobilized and armed, and made into an army decisively, resolutely, thoroughly, and completely to destroy the enemy.'[32] Mao did not expect Chiang to evacuate the islands, neither did he believe that another confrontation would force the Americans to withdraw support fom Taiwan. But he did want to show that the breakdown of talks in Geneva, together with the continued attempts by the United States to isolate China from the international community, would not merely be shrugged off. Accordingly, the bombardment was short-lived and was called off after a few weeks. Mao came round to the view that the status of Quemoy and Matsu was integral to the status of Taiwan. The one could not be resolved without reference to the other. Even if the small islands were evacuated and joined with the mainland, the status of Taiwan would remain outstanding. His long-term objective was still to secure unification. By allowing the offshore islands to remain in the hands of the Nationalists, the Chinese per-petuated the vulnerability of the area. China could still seize the initiative at any time by renewing its challenge.[33]

By the end of the decade both the United States and China had developed entrenched policies towards each other. Of the two nations, the United States was the more inflexible. It had not budged from the position developed after the Chinese intervention in the Korean war. Eisenhower was unwilling to fly in the face of the China bloc, which since 1953 was more effectively organized through its principal lobbying organization, the Committee of One Million Against the Admission of China to the United Nations. He appointed known friends of Chiang, such as Walter Robertson, Assistant Secretary of State, and Arthur Radford of the Joint Chiefs to influential positions. He did not use the weight of the presidential office to combat the campaigns by McCarthy and his sympathizers against the 'China Hands' in the State Department. His support of federal security programmes insulated him from voices that might have been critical of the Nationalist regime on Taiwan. His conviction that a tough policy towards the People's Republic was prudent was reinforced by the stories trickling out of China of mass executions and cruel deportations during the counter-revolutionary campaigns of the early 1950s. Nothing had changed to persuade him to change his mind about the direction of American policy.

However, the President knew where to draw the line: he did stand firm against arguments for removing the Beijing government by force. He rejected the high-risk strategies that men like Robertson and Radford advocated. Despite the rhetorical bluster in the first offshore island crisis, the policy of the Eisenhower administration was one of military restraint. The President believed that China under Mao had no legitimacy because of its disregard for international conventions and principles. He also contended that, because it was communist and provided support and inspiration for communist movements in other parts of Asia, China should be isolated in order to deprive it of international esteem. Non-recognition and the trade embargo remained the central instruments of marginalizing China. By reiterating the belief that the Nationalists on Taiwan really represented the mainland Chinese, the strategy also conveyed a message to non-communist regimes in Asia that American support was dependable. When Eisenhower left office American China policy was more or less as he had found it.[34]

There were voices that called for a revaluation of the policy of ostracism, but these went broadly unheeded. Some scholars pointed out that America's policy of cutting off all contact with China was not compatible with the spirit of free inquiry the United States so fervently claimed to represent. Journalists and reporters were critical of the travel restrictions imposed on them and eventually were able to persuade Dulles to allow about two dozen newsmen to travel to China to report. They argued that the United States should show more confidence in itself by permitting greater contact with China. 'An informed US public is the strongest weapon against Communist China,' insisted William Dwight, president of the Newspaper Publishers Association. There were a few isolated – and brave – voices within the State Department too, but they were easily silenced. Robert McClintock of the Policy Planning Staff warned in December 1957 that the American position was becoming politically and intellectually fragile. McClintock claimed that America's supporters overseas 'held to the fiction that Taiwan represented all China because of the strenuous and unremitting pressure by the United States.' He warned that it was only a matter of time before Communist China was admitted as the sole representative of China in the United Nations. He pleaded with the administration to keep abreast of the alterations in mood and to anticipate the change. 'Unless the

United States accommodates itself to the mutations of time, we shall find that time works against us,' he wrote. A settlement of the Taiwan issue was inevitable one day. McClintock wrote that the United States should base its policy 'more on pragmatism than principle.' The United States could only gain in stature in the Pacific region if it took the initiative and settled its differences with China.[35]

However, the advocates of a settlement with China were few in number. Their limited influence was apparent to Beijing. As far as the Chinese were concerned the United States was still hostage to McCarthyism, the China lobby, and the friends of Chiang Kai-shek. The chances of accommodation with the Eisenhower administration were negligible. Several opportunities for an accommodation had been shunned by the United States, including Zhou Enlai's peace initiative of 1955. China concluded that its options were foreclosed. If they were to be treated as pariahs they would have to look to their own defences. They would confront the United States in those areas where it threatened to upset regional stability. China's hostility was not based purely on the fact that the United States was capitalist. After all, there were other capitalist nations, such as Britain and France, with which China had a *modus vivendi*. China was hostile to the United States because it hindered some of its most fundamental national objectives, particularly the quest for regional security.

The Chinese leadership believed that American policy in the Far East was designed to exclude all Chinese influence. When Eisenhower visited Japan, the Philippines, Korea and Taiwan in June 1960 after the disastrous Paris summit, his visit was lambasted in the Chinese press. The New China News Agency reported that the tour was designed to shore up what it believed was America's crumbling influence in the Far East. It maintained that it revealed Ike's true colours; he was the bearer of 'fire and sword.' The shelling of Quemoy was temporarily resumed to protest against 'US imperialism.' A nationwide Propaganda Week for Opposition to US Imperialist Aggression, Resolute Liberation of Taiwan and Defence of World Peace was hurriedly organized. Special films and exhibitions were mounted as part of this Anti-US Week. In August 1960 Zhou Enlai castigated the United States for its interference in Asian affairs and defended China's militant stance against the United States. He claimed that it was natural for China to feel threatened by the military bases in Okinawa, South Korea and the Philippines. He repeated the charge that military assistance to Taiwan was tantamount to armed intervention in China's domestic affairs. Violent opposition to the United States was as justified as was Abraham Lincoln's opposition to the seceding states of the South. If the parallel was strained, the overall complaint was convincing. American policy was designed to undermine the Communist regime. Eisenhower's bolder peace initiatives had been directed at the Soviets, not the Chinese. American policy towards China remained as inelastic as it had been at the end of the Korean war. But China did not rue that policy. America's containment policy enabled it to lay claim as the champion of oppressed colonial peoples. If anything, the positions were more entrenched when Eisenhower left office than when he took office.[36]

NOTES

1. Memorandum of discussion, NSC in *FRUS, 1952–54, XV: Korea*, 6 May 1953, p. 977; Rosemary Foot, *A Substitute for Victory: The Politics of Peacemaking at the Korean Armistice Talks* (Ithaca, NY, and London, 1990), p. 164.

2. Jeff Broadwater, *Eisenhower and the Anti-Communist Crusade* (Chapel Hill, 1992); Townsend Hoopes, *The Devil and John Foster Dulles* (Boston, MA, 1973); Michael A. Guhin, *John Foster Dulles: A Statesman and his Times* (New York, 1972).

3. Memorandum of conversation, 1 June 1953, *FRUS, 1952–54: XIV*, pp. 199–200; Nancy Bernkopf Tucker, 'A House Divided: The United States, the Department of State, and China,' in Warren I. Cohen and Akira Iriye (eds), *The Great Powers in East Asia, 1953–1960* (New York, 1990), pp. 35–43.

4. William R. Harris, 'Chinese Nuclear Doctrine: The Decade Prior to Weapons Development (1945–1955)', *China Quarterly*, 21 (January–March, 1965), pp. 91–5; John Wilson Lewis and Xue Litai, *China Builds the Bomb* (Stanford, CA, 1988), p. 15.

5. Chen Xiaolu, 'China's Policy towards the United States, 1949–1955,' in Harry Harding and Yuan Ming, *Sino-American Relations, 1945–1955: A Joint Reassessment of a Critical Decade* (Wilmington, DE, 1989), pp. 192–5; Cheng Chu-yuan, *Communist China's Economy, 1949–1962* (South Orange, NJ, 1963).

6. Memorandum of conversation by Director of Office of Chinese Affairs, 30 January 1953; memorandum of conversation by Assistant Secretary of State, FE, 2 February 1953; Chief, MAAG to Chief of General Staff, China, 5 February 1953; memo, Assistant Secretary of State to Secretary of State, 25 March 1953 in *FRUS, 1952–54: XIV China and Japan*, pp. 133, 138–9, 144–5, 162–3; Karl Lott Rankin, *China Assignment* (Seattle, WA, 1964), p. 311.

7. Memorandum of discussion, NSC meeting, 5 November 1953; memorandum of discussion, NSC meeting, 4 February 1954, in *FRUS, 1952–54: XIV*, pp. 265–75, 355–7. For calculations about the possibility of a rift with Moscow, see Gordon H. Chang, *Friends and Enemies: The United States, China, and the Soviet Union, 1948–1972* (Stanford, CA, 1990), pp. 81-115. A useful study of the financial considerations is

John W. Sloan, *Eisenhower and the Management of Prosperity* (Lawrence, KS, 1991), pp. 20–25, 74–9.

8. Statement of Policy by the National Security Council, NSC 166/1, 6 November 1953; Statement of Policy by the National Security Council, NSC 146/2, 6 November 1953, *FRUS, 1952–54: XIV*, pp. 278–330.

9. Memorandum of conversation, 19 May 1954, *FRUS, 1952–54: XIV*, pp. 422–4. An excellent analysis of the background to the Mutual Security Treaty is to be found in Nancy Bernkopf Tucker, 'Cold War Contacts: America and China, 1952–1956,' in Harding and Ming, *Sino-American Relations: 1945–55*, pp. 238–66; Tucker, 'A House Divided,' pp. 45–8.

10. J.H. Kalicki, *The Pattern of Sino-American Crises: Political–Military Interactions in the 1950s* (Cambridge, 1975), pp. 120–31; He Di, 'The Evolution of the People's Republic of China's Policy toward the Offshore Islands,' Cohen and Iriye (eds), *The Great Powers in East Asia*, pp. 222–31; Thomas E. Stolper, *China, Taiwan, and the Offshore Islands: Together with an Implication for Outer Mongolia and Sino-Soviet Relations* (Armonk, NY, 1985), pp. 4–8.

11. Gordon H. Chang and He Di, 'The Absence of War in the U.S.-China Confrontation over Quemoy and Matsu in 1954–1955: Contingency, Luck, Deterrence?' *American Historical Review*, 98 (December 1993), pp. 1500–24; also, Robert Accinelli, 'Eisenhower, Congress and the 1954–55 Offshore Island Crisis,' *Presidential Studies Quarterly*, 20 (Spring, 1990), pp. 329–48.

12. Memorandum of discussion, NSC, 9 September 1954; Special National Intelligence Estimate, 10 September 1954; memorandum of discussion, NSC, 6 October 1954; memorandum of discussion, NSC, 2 November 1954, *FRUS, 1952–1954: XIV*, pp. 585–94, 596, 690–99, 883–7; Rosemary Foot, 'The Search for a Modus Vivendi: Anglo-American Relations and China Policy in the Eisenhower Era,' in Cohen and Iriye, *The Great Powers in East Asia*, pp. 150–59.

13. Dwight D. Eisenhower, *Mandate for Change* (Garden City, NY, 1963), p. 466.

14. Stephen E. Ambrose, *Eisenhower, The President: II, 1952–1969* (London, 1984), pp. 231–5; Kalicki, *The Pattern of Sino-American Crises*, pp. 140–47; Sherman Adams, *Firsthand Report: The Story of the Eisenhower Administration* (New York, 1961), pp. 127–34.

15. Churchill to Eisenhower, undated; Eisenhower to Gruenther, 1 February 1955; memorandum of conversation, Eisenhower and Dulles, 16 February 1955; Dulles to Embassy in UK, 18 February 1955, in *FRUS, 1955–57: II*, pp. 270–72, 190–91, 276–7, 293–4.

16. Chang, *Friends and Enemies*, pp. 137–9; memorandum of discussion, NSC, 10 March 1955, *FRUS, 1955-57: II*, pp. 346–7.

17. Chang, *Friends and Enemies*, pp. 131–42; Kalicki, *The Pattern of Sino-American Crises*, pp. 153–5. Chang has revised his views and has argued recently that 'the absence of war was due more to good luck than to effective deterrence.' See Chang and Di, 'The Absence of War,' pp. 1523–4.

18. NSC 124/2, Statement of Policy by NSC on United States Objectives and Course of Action with respect to Southeast Asia, 25 June 1952, *FRUS, 1952-54: XII*, pp. 127–34.

19. Carlyle A. Thayer, *War By Other Means: National Liberation and Revolution in*

Vietnam, 1954–60 (Sydney and London, 1989); Robert Shaplen, *The Lost Revolution: The US in Vietnam, 1946–1966* (New York, 1966).

20. Melanie Billings-Yun, *Decision Against War: Eisenhower and Dien Bien Phu* (New York, 1988); David L. Anderson, *Trapped by Success: The Eisenhower Administration and Vietnam, 1953–61* (New York, 1991), pp. 17–64; Anthony Short, *The Origins of the Vietnam War* (London and New York, 1989), pp. 102–52. For a rather different twist see Frederick W. Marks III, 'The Real Hawk at Dienbienphu: Dulles or Eisenhower?', *Pacific Historical Review*, 1990, lix, pp. 297–321.

21. *US Department of State Bulletin*, 12 April 1954, pp. 539–42.

22. Quoted in Kalicki, *The Pattern of Sino-American Crises*, pp. 101, 114–22.

23. Some doubt has been raised whether Dulles' infamous refusal to shake hands with Zhou ever happened. A learned and amusing discussion of the incident can be found in Chang, *Friends and Enemies*, fn.41, pp. 318–21. Also, Short, *The Origins of the Vietnam War*, pp. 159–62, 173; Ambrose, *Eisenhower, The President*, pp.204–10; Eisenhower, *Mandate for Change*, pp. 366–72.

24. Qing Simei, 'The Eisenhower Administration and Changes in Western Embargo Policy Against China, 1954–1958'; Rosemary Foot, 'The Search for a Modus Vivendi: Anglo-American Relations and China Policy in the Eisenhower Era,' both in Cohen and Iriye, *The Great Powers in East Asia*, pp. 121–39, 143–8.

25. Memorandum of discussion, NSC, 22 December 1955; National Intelligence Estimate, 5 January 1956, *FRUS, 1955–57, III: China*, pp. 225–7, 238–41.

26. Dulles speech, San Francisco, 28 June 1957, *FRUS, 1955–57: III* (Washington, 1986), pp. 558–66.

27. *Collected Documents of Sino-American Relations, II, part 2* (Beijing, 1960), pp. 2385–404; memoranda of conversations, 14 June, 1 July, 6 July 1955, *FRUS, 1955–57, II*, pp. 595–6, 622–4, 632–4.

28. For developments in this period see: Roderick MacFarquhar, *The Origins of the Cultural Revolution, I: Contradictions among the People, 1956–1957* (New York, 1974); Alexander Eckstein, *China's Economic Revolution* (New York, 1977); Jonathan D. Spence, *The Search for Modern China* (New York, 1990), pp. 541–73; John Gittings, *China Changes Face: The Road from Revolution, 1949–1989* (Oxford, 1989), pp. 17–35, 201–4; Avery Goldstein, *From Bandwagon to Balance-of-Power Politics: Structural Constraints and Politics, 1949–1978* (Stanford, CA, 1991), pp. 92–5.

29. New China News Agency, 18 January 1956; Tientsin Ta Kung Pao, 27 January 1956, both in *Survey of China Mainland Press*, 1956 (hereafter cited as *SCMP*); U. Alexis Johnson (with Jef Olivarius McAllister), *The Right Hand of Power* (Englewood Cliffs, NJ, 1984), pp. 251–63.

30. Kenneth T. Young, *Diplomacy and Power in Washington-Peking Dealings: 1953–1967* (Chicago, 1967), pp. 10–19; Kenneth T. Young, *Negotiating With the Chinese Communists: The United States Experience, 1953–1967* (New York, 1968), pp. 12–22; Robert G. Sutter, *China-Watch: Toward Sino-American Reconciliation* (Baltimore, MD, 1978), pp. 48–50; Acting Secretary of State to Embassy, ROC, 25 November 1955; memorandum of conversation, 4 October 1955; Johnson to Director of Office of Chinese Affairs, 21 October 1955 in *FRUS, 1955–57, III: China*, pp. 185–6, 111–12, 136–8.

31. Franz Schurmann, *Ideology and Organization in Communist China* (Berkeley, CA and Los Angeles, 1966); Meisner, *Mao's China and After*, pp. 204–51.

32. Quoted in Schurmann, *Ideology and Organization in Communist China* , p. 479. See also Chang, *Friends and Enemies*, pp. 190–92; Melvin Gurtov and Byong-Moo Hwang, *China under Threat: The Politics of Strategy and Diplomacy* (Baltimore, MD, and London, 1980), passim.

33. He Di, 'The Evolution of the People's Republic of China's Policy toward the Offshore Islands,' pp. 231–41; Gerald Segal, *Defending China* (Oxford, 1985), pp. 120–28; Ambrose, *Eisenhower*, pp. 482–5.

34. See Broadwater, *Eisenhower and the Anti-Communist Crusade*; David Caute, *The Great Fear: The Anti-Communist Purge under Truman and Eisenhower* (New York, 1978); also, Steven Mosher, *China Misperceived: American Illusions and Chinese Reality* (New York, 1990), pp. 62–85.

35. Memorandum of conversation, 18 February 1957; Dulles to Arthur H. Sulzberger, 30 April 1957; McClintock to Assistant Secretary of State for Policy Planning, 8 February 1957; paper by Robert McClintock, 31 December 1957, in *FRUS, 1955–57: III*, pp. 470–72, 483–6, 520–22, 660–73.

36. New China News Agency, 13, 14, 17, 21 June and 13 August 1960, in *SCMP*, Nos 2279, 2280, 2283, 2286 and 2320, June–August, 1960.

CHAPTER 4

A QUESTION OF CREDIBILITY, 1961–66

All newly elected presidents, particularly if they do not belong to the same party as their predecessor, claim that they will be different. Invariably they promise thorough reviews of inherited policies and ideas, followed by new agendas. John F. Kennedy was no exception. He came to the White House in January 1961 determined to project a positive image. There would be fresh faces and fresh ideas. His presidency would not, he claimed, be a guardianship, but an agency of change. During his campaign and in the transition period he had emphasized that power was being transferred not just from one man to another, but from one generation to the next. The transfer of office from the oldest elected president to the youngest would be accompanied, he insisted, by ideas and policies that reflected that change. His new programmes would differ from those of his predecessor. They would have a distinct identity. Kennedy indicated that he would maintain that freshness by dispensing with old bureaucratic structures and appointing people who were untainted by the constraints of old commitments. Flexibility, the new President claimed, would be the hallmark of his administration. In his celebrated inaugural address he gave notice that old obligations would not necessarily be honoured. 'So let us begin anew ... Let us never fear to negotiate,' he proclaimed. Those remarks, while directed principally at the Soviets, could also have applied to the People's Republic of China.[1]

Any attempt to re-examine policy towards Communist China would have to address the strained relationship of the past decade. The United States had fought a bitter war in Korea and had gone close to the brink of war with China again in defence of the Nationalist-held offshore islands of Quemoy and Matsu. The Eisenhower administration had formalized the containment of China through the Mutual Defence Treaty with Taiwan, the Southeast Asia Treaty Organization and the embargoes on trade and travel with the People's Republic of China. Any innovation by Kennedy in China policy would get a hostile reception from America's Asian allies and their supporters within the United States. Furthermore, there were few influential advocates of change in China policy close to the President. The knowledge and intelligence on China was thin. Policy-makers could point to no obvious evidence of pressure within the PRC for more friendly relations with the United States. Kennedy himself believed that China was intrinsically hostile to the United States and that it would take any opportunity to eliminate American influence from Asia.

While Kennedy continued to employ the rhetoric of dynamism and innovation in foreign policy, he believed that any change of course on China would compomise American interests elsewhere. Also there was no significant public or media pressure to alter policy. A Gallup poll of September 1961 showed that 65 per cent of people were opposed to China's membership of the United Nations and only 18 per cent in favour. Just one month after the inauguration, Robert Menzies, the Australian Prime Minister, became the first Asian Pacific leader to visit the White House. Menzies informed Kennedy that he was under pressure from the Australian left to relax restrictions on trade with China and to encourage further new links. Kennedy had no sympathy with these pressures. He told Menzies that China was an expansionist nation: if recognition were extended and other ties were opened, they would serve to legitimize that aggression. The press speculated that Kennedy might use the occasion to question America's rigid isolation of China, but no such initiative occurred. America's commitment to the international ostracism of China was reaffirmed. The Secretary of State, Dean Rusk, in a closed session of the Senate Armed Services Committee, went out of his way to demonstrate that reports of any change in the US's China policy were false. He depicted China as a 'dangerously radical nation' that preached and encouraged world revolution. The State Department would not countenance closer ties with a nation that sought to destabilize Asia.[2]

There was no significant reconsideration of America's China policy in the early days of the Kennedy presidency. Given Kennedy's narrow electoral mandate and the absence of any significant pressure to change course on China, there was no reason to make any changes. If anything, the reverse was true. Kennedy believed that the United States was beginning to lose its authority in the world. Europe had recovered from the ravages of war, and was creating independent political structures of its own. The Soviet Union possessed a formidable and threatening arsenal of nuclear weapons, and the arms race had done nothing to guarantee American superiority. The emerging nations of the Third World were not automatically choosing to align with the United States. Kennedy believed that the fibre of his country would decline if American power were perceived to be waning. Whether on the sports field, in the bedroom, or in the international arena, Kennedy wanted to be a winner.

Particularly in the early days of his tenure in the White House, Kennedy sought to establish his hallmark of firmness. In the newly independent nations of Asia, he wanted to see stability and political insurgency thwarted. The United States would play an active role in nation building. This meant that in its relations with China there would be no change of policy. He remembered how the Truman administration had been damaged by the 'fall' of China, and how communist triumphs in North Vietnam and North Korea had been attributed to weakness in America's Asian policies. An alteration in China policy would not harmonize with the general posture of toughness and Kennedy's quest for some kind of victory over the communist world. In his final meeting with Dwight Eisenhower just one day before the inauguration, the outgoing President reminded his successor that the Chinese Communists had proved intractable during the civil war when the United States was trying to conciliate between the Nationalists and the Communists. Kennedy understood the importance of first impressions. He would cultivate an image of decisiveness and toughness. Drive would be the watchword of his administration. Drive, however, would not just be channelled into the maintenance of the status quo. He did not want the United States to take on the appearance of a reactionary imperial power, opposed to all change. He believed that liberal political structures could only be realized in the emerging Third World through constructive intervention backed by power. The United States had to offer attractive and convincing alternatives to its communist rivals. Negotiations with the Chinese Communists would not, in his view, enhance America's ability to guide change, particularly in Asia.[3]

The likely direction of Kennedy's China policy could be gauged from his initial appointments. Kennedy had sought advice on appointments from Dean Acheson. The President admired the former Secretary of State for his toughness, and wanted Acheson to suggest people whom he thought would continue the containment policies of Truman. Acheson rooted for Dean Rusk and Kennedy named him Secretary of State. Rusk came to the State Department with a reputation for persistence in his defence of America's allies in the Far East. He was also a survivor. When he was Assistant Secretary of State for Far Eastern Affairs in the Truman administration, Rusk had been strongly opposed to recognition of the People's Republic of China and had advocated a strong commitment to Chiang's regime on Taiwan. He had stood firm on Korea in the military crisis of December 1950. He was one of the few senior staff in the State Department who emerged unscathed from the Republican inquisition over the 'loss' of China. His animosity to the Communist regime in China had not abated. In March 1961 he told a reporter that the Chinese Nationalists were 'a much more genuine representation of the China that we have known.' Throughout his period in office Rusk would reiterate his view that the Chinese posed a greater threat to international stability than the Soviets. He remained firmly opposed to China's admission to the United Nations, and worked assiduously for the appointment of like-minded people to the Far Eastern section of the State Department. At first, there was little significant dissent from Rusk's view. Even Adlai Stevenson, who was appointed US Representative to the UN on the basis of his reputation for flexibility, closed ranks. In the past he had hinted at his support of some kind of 'two-Chinas' policy. But when JFK asked him in 1961 if he favoured China's entry into the UN, Stevenson said he did not.[4]

Kennedy's desire to project an instant image of toughness had its refinements. After all, the march of events creates opportunities for second thoughts. A few of Kennedy's appointees exhibited a guarded and hesitant willingness to improve relations with China. For example, Averell Harriman, who had been a close adviser to Presidents Roosevelt and Truman, serving as ambassador in Moscow and Secretary of Commerce, became an influential source of advice in the Kennedy White House. Harriman was not a hawkish Cold Warrior, but a seasoned diplomat who could distinguish bluster from intent. In April he was instructed by Rusk to go to Laos to find a political solution to the fighting between the warring factions there. Kennedy wanted to prevent a takeover by the communist Pathet Lao in Laos. When Harriman returned he convinced the President that Prince Souvanna Phouma, who had been previously unacceptable to the administration, could provide a solution through a neutral coalition government. The Soviets also were in no mood for a fight, and Kennedy recognized that a peaceful settlement removed Laos from the Cold War confrontation with the Soviets. Harriman was made chief negotiator at the ICC (International Control Commission) talks in Geneva that began the following month, May. Harriman's staff in Geneva believed that a fresh approach to the Chinese might prevent the conflict from degenerating into a war of attrition. Harriman did not think the Chinese posed much of a threat. He even anticipated the forthcoming Sino-Soviet split. Harriman wanted to open talks with the Chinese and probe further in the continuing ambassadorial talks in Warsaw. The State Department objected, but he went ahead anyway. In November 1961 he was made Assistant Secretary for the Far East. In post he promoted people who advocated reconsideration of America's position towards China, and created a separate desk within the State Department for China mainland affairs.[5]

Chester Bowles, Under-Secretary of State, was also appointed because of his well-known liberal credentials and because he might serve as a counterweight to the more stuffy and more hawkish Rusk. Bowles had something of a reputation for idealism. He saw complexity where Kennedy saw, or at least advocated, simplicity. He despised the ravages of McCarthyism and had refused to change his tune to suit the inquisitors. He had shown a special interest in China and had considered the Eisenhower administration's approach to East Asia blinkered. He recognized the existence of diversity and tensions in the communist world, and believed that America could take advantage of those divisions. Addressing the National Press Club on 15 August 1961 he told reporters that China's expansionist tendency was the consequence of the ruthless dictatorship under which it suffered. The United States had to learn that its foreign policy stemmed from a political dynamic. America was ignorant of Chinese affairs. Nothing lasts, he warned; Americans had to prepare for the changes that he believed were inevitable in China. Bowles was clearly trying to qualify the hard line of his political superiors.[6]

By and large no significant steps were taken in the first two years of the Kennedy administration to review policy towards Communist China. There were no urgent political reasons for change. The pro-Chiang lobby, particularly the forceful Committee of One Million, was far more influential than the small number of people who urged a fresh initiative on the issue of contacts with the Chinese Communists. A door was kept ajar by both sides through the ambassadorial talks that were held from time to time in Warsaw. While the talks served as useful listening posts, they did little to change mutual perceptions. The Chinese government would entertain no change in policy until the United States withdrew its support from the Nationalists on Taiwan. Recriminating statements on both sides served to reinforce old attitudes. The change-over in the White House did not affect the desultory pattern of discussion. Neither side budged or seemed likely to budge.[7]

If anything, there was a hardening of attitudes. The Chinese leadership gave no indication after Kennedy was elected in November that there might be a new initiative. As far as the Beijing government was concerned, the changes in Washington were cosmetic. Kennedy's policies, one commentator wrote, 'smack of gun-power ... The reactionary nature of the new tool of monopoly capital differs little from the Republican government either in its policies at home or abroad.'[8] The Chinese believed that the new President's gestures for peace were a smokescreen. A Chinese military periodical informed soldiers in the People's Liberation Army that 'it is better to maintain a frozen relationship between China and the United States, with a continued impasse for many years.' One day, the article predicted, there would be a solution of the problems, but such a solution was far away, notwithstanding the continuing discussions in Warsaw. America would not change while it was in Kennedy's charge. 'We must be very watchful of this smiling tiger, which looks "relaxed internally but intense externally",' it warned.[9]

The Chinese leadership saw no reason to alter its policies towards the United States. The change of presidential office in Washington coincided with the ending of China's disastrous Great Leap Forward. By the end of 1960 China's leaders recognized that the attempt to accelerate the pace of industial investment and to reorganize China into people's communes had failed. They had tried to move too fast. The dragooning of mass will and energy could not and did not generate economic growth. The Great Leap Forward had created an official cult of exertion and exhaustion. It had been an attempt to demonstrate that change could be realized through inspiring people. In Mao's view economic and national development were attainable through motivation. Economic progress, he insisted, could only be achieved through single-minded effort. Such effort required socialist solidarity. It would be assisted through aid and encouragement from other socialist regimes and through a united front against the external enemies of China. In Mao's opinion, the principal threat to China's unity was the United

States. It had conspired to isolate China from world markets and Western technology and used military threats to prevent national unification. As a revolutionary, Mao insisted that America's hostility could be turned to advantage. In August 1958 he had said that 'as for the embargo, the tighter the better ... To have an enemy in front of us, to have tension, is to our advantage.'[10]

Not all China's leaders agreed, however. The Defence Minister, Peng Dehuai, attacked the Great Leap Forward for undermining modern industrial development and endangering the Sino-Soviet alliance. Mao recognized that if Peng's criticisms were accepted his leadership of the party would be undermined. His critics did not follow Peng into the fray. They lamely continued to support the Great Leap and closed ranks around Mao, who continued to insist on national independence and China's unique path to socialism. Maurice Meisner has argued that the abject failure of the Great Leap resulted in a deep personal crisis for Mao. His vision had wrought disaster. His attempts to initiate new revolutionary campaigns had been thwarted and control over the party between 1960 and 1962 had fallen to a group of men, the 'Thermidorians,' who were less interested in change than in political stability and economic efficiency. They did not want further chaos. It was time for political consolidation and a proper addressing of the food shortages that had arisen. Liu Shaoqi oversaw the economic recovery programme. He advocated the use of the central bureaucratic state apparatus to achieve a cutback in industrial enterprise and a revival in agricultural production. The reformers, particularly Liu Shaoqi, Zhou Enlai and Deng Xiaoping, believed that planning, combined with some assistance from the Soviets, would succeed in reversing the setbacks created by the blind policies of the Great Leap. It was this public abandonment of the Great Leap and the reassessment of all its implications within the Chinese leadership that persuaded some members of the Kennedy administration that it had a chance to exploit China's current economic and political difficulties.[11]

One of the first issues to confront the Kennedy administration with regard to China was the serious food shortage arising from the policies of the Great Leap Forward. The administration realized that China's famine presented an opportunity to reconsider policy towards China. In an early news conference Kennedy had stated pointedly that he would consider any plea for food, 'regardless of the source.' Chester Bowles believed that if America shipped food to China it might respond by

moderating its course. It was known that the Chinese leadership was
divided on the means of economic regeneration. Appropriate food
shipments might just reinforce the hands of Liu Shaoqi and the advocates
of bureaucratization. The granting of export licences for food would
also give the Kennedy administration the opportunity to show that it
was flexible towards the Third World, and that humanitarian considerations would play an important role in the formulation of foreign
policy. Respected academics were arguing that the stability of the regime
in Beijing was fragile, and that the realities of the food shortages
contrasted with the leadership's assertions that the needs of the masses
were always the principal consideration of policy. However, Bowles'
receptivity to the use of food supplies as a means of moderating China's
policy met resistance from Rusk and the State Department. In November 1961 there was a major reshuffle in the State Department, the so-
called 'Thanksgiving Day Massacre,' and Bowles was asked to resign.
He became a roving ambassador but he still continued to press for the
provision of food. However, the administration lost whatever enthusiasm
it might have once felt. The Chinese themselves showed no interest.
Pressure from the State Department, the pro-Taiwan lobby, and the
European desk officers who wanted to see a further wedge driven
between China and the Soviet Union convinced the President that the
time was not right for a change in America's China policy.[12]

One reason for the administration's apparent floundering lay in the
uncertainty arising from the deteriorating relationship between the
People's Republic of China and the Soviet Union. That deterioration
would have a direct impact on Sino-American relations. Difficulties
between the Soviets and the Chinese had arisen in the early days when
Mao came to power, but they were swept under the carpet as both
nations closed ranks in the adjustment to the Cold War. The origin of
the conflict lay in China's sense that Soviet assistance was usually
inadequate and always grudging. From 1949 onwards, technical assistance
and direct military aid were always less than the Chinese wanted. But
matters started to get worse in 1956, when Khrushchev denounced
Stalin and the whole cult of personality. In addition Khrushchev declared
his belief in peaceful coexistence between states with different economic
systems. He argued that there would be a peaceful transition from
capitalism to communism, and that armed struggle was unnecessary and
too dangerous. He refused to become involved in the disputes over
Quemoy and Matsu and the future of Taiwan. He made it clear that he

wanted to concentrate on raising living standards in the USSR. Consequently, he gave only small amounts of aid for the alleviation of food shortages in China. Finally, in September 1960 the Soviets withdrew all their 1,600 specialists and advisers working in China, including weapons experts.[13]

The rift between the Soviet Union and China was regarded by Maoists as a feature of the continuing international class war between the imperialists and the oppressed. China believed that there should be no let-up in the struggle. In its view there could be no compromise on the matter of liberation for the world's oppressed. Class struggle was a continuing process. In Asia and Africa it had reached a crucial stage, where the last vestiges of Western colonialism were on the verge of being overthrown. The process should not be halted in its steps. The Chinese accused the Soviets of betraying revolutionary efforts elsewhere, and announced that they would provide instead the support that the Soviets witheld. Beijing would supplant Moscow as the inspiration and guide of the world's insurgent forces. The Chinese Communists, who had long experience of years of struggle in the countryside, considered themselves a more appropriate model for the revolutionary forces of the Third World. They believed they were more attuned to the problems of Asia than the Soviets, and that they could be particularly serviceable to the Asian peasantry. Equally important, they recognized that the Soviets' possession of superior technological resources would enable them to exert greater influence. They would provide training and material assistance, particularly to those involved in insurgency along their own borders in Vietnam and Laos. Their public rejection of the predominant international system and their call for a united revolutionary front in Asia inevitably strengthened the case in Washington for continued confrontation with China.[14]

Relations between China and the Soviet Union went downhill at the end of 1962. The Chinese leadership was highly critical of Khrushchev's climbdown during the Cuban missile crisis. In October 1962 Zhou Enlai left the 22nd Congress of the CPSU early as a result of the Congress's veiled criticisms of China. Within a few months each side was openly denouncing the other. On 31 December 1962 the *People's Daily* published a stinging condemnation of Palmiro Togliatti, the Italian Communist leader, and 'other comrades' for not supporting 'class struggle on a world scale.' Oppressed peoples, such as the Vietnamese, the newspaper asserted, should not risk their national independence for the sake of 'peaceful existence.' An attempt was made to patch things up, but it failed. In June 1963 the Central Committee of the CCP issued a general statement, defending its stance against the Soviets. It stated that peaceful coexistence 'discards the historical mission of proletarian world revolution.' Socialists had to understand that the contradictions within societies characterized by oppression could not be resolved without revolution.[15]

The open rupture in the communist alliance prompted a great deal of speculation among government officials and scholars in the United States. Most specialists, as Gordon Chang has pointed out, were circumspect about the conclusions they could draw. The ideological disagreements appeared obscure, and were not easy for Americans to understand. Some observers believed that the basis of the feud was personal and that it would change once Mao or Khrushchev left office. It would be unwise to base policy on a split that seemed esoteric and that might well only be temporary. To confuse things further, the split was in part a disagreement on how to confront the United States. Analysts found it difficult to develop a strategy of accommodation to nations that based national ideology on their antagonism to American power. Zbigniew Brzezinski, then at Columbia University, argued that Soviet communism was dangerous because of its military potential, and that Chinese communism was dangerous because it promoted revolution and international instability. Walt Rostow did not want the opportunity to slide. He wrote that the split was of great historical significance and provided the USA with an unprecedented opportunity, but he added that 'no one knows what to do about it.' Since China sent no smoke signals – and the discussions in Warsaw were getting nowhere – Washington believed that until things became clearer the best course was to pursue a *modus vivendi* with the Soviets. The Chinese, it seemed, were in no mood to negotiate.[16]

There was one issue in particular in which the United States and the Soviet Union shared a common concern. Both Kennedy and Khrushchev were wary of China's potential as a nuclear power. China had embarked on an ambitious programme of nuclear weapons development. Its nuclear scientists had worked for years on research and development, with little interference from the central bureaucratic authorities. China wanted atomic weapons to counteract America's practice of resorting to nuclear diplomacy and to reinforce its own defence capability. It also wished to enhance its own standing in Asia and the communist world. The Chinese believed that if socialist countries possessed nuclear weapons, they would be safer. They also contended that sole possession by the Soviets gave the Russians power to dominate the socialist camp. The Chinese had criticized the Soviets for regarding nuclear weapons principally as instruments of deterrence. They could be effectively used, they argued, in wars of national liberation. They were not about to surrender control, just as their years of research endeavour were nearing fruition.[17]

There is evidence that one of Kennedy's motives for securing a treaty that banned atmospheric testing of nuclear weapons was his desire somehow to stop the Chinese developing their own atomic defences. He instructed Averell Harriman, who led the American negotiating team, to try to get China to accede to the treaty, even though the United States did not even recognize China. Kennedy had come to the conclusion that China presented the greater danger to peace in the long term. He believed that a test ban treaty with the Soviets might induce the Chinese to reconsider their quest for independent nuclear weapons, if only because it would make them feel less threatened. If tests were banned, the Chinese could not justify continued testing on the grounds that their rivals were testing too. The Russians, Kennedy thought, might try to exert pressure on the Chinese to accede to the treaty. The test ban yielded an extra dividend. Kennedy understood that a test ban treaty engaged the Soviets in the containment of China. They could either influence China and persuade it to join the international condominium for the control of weapons development. Or else the Russians' very endeavour would antagonize Beijing, and so exacerbate Sino-Soviet relations even further. Given the opprobrium expressed by the two communist powers for each other, it was unlikely that Khrushchev would prevail over the Chinese. Thus the test ban treaty came to be seen as an effective and potent device for isolating China and accelerating the disintegration of Sino-Soviet understanding. Indeed, Gordon Chang has testified that the United States considered joint military action with the Soviets against Chinese nuclear installations. The Americans guessed correctly that the Chinese were only months away from testing their own nuclear device: if they could not get the Chinese to sign the treaty, they would contemplate a pre-emptive attack. In the end the idea was dropped. It was unlikely that the Soviets would agree to the scheme; and a unilateral attack would draw the Russians and Chinese together again.[18]

The test ban treaty served to push back the prospect of any overture to the People's Republic of China. The refusal of the Chinese to ratify the treaty convinced the Americans that China was not interested in peace and that it was prepared to risk war to achieve a socialist millennium. Kennedy regarded the test ban as a triumph, not only because it brought the testing of weapons under Soviet–American scrutiny but because it placed greater strains on the communist bloc. The Chinese pushed ahead with their own weapons programme. A Chinese government statement of August 1963 declared that while the tripartite test ban treaty 'created an illusion of peace,' it actually increased the chances of nuclear war. It did nothing to halt the continued development of weapons. The Americans, claimed China, aimed to use smaller tactical weapons in their wars against non-nuclear socialist countries. Every country had a right to defend itself. 'So long as the imperialists refuse to ban nuclear weapons, the greater the number of socialist countries possessing them, the better the guarantee of world peace,' it proclaimed. Indeed there is evidence to suggest that the test ban treaty reinforced the hands of the military faction in China, who were intent on making the nation more self-reliant and prepared for the possibility of war with the United States.[19]

China's continuing nuclear weapons programme and the successful detonation of an atomic device on 16 October 1964, convinced policy-makers in Washington that China threatened the strategic balance in Asia. However, China's entry to the nuclear club did not make much difference to the direction of American policy. China policy had not budged in any significant way since 1950. The United States had not reassessed its own interests in Asia and continued to believe that its ties with Taiwan served to protect those interests. Successive policy-makers believed there was no advantage to be had in a reorientation. China's modest nuclear armoury was no match for America's sophisticated arsenal. The new military balance in the 1960s was not in itself responsible for the continuing suspicion of Beijing. Indeed, Washington was realistic in its evaluation of China's ability to threaten the United States militarily. It recognized that China was no match in nuclear capability. It also believed that, despite the bluster from Beijing, the armed forces were in no position to wage war against either of the two superpowers.

Washington did believe, however, that the limitations of China's military capability served to encourage it in its interventions in bordering nations. In a revealing speech to the National Legislative Conference in Honolulu on 20 August 1963, Roger Hilsman, Assistant Secretary of

State for Far Eastern Affairs, said that 'the power of China dwindles.' China's factories, said Hilsman, could not produce enough goods. Its air force was almost obsolescent and it was finding it difficult to obtain military hardware. China could not, he insisted, become 'a major modern military power ... in the foreseeable future.' Hilsman's remarks raise the question of why the United States still continued to oppose any trade or ties with China, given its perceived weakness. Hilsman provided an answer. He argued that it was the very weakness of China that drove it to assist revolutionary movements elsewhere. It became involved in insurgency along its borders in Southeast Asia for the very reason that it could not achieve any of its national goals through traditional military and economic endeavour. In December 1963 Hilsman explained that the basis of American policy was not just the defence of vital territory, but also the modification of political behaviour. The USA was keeping the door open 'to the possibility of change,' he explained. He asserted that the Chinese government did not represent the wishes of the Chinese people. The Beijing leadership dealt in phantoms. Diplomacy, he said, could not work where there was 'no ground of common interest.'[20]

America's growing involvement in the revolutionary wars of Southeast Asia in the Kennedy years was often justified by reference to China's disconnection from the traditional Cold War framework. The United States believed that the weakness of Chinese military forces, combined with the widening rift with the Soviet Union, served to energize it into intervention along its periphery. Ironically, Washington did not confront the other conclusion it had drawn: namely, that China was too weak to pose a military threat to the security of the United States.

The story of America's escalating involvement in the Vietnam conflict is well known and will not be retold in these pages. What follows is an examination of the Chinese dimension in the pattern of American decision making. American policy-makers and scholars frequently asked who the real enemy in Vietnam was. Unsurprisingly, their answer depended on the occasion and the person making the reply. One conclusion came up time and again, however. They consistently maintained that the Vietnamese communists could not have waged an effective war without the active assistance of China. Policy-makers asserted that the strategy of the North Vietnamese provided a showcase for Chinese policy. The spectre of Beijing was never far from Kennedy's mind. He believed that the Chinese saw the conflict in Vietnam as a testing ground for their commitment to wars of national liberation. He knew that the communist world was fragmenting – the Sino-Soviet split was a public affair. He also was aware that China was militarily weak. Yet despite the apparent vulnerability of China, and the possibility that Asian communists might also be fragmented, the Kennedy administration saw the conflict in Vietnam as a prototype for future struggles in Asia. The United States wanted to present an alternative agenda to Southeast Asia; but it was crucial to avoid a direct confrontation with China. Kennedy and Lyndon Johnson, his successor, wanted to contain China, but they did not want to risk war with it. They did not want a repeat of the Korean experience. The struggle in Indo-China provided them with an opportunity to counter Beijing's claim to be the protector of the Third World. Involvement in Vietnam also gave policy-makers the illusion that they could gauge Chinese thinking at what they thought was close quarters.

Washington had become preoccupied with the plausibility of American potency. The failure of the Bay of Pigs operation in Cuba and the Berlin confrontation in spring of 1961 galvanized Washington into demonstrating that American influence and power were not in decline. Southeast Asia was to be elevated into a key testing ground of US influence. If the United States could keep the Pathet Lao out of power in Laos and prop up the Diem regime in South Vietnam against the growing challenges of the communist National Liberation Front, it would be able to claim crediblity as a power that could stem the tide of communism. It could also play a formative role in political development and nation building throughout the world. As is well documented, the preoccupation with credibility grew as events escalated in Vietnam. The worth of America's commitments and the essence of its power had to be demonstrated. When it perceived failure, the United States responded by stepping up its obligations. It felt compelled to demonstrate its ability to sustain its client in South Vietnam. It also wished to show that it could overcome challenges from wars of national liberation and their sponsors.

The Kennedy administration believed that the war in Vietnam could not be fought without the aid of China. Zhou Enlai had stated publicly in Beijing in September 1960 that the unification of Vietnam was a sacred right, and that it was a prerequisite to peace in Indo-China and Asia. William Bundy said Kennedy believed that the US was the only power that could resist 'multiple Communist threats.' The vision of China, said Bundy, was never far from the President's mind. Kennedy knew he had to be careful; a rapid intensification of the conflict might encourage China to enter the struggle more overtly. But Kennedy also felt that failure by the United States to act might encourage Chinese intercession even more. A Special Intelligence Estimate of 21 February 1962 stated that the long-range objective of the Chinese communists was the elimination of US influence in Southeast Asia. They would not risk outright war for this objective but they would employ subversion to minimize the risks of Western intervention. It claimed that the Chinese were calculating and cautious in their strategy. They would calibrate their military activities to reduce the risk of counteraction by the United States. In short, the administration held that its resistance to the revolution in Southeast Asia was in part a matter of Sino-American relations, even though it did not believe that the Chinese threat was immediate. China would exhibit a persistence that would be matched by the United States.[21]

Officials in Washington believed that the North Vietnamese were fighting alongside the indigenous communist forces of the South, the National Liberation Front, or Vietcong. They acknowledged that the principal force for insurgency came from within Vietnam and not from outside. But they also insisted that the insurgency could not succeed without the aid of the Soviets and Chinese. Roger Hilsman informed Dean Rusk in December 1962 that Moscow and Beijing had 'overriding influence over any major decision' in Hanoi. But he admitted that there was little evidence of active military support. Indeed, members of the administration recognized that North Vietnam's acceptance of Chinese help with hardware was guarded. Hanoi was aware of the historic animosity between the Vietnamese and the Chinese. The Deputy Director of the Vietnam Task Force told Harriman that 'As orientals they do not naturally band together to face a common danger. This tendency to look out for themselves is accentuated by Communist training to act as separate cells and cadres.' Hilsman even contemplated a media offensive to wean Hanoi away from Beijing. He wrote to Ed Murrow, Director of the US Information Agency, that Ho Chi Minh was attempting to straddle the Soviet Union and China. He thought that support for Ho inside Vietnam might even evaporate if he veered too closely to the Chinese. He suggested that the USA should broadcast news of all visits between Chinese and North Vietnamese officials in the hope of driving a wedge between the two.[22]

The United States involved itself in Vietnam to provide a counterweight to China's claim that it acted as the standard bearer of revolutionary change. But in identifying Communist China as one of the principal challenges in Vietnam, the United States tied its hands to the policies of the marginalization and isolation of China that had been developed and laid down by Truman and Eisenhower. If China posed the major threat to peace and security in Asia, policy-makers reasoned, it made little sense to turn the tables and to explore avenues of co-operation. If it had not been in American interests to admit China to the United Nations or to recognize it in the 1950s, it was even less prudent in the early 1960s, when the administration insisted that the insurgency in Southeast Asia was being orchestrated from Beijing. China, said Roger Hilsman, sought eventual control of all Asia. America could not recognize it as long as it held this ambition. The United States had to support and encourage regimes, such as those in Taiwan, South Korea and South Vietnam, to keep alive the prospect of liberal democracy in Asia, however imperfect. The administration tended to interpret every visit, communication and export item as evidence of China's expansionist designs. They were helped in this respect by the Soviets, who managed to deflect their support of the DRV through their calls for peaceful coexistence. An army report to the Joint Chiefs of Staff in January 1963 reported that the growth in strength of the Vietcong was due to the increased level of imports of Chinese infantry weapons.

However, Washington did not think that China's commitment was without any ceiling. It did not believe that the Chinese would send regular troops to Vietnam, particularly as their supplies of weapons were achieving their national purposes anyway. Reports tended to inflate the impact of Chinese weaponry. One estimate in 1964 showed that while 20 per cent of weapons recovered from the VC originated in the PRC, 31 per cent had been made in the United States! Captured or diverted American small arms were a mainstay of the insurgents, particularly before the large-scale escalation in early 1965. By then it was the Soviets and not the Chinese who provided North Vietnam with the wherewithal to engage large units in combat. Thus while the Chinese supplied arms – in mid-1962 they had agreed to furnish Ho with 90,000 weapons – those weapons were not the lifeblood of the Vietnamese communists.[23]

The situation in Southeast Asia changed dramatically after Kennedy's assassination in November 1963. The overthrow of President Ngo Dinh Diem, just three weeks earlier, left a political vacuum in South Vietnam. The succession of governments that followed in Diem's wake were unable to sustain military operations against the insurgents; indeed government in the Republic of Vietnam had almost come to a standstill. In Laos the international agreement of 1962 was under attack from all factions and in Cambodia Prince Norodom Sihanouk renounced American aid. In Indonesia Achmed Sukarno established closer ties with China in his quest to overcome opposition to his regime. The new administration of Lyndon Johnson believed that China would take full advantage of its opportunity to exploit the turmoil in the region. Johnson was determined to uphold Kennedy's commitments and to demonstrate to his critics that he could hold the line. His immediate concern was to prevent further deterioration which, he believed, would play straight into the hands of the Chinese. He decided to intensify the level of American assistance. He appointed General William Westmoreland to head the Military Assistance Command in Vietnam and began to plan for a strategic show of force that would compel the Vietcong to give up the insurgency. The Americans became increasingly convinced that if they could not change matters in the south, they could take the struggle north. Inevitably the direct engagement of North Vietnam, with its Chinese border, confronted the administration with the prospect of direct hostilities with China.[24]

Until 1964 the United States had developed a policy which, it believed, minimized the risk of engagement with the People's Republic of China. Despite their implication of China, Kennedy and Johnson did not want to see an internationalization of the war. They were sufficiently confident that they would avoid the errors made in the Korean conflict. When the situation deteriorated in the South, military planners continued to advise that the United States could risk escalation without fear of a parallel intervention by China. They contended that China was not prepared to risk its own development programmes for an uncertain foray into an area which had shown hostility to its Chinese neighbour in the past. At a conference in Honolulu in June 1964 various contingency plans for air strikes were discussed and planned. The Joint Chiefs urged the administration to take bolder risks in Indo-China. General Maxwell Taylor claimed that he did not visualize a 'yellow horde' of Chinese pouring into Southeast Asia. CIA Director John McCone was less confident. He warned that China would feel threatened by an escalation in the air. However, his view did not prevail. McNamara supported Taylor's contingency plans, and insisted that a Chinese intervention was improbable.[25]

When Congress passed the Gulf of Tonkin resolution authorizing the President to 'take all necessary measures to repel any armed attacks' on 7 August 1964, the plans for the bombing of the North were activated. President Johnson's decision to seek Congressional authorization for an escalation of the conflict was based on his continued conviction that the Chinese would not intervene with their armed forces. He did not see the war in Vietnam as simply a war of containment, and assumed that China would see it that way too. It was a war that sought to establish the credibility of the United States as a military power, as an ally, and as the standard bearer of a liberal order. The US would provide an alternative to revolutionary socialism in Asia. Lyndon Johnson recognized that aerial warfare and the dispatch of ground troops raised the level and the degree of the American commitment. But in his view, the escalation of means did not mean that his objectives had changed. He was anxious to convey to Beijing that he regarded the intervention as limited in its goals. The Chinese, Walt Rostow told McNamara, 'should feel they now confront an LBJ who has made up his mind ... I believe it quite possible to communicate the limits as well as the seriousness of our intentions.'[26] Johnson himself told Walter Cronkite in a CBS interview in 1970 that he had asked Congress for a resolution rather than a declaration of war, in case North Vietnam had a secret defence treaty with China that required it to go to its assistance in the event of war. Johnson wanted to demonstrate the seriousness of his intentions, but he wanted to calibrate the military response. He authorized the air strikes that had been planned. However, US aircraft and naval ships were instructed to target North Vietnamese craft and not their bases. The Commander-in-Chief, Pacific Fleet (CINCPAC) had orders to ensure that all naval aircraft flew at least fifty miles from Chinese territory and that North Vietnam was the sole object of retaliation. But the Defense Department recognized that things could go wrong and that it might miscalculate for a second time since 1950. It developed plans for a possible war with China. If China did attack American bases, the US would retaliate. The plans, codenamed OPLAN 32–64 and 39–65, provided for 'massive US naval and air power against Communist China and her satellites' and 'either non-nuclear or nuclear options.'[27]

By the beginning of 1965 Johnson and his advisers agreed that continuing instability in the South justified a sustained bombing campaign against the North. Operation Rolling Thunder, a programme of gradually intensified air attacks, was undertaken. The bombing had little effect. Unsurprisingly, communist forces initiated reprisals and began to attack the air bases from which the aircraft took off on their bombing missions. The Joint Chiefs and the Defense Department called for ground combat troops in retaliation against NLF raids and to defend American military personnel. Washington's policy-makers would not countenance the prospect of a defeat of the Republic of Vietnam. Credibility became the justification that unified all the major players. They were confident that American power and example would stem the tide of communist insurgency. An escalation of the American commitment would buy time for the Republic of Vietnam (RVN) and convince the communists that they could not win. The Joint Chiefs of Staff argued that with sufficient ground troops the United States could even defeat them. Johnson agreed in principle and in July 1965 announced that he had authorized the sending of 50,000 additional troops to Vietnam. He knew that these would not be enough, but did not want to admit that an open-ended commitment would endanger the Great Society programme and that it might open up the prospect of a long, drawn-out war.

Johnson escalated gradually; by the end of 1965 there were nearly 185,000 troops in Vietnam. He did not reveal his anxiety that the involvement would spiral for one other reason. He did not want to provoke the Soviet Union or China into action of their own. Military policy was devised in such a way that there was no one step that could be singled out as the threshold of a larger war. The administration's main objective was to display its determination to uphold the Saigon regime. It believed that if it failed, the main beneficiary would be China.

Dean Rusk, the Secretary of State, believed that China's revolutionary ideology would threaten peace and welfare in Asia. If its record were kept in the limelight, its claim to leadership would, he believed, be rejected. China's credibility as a viable force for the Third World had to be challenged. China had opened up hostilities against India in 1962, had refused to renounce the use of force in the Taiwan Strait, had not observed the accords on Laos, and had refused to sign the nuclear test ban treaty. Above all, it had broken with Moscow on the grounds that the Soviets were too conciliatory and were prepared to renounce the use of violence in the overthrow of capitalism. The movement towards recognition and the eventual admission to the United Nations was growing in the international community. Beijing was campaigning actively to achieve leadership among the newly independent nations. In January 1964 Premier Zhou Enlai toured Africa and secured recognition from fourteen African nations. In the same month France recognized the PRC. Dean Rusk was furious, and condemned France on the grounds that it encouraged China's policy of supporting national liberation movements. He rejected the view it would be easier to deal with China if it were a member of the UN. In October 1964 China successfully detonated its first atomic device and could claim great power status. Rusk was convinced that the United States should continue to try to deny China international legitimacy. After the November elections Rusk expressed his frustration with the ambassadorial talks and said they had got nowhere; recognition would constitute a betrayal of Taiwan and would reward China's support of armed insurgency. China's militant championship of world revolution would 'destroy the structure of international life as written into the United Nations Charter.' He believed that America's military might had forced the Soviet Union to moderate. The same policies would have to be employed with China.[28]

One reason that Washington made Vietnam a test case of its resolve was that, in its view, China was doing the same. The United States would not only match China; through an intervention in Vietnam it would expose China's fragility and isolate it from its potential allies. The application of American power in Vietnam would demonstrate to the Chinese the dangers of continuing confrontation, just as the Cuban missile crisis had convinced the Kremlin of the need to establish a working relationship with the United States. Dean Rusk stated on the *Today* programme in January 1967 that 'if the second generation in China can show some of the prudence that the second generation in the Soviet Union show, then, maybe, we can begin to build a durable peace there.' Robert McNamara was equally insistent that China held the key to peace in Southeast Asia. He stated that the US was not dealing with the last remains of a colonial struggle in Vietnam. Communist China, he stated, 'publicly castigated Moscow for betraying the revolutionary cause whenever the Soviets sounded a cautionary note. It has characterized the United States as a paper tiger and has insisted that the revolutionary struggle ... could be fought without risks ... Peiping thus appears to feel that it has a large stake in demonstrating the new strategy, using Vietnam as a test case.' Thus 'the stakes in South Vietnam are far greater than the loss of one small country to communism.'

Officials did not believe that China posed an immediate threat; they were aware that the North Vietnamese were in receipt of aid from Moscow too and that China's military capability was limited. 'A unified mainland China today,' said William Bundy, threatened Asia 'not necessarily drastically, or at once.' The threat was slow and inexorable 'through the technique of spurious national movements.'[29]

However, some officials in Washington began to argue that the element of patience in China's military philosophy provided the United States with an opportunity to reconsider America's policy towards China. They did not understand at the time that China's hesitant support of the Vietnamese insurgents was motivated by its desire to deny the Soviets an incentive for arming the North. The administration believed that China was just playing for time. It was waiting for the enemy to be ground down slowly in a drawn-out people's war.

The United States could use the same breathing space to see if there was some room for manoeuvre. Policy-makers also could not ignore the fact that support in the United Nations General Assembly for the admission of China was growing. In February 1965 Marshall Green, Assistant Secretary of State for Far Eastern Affairs, told a conference on Sino-American relations at Princeton that while American policy in Vietnam sought to convince China that 'its external adventures are risky,' the United States wanted to develop policies that would nurture change within China. Restrictions on postal deliveries and travel for newsmen were to be eased. The government, he said, was exploring new ways to open up contacts, but he warned that 'it takes two to tango.' Dean Rusk, who had been most vigorous in laying the fault for the war in Vietnam at the feet of China, stated that Chinese leaders 'have been somewhat more cautious and prudent in their actions than they have been in their words.' A number of small changes were made in order to show that the United States was not completely inflexible. In 1966 American officials began referring to China's capital as Peking [Beijing], rather than Peiping, the term favoured by the Nationalists. In the spring of 1966 China indicated to Washington that it would not become involved in Vietnam, provided that the United States refrained from invading North Vietnam and bombing the North's Red River dikes. Johnson signalled acceptance of these conditions, and in a major speech in July 1966 he revealed his hope that contacts between Washington and Beijing would increase in time.[30]

The small shift in tone by the administration mirrored the change in some other areas of American public life towards China. In 1966 the Council on Foreign Relations brought a three-year project on Sino-American relations to a conclusion. The consensus of opinion was that the United States should review its policies. In March 1966 the Senate Foreign Relations committee held extensive hearings on the adminis-tration's China policy. The Democratic chairman of the committee, J. William Fulbright of Arkansas, reflected that China's supposed militancy might well be the result of past 'ravages of the West.' If that was the case the West should perhaps act to reassure China that the imperial ambitions of the nineteenth and early twentieth centuries no longer applied. A number of distinguished academics and public officials testi-fied, and the majority echoed Fulbright's sentiment and called for a reassessment of American policy. A. Doak Barnett warned that it was difficult for China to disentangle America's involvement in Vietnam from earlier western intrusions in East Asian affairs. John Fairbank, probably America's most distinguished historian of China, warned that the United States had failed to understand China's sense of wounded pride. 'Ameri-cans were conscious of their own good intentions,' he testified, 'and less conscious of the humiliation that their superior circumstances often inflicted upon their Chinese friends.' The Chinese saw America's involve-ment in Vietnam as just another version of American interventionism. Morton Halperin defended America's involvement in Vietnam, but warned that China needed assurance that it was not the ultimate target of the war. Donald Zagoria said that America's tactics of leaning on China to use its influence to persuade the North Vietnamese to seek a negotiated settlement was based on a fundamental misunderstanding. The Vietnam conflict gave the Chinese an opportunity to weaken the US by protracting the war. Hans Morgenthau said it was pointless to try to undermine Chinese influence in Asia. If the USA wanted to contain Beijing it should employ the same means that it used against the Kremlin: namely, the threat of nuclear war. Fighting wars on its peri-phery was bound to raise the level of China's nervousness about America's intentions.[31]

By 1966, when the Senate hearings were conducted, China appeared to be fully committed to the NLF's war effort in Vietnam. When the first major contingent of American troops was dispatched to South Vietnam in the summer of 1965, China responded by increasing the flow of aid to the North. Some one thousand tons of supplies began to arrive daily from China; at the time this was equivalent to about one-third of all the country's external aid. The bulk of North Vietnam's military hardware reached it through the rail link with China, though a substantial proportion of the deliveries originated in the Soviet Union. Chinese troops moved to the border and Chinese repair crews kept the vital rail link to the Democratic Republic of Vietnam open. By the spring of 1966 the PRC had dispatched some 50,000 military personnel, mainly engineers and maintenance staff, to the area as part of its commitment to the North's cause. It also began its little-known programme of investment in military industries in the mountainous inland region of the Southwest as part of a 'third front' policy of securing itself against an American threat from Vietnam. Yet it is important to note that these deployments were not publicized. As will be seen, China wished to show solidarity with North Vietnam, but it did not wish to be drawn into a major and uncontrolled conflict. Mao believed that the greatest threat to his country's military security came from the Soviet Union, not from the United States. Within two years he authorized investment in military industries to be switched to the northern border areas. He was afraid that a military confrontation with the United States would divert resources from the Soviet front. He also did not want the People's Liberation Army to be further empowered, as that might strengthen the hands of his political rivals.[32]

China urged the insurgents to intensify the struggle against the government of South Vietnam and its American protectors. It did so not only to pursue its goal of a socialist world order but also because it perceived that America's intensification of the war in Indo-China, and especially the bombing of the North, presented a new threat to its security. American action seemed to confirm its canon that the United States sought hegemony in the region. It had no reason to trust Washington's reassurances that it would not extend the war to mainland China. It believed that a new phase in the struggle had begun and that China could demonstrate the effectiveness of its military doctrines, as well as its claim to the leadership of the socialist Third World. Lo Ruiqing, Chief of Staff in the Chinese People's Liberation Army, wrote in the *Red Flag*, the CCP's main theoretical journal, that China could place no faith in reassurances and deals. The interest of the world proletarian revolution dictated that China should assist all revolutionary struggles. The struggle in Vietnam would affirm the efficacy of the doctrine of people's war. 'Victory in war,' he wrote, 'does not depend on new weapons of one kind or another, or on a particular technical arm. It depends on the close integration of the armed forces and the civilian masses, the joint efforts of the people at the front and in the rear ... All revolutionary wars support each other.' He reassured the Vietnamese that China was 'prepared to send our men to fight together with the people of Vietnam when they need us.' In March 1966, when Kemusu Suharto's generals successfully led the coup in Indonesia against Sukarno, China's strategy of heading a new communist axis in Asia suffered a serious setback. As a result, the Chinese elevated the importance of the struggle in Vietnam even more. In their opinion it offered the last and best opportunity to bring about a serious defeat of the Americans in Asia.[33]

Despite the special encouragement from China, North Vietnam accepted assistance from the Soviet Union too. Hanoi regretted the schism between the Soviets and the Chinese, particularly since strategy in the Vietnam war was one of the root causes of that division. However, Hanoi also realized that Sino-Soviet disunity could be converted into an advantage. It needed supplies from both Moscow and Beijing. It tried to disengage itself from the polemics that were being fired across the bows. In May 1965, only three months after Soviet Premier Aleksei Kosygin had visited Hanoi, Ho Chi Minh travelled to Beijing to arrange for the continuing flow of arms deliveries. The North Vietnamese valued Chinese support. They knew that the various bombing halts called by Washington were done in the hope of securing the mediation of Moscow, which wanted to see an end to the escalation in Indo-China. As their objective was national unification, they did not intend to give up the fight. A document belonging to the Central Office for the South Vietnam Communist Party showed that the NLF also endorsed China's strategy of continuing the fight. General Nguyen Vinh of the Lao Dong (Workers) Party told his men 'to bog down the enemy, and [to] wait until a number of socialist countries acquire adequate conditions for strengthening their main force troops to launch a strong, all-out, and rapid offensive. ... What we should do in the South today is to try restraining the enemy and make him bogged down, waiting until China has built strong forces to launch an all-out offensive.' The evidence for a planned Chinese intervention was thin, but General Vinh's speech demonstrates the importance given to the prospect of active military assistance from China.[34]

The war in Vietnam was something of a test for Mao's military doctrine. Inevitably, perhaps, the Vietnamese insurgency prompted the

Chinese to re-examine the application of its own revolutionary ideology. On 3 September 1965, the twentieth anniversary of China's V-J Day, China's Defence Minister, Lin Biao, published his *Long Live the Victory of People's War!* Lin Biao's polemical essay drew on the experiences of the Chinese Communist resistance to Japan in the Second World War to highlight the options open to the Vietnamese in their struggle against the United States. The Vietnamese, said Lin, should imitate Chinese strategy. China had relied on the tenaciousness of its peasantry for victory in the 'people's war.' He repeated Mao's adage that 'all reactionaries are paper tigers,' and predicted that the persistence of the NLF would bring victory, irrespective of the superiority in weapons technology of the enemy. 'No force,' he wrote, 'can alter its general trend towards inevitable triumph.' He believed that America's intervention in Vietnam actually helped the cause of international socialism. 'The more they expand the war,' he continued, 'the greater will be the chain reaction. The more they escalate the war, the heavier will be their fall and the more disastrous their defeat. The people in other parts of the world will see still more clearly that US imperialism can be defeated, and that what the Vietnamese people can do, they can do too.' He promised that the support of China was 'unshakable' and that it would back the Vietnamese people until 'every single one of the U.S. aggressors is driven out of Vietnam.'[35]

Lin Biao's document appeared on the surface to be an uncompromising and open-ended offer of support to the Vietnamese communists. But a closer reading shows that its main message was that revolutionaries should be self-reliant. *Long Live the Victory of People's War!* was saying that victory would come about through persistence and the conjunction of military and political organizations. People's war would result in ultimate victory. Peace negotiations were pointless, as they would surrender a victory that would inevitably come. Chinese intervention was unnecessary, as was the military assistance of the Soviet Union. Lin was indicating that China could make a strategic withdrawal without sacrificing the prospect of victory. A retreat from others' wars of liberation would enable China to concentrate on its own developments.[36]

However, for most policy-makers in Washington *Long Live the Victory of People's War!* confirmed their worst fears about China. Parallels were drawn with Hitler's *Mein Kampf*. Averell Harriman believed that Lin's work showed 'what the intentions of Communist China are, what sort of world it wants, and how that world is to be created.' Arthur Gold-berg, US Representative to the United Nations, described it as a 'modern imperialism ... the antithesis of everything this organization [the UN] stands for.' So just as pressure was building up within selected circles in the United States for a reassessment of American policy, the People's Republic of China itself was about to embark on the greatest internal convulsion of its mercurial history. Washington interpreted Lin's document as the start of a new stage in communist militancy.[37]

Notwithstanding anxiety in the United States, the plain truth was that Mao had no intention of going to war with the United States over Vietnam. Indeed, some commentators have argued that it was an opening salvo by Mao for a *modus vivendi* with the United States! Mao felt that his power was actually dwindling. Drift within the national leadership, together with the setbacks in Indonesia and Vietnam, made Mao turn inwards for political strength. China was about to plunge into its own chaotic experience of militant self-reliance, the Cultural Revolution. What Washington did not immediately realize was that this new phase of revolutionary zeal, inspired by Mao Zedong, also marked the begin-ning of a new period of self-imposed isolation. The doctrine of people's war was a doctrine of self-reliance. For China that would mean a concentration on domestic issues and a change in strategic orientation. Revolutionary movements overseas would receive moral encouragement, but little more. Its hostility to the Soviet Union would reach new heights. Ironically, China's prospective retreat would make it easier for the United States to oppose small-scale people's wars. Yet like China, the United States would experience its own version of domestic upheaval. On the eve of those disturbances, neither nation believed that the barriers between them could be bridged. However, one of the ironies of their troubled affair was that the two countries, shaken by the divisions within their own societies, would emerge from the turbulence convinced that a rapprochement would now serve their interests.[38]

NOTES

1. Pierre Salinger, *With Kennedy* (London, 1967), pp. 63–80; Theodore C. Soren-sen, *Kennedy* (New York, 1965), pp. 227–51; David Burner, *John F. Kennedy and a New Generation* (Boston, MA, 1980), pp. 57–65; Edwin O. Guthman and Jeffrey Shulman, *Robert Kennedy: In His Own Words: The Unpublished Recollections of the*

Kennedy Years (New York, 1988), pp. 33–57; David Brinley, 'The New Men', in Lester Tanzer, *The Kennedy Circle* (New York, 1961), pp. xi–xix.

2. Timothy Maga, 'Pay any Price, Bear Any Burden: John F. Kennedy and Sino-American Relations, 1961–1963', in Priscilla Roberts (ed.), *Sino-American Relations Since 1900* (Hong Kong, 1991), pp. 469–74; Leonard A. Kusnitz, *Public Opinion and Foreign Policy: America's China Policy, 1949–1979* (Westport, 1984), pp. 97–100; James C. Thomson, Jr., 'On the Making of U.S. China Policy, 1961–1969: A Study in Bureaucratic Politics,' *China Quarterly*, 50 (April–June 1972), pp. 221–2.

3. Arthur Schlesinger Jr., *A Thousand Days: John F. Kennedy in the White House* (London, 1965), pp. 148, 193; Thomas G. Paterson, 'Introduction: John F. Kennedy's Quest for Victory and Global Crisis,' in Thomas G. Paterson (ed.), *Kennedy's Quest for Victory: American Foreign Policy, 1961–1963* (New York and Oxford, 1989), p. 10; Richard J. Walton, *Cold War and Counterrevolution* (New York, 1972), pp. 34–8; Thomas Brown, *JFK: History of an Image* (Bloomington, 1988), pp. 6–23; Michael R. Beschloss, *Kennedy v. Khrushchev: The Crisis Years, 1960–63* (London, 1991), pp. 42–4, 63–5; Thomas Reeves, *A Question of Character: A Life of John F. Kennedy* (London, 1991), pp. 221–44.

4. Herbert S. Parmet, *JFK: The Presidency of John F. Kennedy* (Harmondsworth, 1984), p. 67; Walter Isaacson and Evan Thomas, *The Wise Men: Six Friends and the World They Made* (New York, 1986), pp. 589–94; James Fetzer, 'Clinging to Containment: China Policy,' in Paterson (ed.), *Kennedy's Quest for Victory*, pp. 180–81; Rusk reply, 3 March 1961, U.S. Department of State, *American Foreign Policy: Current Documents, 1961* (Washington, DC, 1965), p. 946.

5. Isaacson and Thomas, *The Wise Men*, pp. 616–18; Theodore C. Sorensen, *Kennedy* (New York, 1965), p. 643; Parmet, *JFK*, pp. 131–55; also, Kenneth T. Young, 'American Dealings with Peking,' *Foreign Affairs*, 45 (October 1966), pp. 77–87; Robert Blum, *The United States and China in World Affairs* (New York and London, 1966), pp. 126–8.

6. Gordon H. Chang, *Friends and Enemies: The United States, China, and the Soviet Union, 1948–1972* (Stanford, CA, 1990), pp. 217–20; David Halberstam, *The Best and the Brightest* (New York, 1972), pp. 22–31; Chester Bowles, 'Is Communist Ideology Becoming Irrelevant?' *Foreign Affairs*, July 1962, vol. 40, pp. 553–65.

7. Kenneth T. Young, *Negotiating with the Chinese Communists: the United States Experience, 1953–1967* (New York and London, 1968), pp. 236–48; A. T. Steele, *The American People and China* (New York and London, 1966), pp. 221–5; also, Stanley D. Bachrack, *The Committee of One Million: 'China Lobby' Politics, 1953–1971* (New York, 1976).

8. Kuang-ming Jih-pao in *Survey of China Mainland Press*, 18 November 1960.

9. Harold C. Hinton (ed.), *The People's Republic of China, 1949–1979: A Documentary Survey, II, 1957–1965: The Great Leap Forward and its Aftermath* (Wilmington, DE, 1980), pp. 898–902; A. M. Halpern, 'Communist China's Foreign Policy: The Recent Phase,' *China Quarterly*, 11, July–September 1962, pp. 89–104.

10. 'Talks at the Beidaihe Conference, 17 August 1958', in Roderick MacFarquhar, Timothy Cheek and Eugene Wu, *The Secret Speeches of Chairman Mao: From the Hundred Flowers to the Great Leap Forward* (Cambridge, MA, 1989), pp. 402–3; Lynn T. White, *Policies of Chaos: The Organizational Causes of Violence in China's Cultural*

Revolution (Princeton, NJ, 1989), pp. 148–79; also, Franz Schurmann, *Ideology and Organization in Communist China* (Berkeley, CA, and Los Angeles, 1966).

11. Maurice Meisner, *Mao's China and After: A History of the People's Republic,* rev. edn (New York, 1986), pp. 257–72; Lowell Dittmer, *Liu Shao-ch'i and the Chinese Cultural Revolution: The Politics of Mass Criticism* (Berkeley and Los Angeles, CA, 1974), pp. 42–4.

12. Kennedy news conference, 25 January 1961 in *American Foreign Policy, 1961*, p. 945; Hans Morgenthau, 'The Roots of America's China Policy'; Michael Lindsay, 'A New China Policy: Difficulties and Possibilities,' both in *China Quarterly,* 10, April–June 1962, pp. 45–50, 56–63; Roger Hilsman, *To Move a Nation: The Politics of Foreign Policy in the Administration of John F. Kennedy* (New York, 1967), p. 317; Chiao Chiao Hsieh, *Strategy for Survival: The Foreign Policy and External Relations of the Republic of China on Taiwan, 1949–79* (London, 1985), p. 129; John M. Newman, *JFK and Vietnam: Deception, Intrigue, and the Struggle for Power* (New York, 1992), p. 141.

13. Particularly useful for the background of the Sino-Soviet dispute are Donald Zagoria, *The Sino-Soviet Conflict, 1956–1961* (Princeton, NJ, 1962); Donald Treadgold, ed., *Soviet and Chinese Communism: Similarities and Differences* (Seattle, WA, 1967); Herbert J. Ellison, ed., *The Sino-Soviet Conflict: A Global Perspective* (Seattle, WA, 1982); Roy Medvedev, *China and the Superpowers* (Oxford, 1986).

14. Robert A. Scalapino, 'Moscow, Peking and the Communist Parties of Asia', *Foreign Affairs,* 41, Jan. 1963, pp. 323–43; Zbigniew Brzezinski, 'Peaceful Engagement in Communist Disunity,' *China Quarterly,* 10, April–June 1962, pp. 64–71; Michael B. Yahuda, *China's Role in World Affairs* (London, 1978), pp. 23–9; Richard Lowenthal, 'Communist China's Foreign Policy,' in Tang Tsou (ed.), *China in Crisis, II: China's Policies in Asia and America's Alternatives* (Chicago, IL, 1968), pp. 2–3.

15. *People's Daily,* 31 December 1962; letter, Central Committee of CCP to Central Committee of CPSU, 14 June 1963, in Hinton, ed., *PRC: Documentary Survey, 1949–79, II,* pp. 1056–62, 1121–35; F. Charles Parker IV, *Vietnam: Strategy for a Stalemate* (New York, 1989), pp. 19–33.

16. Chang, *Friends and Enemies,* pp. 217–21; Zbigniew Brzezinski, 'Threat and Opportunity in the Communist Schism,' *Foreign Affairs,* 41, January 1963, pp. 513–25.

17. John Wilson Lewis and Xue Litai, *China Builds the Bomb* (Stanford, CA, 1988), pp. 223–6; Morton H. Halperin, 'China and the Bomb: Chinese Nuclear Strategy,' *China Quarterly,* 21, January–March 1965, pp. 74–86; Samuel B. Griffith II, 'Communist China's Capacity to Make War,' *Foreign Affairs,* 43, January 1965, pp. 217–36.

18. Chang, *Friends and Enemies,* pp. 228–52; Schlesinger, *A Thousand Days,* pp. 771–6; Medvedev, *China and the Superpowers* , pp. 39–40.

19. Statement in Hinton (ed.), *PRC, 1949–79: A Documentary Survey, II,* pp. 1137–41; Glenn T. Seaborg and Benjamin S. Loeb, *Kennedy, Khrushchev, and the Test Ban* (Berkeley, CA, 1981), pp. 180–82; Peter Kien-hong Yu, *A Strategic Model of Chinese Checkers: Power and Exchange in Beijing's Interactions with Washington and Moscow* (New York, 1984), pp. 64–8.

20. Hilsman, Address before the Legislative Conference, Honolulu, 20 August 1963; Hilsman, Address before the Commonwealth Club, 13 December 1963 in *American Foreign Policy, 1963*, pp. 753–61.

21. Speech, Zhou Enlai, 2 September 1960; Special National Intelligence Estimate, No. 10–62, 21 February 1962 both in Gareth Porter, ed., *Vietnam: The Definitive Documentation of Human Decisions, II* (Philadelphia and London, 1979), pp. 72, 150–52; William Conrad Gibbons, *The US Government and the Vietnam War: Executive and Legislative Relationships: II, 1961–1964* (Princeton, NJ, 1986), pp. 98–99.

22. Hilsman to Rusk, 3 December 1962, Senator Gravel Edition, *The Pentagon Papers, II: The Defense Department History of United States Decisionmaking on Vietnam*, 4 vols. (Boston, MA, n.d.), pp. 693–4 (hereafter cited as *Pentagon Papers*); Wood to Harriman, 11 May 1962, *FRUS, 1961–1963, II: Vietnam, 1962*, p. 387; Hilsman to Murrow, 6 May 1963, *FRUS, 1961–1963, III: Vietnam, 1963*, pp. 271–2.

23. Hilsman, Address, Tampa, 14 June 1963, *Pentagon Papers, II;* report, Chief of Staff, US Army to JCS, January 1963; Saigon Embassy to State Dept., 8 February 1963, both in *FRUS, 1961–1963,III*, pp. 74–80, 109; Larry Cable, *Unholy Grail: The US and the Wars in Vietnam, 1965–8* (London and New York, 1991), pp. 33–5; Parker IV, *Vietnam*, pp. 84–5; R.B. Smith, *An International History of the Vietnam War: II, The Struggle for Southeast Asia, 1961–65* (London, 1985), p. 88.

24. The literature on America's involvement in Vietnam is vast and is growing. The best introductions include: George C. Herring, *America's Longest War: The United States and Vietnam, 1950–75* (New York, 1979); Gabriel Kolko, *Vietnam: Anatomy of a War, 1940–1975* (London, 1985); Guenther Lewy, *America in Vietnam* (New York, 1978); Larry Berman, *Planning a Tragedy: The Americanization of the War in Vietnam* (New York, 1982); Herbert Y. Schandler, *The Unmaking of a President: Lyndon Johnson and Vietnam* (Princeton, NJ, 1977); Stanley Karnow, *Vietnam: A History* (New York, 1986); Leslie H. Gelb and Richard K. Betts, *The Irony of Vietnam: The System Worked* (Washington, DC, 1979); John Dumbrell, *Vietnam: American Involvement at Home and Abroad* (Halifax, NS, 1992); T. Louise Brown, *War and Aftermath in Vietnam* (London, 1991); William S. Turley, *The Second Indochina War* (Boulder, CO, 1986); James S. Olson and Randy Roberts, *Where the Domino Fell: America and Vietnam 1945 to 1990* (New York, 1991).

25. Honolulu conference, 1–2 June 1964, *Pentagon Papers, III*, pp. 173–5.

26. Rostow to McNamara, 16 November 1964, *Pentagon Papers, III;* also, Gibbons, *The US Government and the Vietnam War.*

27. Edward J.Marolda and Oscar P.Fitzgerald, *The US Navy and the Vietnam Conflict: II, From Military Assistance to Combat, 1959–1965* (Washington, DC, 1986) pp. 443–4; Honolulu Conference, 1–2 June 1964; paper, 'Likely Developments and Problems … at Some Point,' 10 November 1964, both in *Pentagon Papers, III.*

28. Rusk, news conferences, 2 January 7 February, 11 November, 23 December 1964 in Dept. of State, *American Foreign Policy: Current Documents, 1964* (Washington, DC, 1967), pp. 871–2, 875, 886–7; Rusk, news conference, 23 December 1964, *Pentagon Papers, III*, p. 724; Hsieh, *Strategy for Survival*, pp. 130–31; Thomas J. Schoenbaum, *Waging Peace and War: Dean Rusk in the Truman, Kennedy and Johnson Years* (New York and London, 1988), pp. 391, 416–25; B.M. Jain, *India and the United States, 1961–1963* (New Delhi, 1987), pp. 120–25.

29. McNamara, 'United States Policy in Vietnam;' McNamara, 'Buildup of US Forces in Vietnam,' in *Department of State Bulletin*, 13 April 1964 and 30 August 1965; Bundy address, 27 May 1965 in *Pentagon Papers III*, p. 741; Rusk interview, 12

January 1967 in *Pentagon Papers IV*, pp. 662–3; Joseph A. Califano, Jr., *The Triumph and Tragedy of Lyndon Johnson* (New York, 1991), pp. 41–6.

30. Address, Green, 26 February 1965, Dept. of State, *American Foreign Policy, 1965*, pp. 721–6; Rusk replies, ABC TV, 27 April 1966, Dept. of State, *American Foreign Policy, 1966*; Frank E. Rogers, 'Sino-American Relations and the Vietnam War, 1964–6,' *China Quarterly*, 66, June 1976, pp. 306–9; Chang, *Friends and Enemies*, pp. 272–3.

31. *China, Vietnam, and the United States: Highlights of the Hearings of the Senate Foreign Relations Committee* (Washington, DC, 1966), pp. 4–12, 16–27, 38–42, 76–81, 93–9, 180–83.

32. Andrew Hall Wedeman, *The East Wind Subsides: Chinese Foreign Policy and the Origins of the Cultural Revolution* (Washington, DC, 1987), pp. 78–83; Barry Naughton, 'Industrial Policy during the Cultural Revolution: Military Preparation, Decentralization, and Leaps Forward,' in William A. Joseph, Christine P.W. Wong and David Zweig, eds., *New Perspectives on the Cultural Revolution* (Cambridge, MA, and London, 1991), pp. 153–81; Parker, *Vietnam*, pp. 95–101.

33. Smith, *International History of the Vietnam War, II*, pp. 127–8; Smith, *International History of the Vietnam War, III*, pp. 134–6; Lewy, *America in Vietnam*, p. 392; Gary R. Hess, *Vietnam and the United States: Origins and Legacy of a War* (Boston, MA, 1990), pp. 92–4; Lo Jui-ch'ing, 'Commemorate the Victory over German Fascism! Carry the Struggle against US Imperialism Through to the End!' in Hinton (ed.), *The People's Republic of China, II*, pp. 1207–12; Harry Harding and Melvin Gurtov, *The Purge of Lo Jui-ch'ing: The Politics of Chinese Strategic Planning* (Santa Monica, CA, 1971), pp. 22–3.

34. Summary of Speech by Gen. Nguyen Van Vinh, COSVN Congress, April 1966 in Porter (ed.), *Vietnam: The Definitive Documentation*, pp. 418–19; *Peking Review*, 12 November 1965; speech by P'eng Chen in Hinton (ed.), *The People's Republic of China, II*, pp. 1215–19; Kolko, *Vietnam*, p. 158; Smith, *An International History of the Vietnam War, II*, pp. 135–6.

35. Lin Biao, *Long Live the Victory of People's War!* (Beijing, 1965); also, 'China Stands Ready to Smash US War Schemes,' *Peking Review*, 6 August 1965.

36. David Mozingo, *China's Foreign Policy and the Cultural Revolution* (Ithaca, NY, 1970), pp. 26–7; Richard Lowenthal, 'Communist China's Foreign Policy,' in Tang Tsou (ed.), *China in Crisis, II: China's Policies in Asia and America's Alternatives* (Chicago, IL, 1968), pp. 2–3; Jaap van Ginneken, *The Rise and Fall of Lin Piao* (Harmondsworth, 1976), pp. 39–41; Jürgen Domes with Marie Luise Näth, *China After the Cultural Revolution: Politics between Two Party Congresses* (London, 1975), pp. 209–14; Lo Jui-ch'ing, 'The People Defeated Japanese Fascism and they Certainly Can Defeat US Imperialism too,' in Hinton (ed.), *The People's Republic of China, II*, pp. 1241–6.

37. Statements by Goldberg and Harriman, Department of State, *American Foreign Policy, 1965*, pp. 747–50; Address, Goldberg, 4 March 1966, *Pentagon Papers, IV*, pp. 645–66.

38. Wedeman, *The East Wind Subsides*, pp. 149–69.

CHAPTER 5

THE EAST WIND MEETS THE WEST WIND: FROM THE CULTURAL REVOLUTION TO THE BEIJING SUMMIT, 1966–72

The participation of the United States in the Vietnam conflict rested on a profound irony. While the Johnson administration insisted that its intervention was motivated largely by its wish to contain an expansionist Communist China, Mao Zedong had rejected the idea of active Chinese involvement in the war. The United States either did not know or did not believe that China's leaders were deeply divided over foreign policy. The debate within China on relations with the United States and the Soviet Union rent the leadership asunder and was a major contributory factor in the Great Proletarian Cultural Revolution, which became the fiercest power struggle experienced in the history of Communist China.

On the face of it, the Cultural Revolution was a magnified but recognizable version of earlier campaigns against 'imperialists' or 'capitalist roaders.' All people singled out as opponents of Mao's leadership were labelled sympathizers of the capitalist West. The slogans of demonstrating Red Guards and the rhetoric of the Beijing leadership were laced with vengeful references to the collaborationist tendencies of all opponents of Chairman Mao. The press fed its readers with a daily diet of anti-American invective and predicted an utter defeat of American forces in Vietnam. Because these claims stretched the credulity of most Americans, the United States increasingly came to believe that the Soviets were a moderating force within the communist world and constituted an obstacle to a new wave of international insanity. The anti-imperialist rhetoric and the corresponding calls for 'people's war' convinced Americans that the Vietnamese communists owed their allegiance to Beijing. The reality was different. It was the Soviets, not the Chinese, who viewed the Vietnam conflict as a rallying ground for the communist world and who calculated that the unification of Vietnam would serve to destabilize their Chinese rivals.

Mao Zedong recognized that divisions within the party leadership were exacerbated by the difficult foreign policy choices confronting it. The Chinese leadership was broadly divided between two groups. One group was dominated by Liu Shaoqi and Deng Xiaoping, the other by Mao and the Defence Minister, Lin Biao. The failure of the Great Leap Forward had convinced the faction headed by Deng and Liu that the solution to China's chronic problems of food shortages and industrial backwardness was the development of an efficient modernization programme. They wished to subordinate issues of ideology to the more immediate concerns of improved production and efficient party management. Mao, on the other hand, still believed that selfishness undermined the progress to pure communism and that only a concerted and zealous programme of self-denial and political education would create the conditions for the attainment of a socialist society. He believed the party had become an entity of its own, and was more concerned with problems of internal organization than with substantive issues of ideology. At the Tenth Plenum of the Central Committee held earlier in September 1962 Mao condemned the trend towards private land ownership and 'bourgeois' tendencies in literature and art. He called for a mass movement of socialist education in rural areas. Lin Biao endorsed Mao's position and was instrumental in making the People's Liberation Army the vehicle of the new socialist revivalism. The ensuing Socialist Education Movement was designed to halt the slide towards 'capitalism,' particularly in the countryside. Army cadres were dispatched to form new work teams and put together study materials on socialist ideology and class struggle. Intellectuals were instructed to play a full role in the militant enlightenment of the masses.

Mao thought that a new drive would rejuvenate the party rank and file, eliminate the competition between cadres, and revive the flagging mass enthusiasm for socialism. He and his followers believed that a spiritual revival was the key to China's national salvation. However, the movement did not produce the desired result of national rededication. The Socialist Education Movement actually hurt Mao politically, as it failed to eliminate competition among cadres and to revive the mass enthusuiasm for socialism. Despite Mao's towering authority, the Communist Party of China consisted of various political machines and coalitions based on the principle of mutual support. Mao believed that the Party was becoming like so many other parties, a vehicle for the perpetuation of political careers rather than a machine for engineering social progress. The most formidable leaders of the party, Liu Shaoqi and Deng Xiaoping, managed to tighten their grip of the party apparatus, including the control of the leading newspaper, the *People's Daily*. Liu Shaoqi had developed a quite different approach to party organization. Unlike Mao, Liu was a coordinator of policy, not a visionary. Mao believed that indoctrination and zeal were the keys to national and political unity. Liu, on the other hand, relied on the management of men, attained through a combination of tight party regulation and consensus. Mao saw himself as the provocateur, Liu as the agent of economic efficiency and administrative rationality.[1]

The debate over the role of ideology in policy-making was closely linked with the problem of international strategy. Mao and Lin Biao believed that China's security interests were best served through the encouragement of socialist revolution in the Third World (or intermediate zone, as they preferred to call it) but they did not believe that Chinese armour was necessary to ensure success. They also insisted that the Foreign Ministry and its agencies were proper instruments for propagating socialist thought abroad. They rejected the option of active military intervention in other struggles on the grounds that communism would inevitably prevail and that the forces of anti-imperialism would naturally unite behind China's leadership. In Mao's own famous dictum of November 1957: 'There are two winds in the world today, the East Wind and the West Wind ... I believe that the East Wind is prevailing over the West Wind. That is to say, the forces of socialism have become overwhelmingly superior to the forces of imperialism.' And, as has been seen, Lin Biao had argued in *Long Live the Victory of People's War!* that victory was inevitable and that self-reliance would enhance the prospects of that ultimate victory. Mao also recognized that the Soviets were already heavily committed to assisting the North Vietnamese and that Chinese aid could serve to strengthen the Soviets' power in Southeast Asia. The schism with Moscow precluded coordinated assistance to the Vietnamese communists. Beijing did not want to become involved in a competition with Moscow for influence in Hanoi.[2]

China was convinced that time was on its side. It was an article of faith that in the underdeveloped world anti-imperialism would triumph and the tide of communism would advance. As more nations achieved communist government, international pressure would grow for the integration of the PRC into the community of nations. China did not see any advantage in taking military action for goals which, it believed, would materialize anyway in the course of time. Thus when Lyndon Johnson in June 1965 authorized US forces to undertake offensive operations in Vietnam, China rejected cooperation with the Soviets and turned down their request for air bases in southern China. In September a US plane was shot down over Hainan island, but China's reaction was quite subdued. Despite its anti-American rhetoric, China did not appear to be prepared for war along its southern borders. Indeed, half of the PLA's main force in the autumn of 1965 was deployed along the east coast, opposite Taiwan.[3]

But a series of reversals occurred in the summer and autumn of 1965 which may have shaken China's confidence. Lin Biao's *Long Live the Victory of People's War!* can be read in the light of these setbacks. A major diplomatic initiative to reconvene a second Afro-Asian conference in Algeria failed. The countries of the Third World were critical of Indonesia's call for a general withdrawal from the UN, and were all too aware that aid from the Soviet Union was more valuable than the rhetorical encouragement of Beijing. In September Nasser cracked down on Maoists in Egypt. In October the abortive coup in Indonesia paved the way for the bloody destruction of the Indonesian Communist party and the disintegration of Sukarno's political base. In January 1966 Bokassa overthrew the government of the Central African Republic and immediately broke off diplomatic relations with China. Beijing's political influence was on the wane, and Mao's hope of making China the leader of the Third World was in tatters.

A combination of reversals in foreign policy, a growing sense that the Chinese revolution was going flabby and losing direction, and a paranoia that resembled the worst forms of Stalinism prompted Mao to undertake his violent and gruelling shake-up of the Chinese political system, the Great Proletarian Cultural Revolution. Mao saw a direct relationship between China's problems abroad and the drift that was deemed to characterize Chinese politics in the middle of the decade. He believed that a regeneration of his revolution would make it dynamic again. A purge of the old party leaders would eliminate challenges to his authority and leave him in full command. In foreign policy it would undermine men like Liu who sought to heal the split with the Soviets. He sensed that a full reorientation of the political life of China would resolve such outstanding issues as the leadership succession, foreign policy, and the Vietnam war. But as things turned out, the Cultural Revolution became an improvised revolution without clear direction. It passed through several stages. Each stage had its own unique features, and everybody involved had to adjust to the volatile, and changing circumstances to form new alliances in the hope of prevailing. Nobody quite knew where they were going; it is highly doubtful if Mao himself knew.[4]

The trigger for the Great Proletarian Cultural Revolution was a play, *Hai Jui Dismissed From Office*, written in 1961 by Wu Han, vice-mayor of Beijing. Mao used the publication of the play to unleash his vindictive purge. He claimed that the play was a veiled political attack on his leadership. The fabricated literary controversy rapidly developed into a full-blown ideological and political struggle over the structure and authority of the Communist Party. By February 1966 two groups emerged in the debate over Wu Han's play. One group consisted of the senior party officials and intellectuals who gravitated around Liu Shaoqi and Deng Xiaoping. The other group, centred around Mao, called for socialist purification and did not have close links with the party bureaucracy. They were also aware of the opportunities that arose from spreading their views and distancing themselves from the old guard. The Maoists maintained that a conspiracy to overthrow Chinese communism existed. The traitors had to be driven out in order to save socialism. They endorsed Mao's view that lethargy had set in and that the party had become a self-serving interest group. They believed that they would become the beneficiaries of new purges in the party structure, no matter how chaotic or brutal they were. Thus within the party leadership factions were drawn along lines of ideology and personal ambition.[5]

Events moved fast and unpredictably. To begin with, most manoeuvrings and criticisms took place within the party hierarchy. But soon the conflict spread to the Chinese masses, as the Maoist leadership called on them to subject party officials to mass self-criticism. At first work teams were sent out to schools and universities to organize and anchor these public apologies. But things backfired when radicals and young people with few attachments to the party organization took matters into their own hands. At the end of July Mao ordered the withdrawal of the work teams and stressed that the Cultural Revolution should be led by 'revolutionary teachers, students and neutrals, who are the only people in the schools who know anything at all.'[6] Soon squads of young students were issued with armbands and copies of the 'Little Red Book' of Chairman Mao's quotations. These 'Red Guards' were the vanguard of the Cultural Revolution, and rapidly became a law unto themselves. Mao gave them almost free rein to punish, humiliate and destroy all those individuals and institutions that did not share his vision. Unsurprisingly, the Red Guards used their sudden and un-disciplined authority to settle old scores. Teachers, party administrators, lower-level cadres and even parents were subjected to humiliations and torture. Many died or were driven to suicide. The Red Guards had been told that their actions against their former political masters were a form of class struggle. The Chinese had grown accustomed to political labelling of one sort or another. The activists believed that their en-deavours were just a continuation of earlier political campaigns. For some of them, the Cultural Revolution was a struggle for personal freedom. The party hierarchy had represented difficult work assignments and slow promotion prospects for many former underlings. They justified their administrative violence as a proper instrument for rectifying their grievances. The Cultural Revolution unleashed frustrations and provided opportunities to people who believed that they had been disadvantaged by the political structure. It also enabled them to prove their loyalty to the state that had so much power over them. The result was tumult, as different groups competed with one another to display and reap the benefit of that loyalty.[7]

From the summer of 1966 to late 1967 China was in chaos. Schools and universities closed down so that students could join the Red Guards. Workers concentrated their efforts on studying the quotations of Chair-man Mao and attending mass meetings. Visitations from the radical groups, many of them sadistic, often spelled assault, exile, depression or suicide. Countless thousands were beaten, and many died of their injuries. The Red Guard units took to the countryside to spread the word to the peasantry. Normal life effectively ground to a halt. In the provinces the struggles became almost mini civil wars, as Red Guards seized local offices in order to winkle out 'power holders taking the capitalist road.' In February 1967 an 'adverse current' guideline was issued. It sought to limit the number of power seizures and to provide some protection to party bureaucrats and the apparatus of state. The People's Liberation Army became the principal instrument for estab-lishing order. The PLA was a combat force that needed organizational integrity and a hierarchical command structure. It was a professional army committed to the defence of China and the preservation of civil order: it recognized that radicalization and chaos undermined its very being. Tension grew between the PLA and the Cultural Revolution groups, and by the summer of 1967 they were in open conflict with one another for control of the destiny of the Cultural Revolution. In Wuhan, after the PLA arrested 500 leaders of the Red Guard, clashes broke out and over 1,000 people were killed by the army. A senior member of the Cultural Revolution leadership from Beijing was kidnapped from his hotel and only released when military reinforcements, including airborne units, were dispatched from the capital.[8]

Mao realized that China was on the brink of civil war. The Cultural Revolution had misfired. He had probably originally intended to revolutionize the existing ruling structure; instead he had come close to destroying it. Having initiated the attack on the Communist Party Mao now ordered its reconstruction. Workers, rather than students, were acclaimed as the vanguard class. They were sent into the schools, universities, factories and party organs to restore order and to initiate fresh study classes of Mao's thought. Special investigative teams were instructed to reconcile warring factions and to instil a renewed sense of unity. Slowly the rhythms of life were restored. At the Ninth Party Congress of April 1969, the chapter of the Cultural Revolution was officially closed.[9]

The Cultural Revolution had a greater impact on the management of Chinese foreign policy than on its substance. The Foreign Minister, Chen Yi, had to perform something of a juggling act. He paid lip-service to the aims of the Cultural Revolution but was courageous enough to stand up for his brief, which was to protect China's interests abroad. He was mindful of the fact that China's revolutionary course had little support among its traditional Afro-Asian supporters. He affirmed repeatedly that Mao Zedong Thought was distinctive to China's revolutionary experience and was not exportable. He made a number of self-criticisms in the hope of staving off the radicals. But the Foreign Ministry fell victim to their intrusions. In January 1967 anti-Chen forces gained a foothold by setting up a Red Guard Revolutionary Rebel Liaison station. On 29 May 300 Red Guards raided the ministry and forcibly removed classified materials. Throughout the summer the ministry barely functioned. Red Guards insisted on recalling embassy staff from overseas, and called on the remainder to make revolution abroad. By the end of 1967 virtually every Chinese embassy was without an ambassador. The skeleton staff remaining was required to take to the streets to wave 'Little Red Books' to bemused passers-by. In Beijing tens of thousands of demonstrators surrounded the Soviet embassy and plastered it with posters inciting people to 'Shoot Brezhnev.' The chargé d'affaires of the British embassy in Beijing, Donald Hobson, was dragged out and beaten. Diplomatic incidents were provoked with at least thirty-two different countries. However, the Foreign Ministry survived the turmoil better than most government departments, protected by Zhou Enlai. Chen Yi's opponents were eventually ousted. Despite the Maoist jeering and the outbreaks of sporadic violence abroad, the foreign policy of China suffered little lasting damage. Chen Yi had jealously guarded his belief that it was not the function of the Foreign Ministry to propagate Mao's thoughts. By and large the Cultural Revolution remained an internal phenomenon and was not concerned with a major restructuring of foreign policy. There were no new military adventures, and support for the Vietnamese communists increased only in the vehemence of China's rhetoric.[10]

China's self-destructive descent into violence and disorder did not advance its cause among its friends in the United States. Indeed, one of its aims was to demonstrate that its revolutionary ideals would not be compromised or held in abeyance for the sake of recognition. Surprisingly, perhaps, the Cultural Revolution did not drive an additional wedge between the two countries. The United States was not involved in any of the incidents involving Red Guard 'diplomacy.' In all probability the Cultural Revolution did little to change attitudes already held. Lucian Pye predicted in early 1967 that the upheavals would expose China's poor resources and would lead eventually to a movement for moderation. Public opinion polls showed a continuing shift in favour of greater contacts between the United States and China, even though by late 1967 China was held in lower esteem than any other nation in the world. The young in particular believed that the Vietnam war should not be permitted to stop progress towards some kind of rapprochement. The changes in opinion discussed in the previous chapter did not undergo significant alteration as a result of the Cultural Revolution. Many people contended that China's isolation had probably enhanced the propensity for turmoil, and that the convulsions would in any case burn out.[11]

The Johnson administration was in two minds about events in China. It continued to justify its intervention in Vietnam as an essential part of its containment of Communist China. On 12 October 1967 Dean Rusk was asked by John Finney of the *New York Times* why the security of the United States was at stake in Vietnam. Rusk replied that the prospect of 'a billion Chinese on the mainland armed with nuclear weapons' was dangerous, as 'Peking has nominated itself by proclaiming a militant doctrine of the world revolution and doing something about it.' The USA could not, he said, stand by. 'It gets tough ... we are tested, and we find out what kind of people we are.' Vice-president Hubert Humphrey added three days later that 'the threat to world peace is militant aggressive communism, with its headquarters in Peking.' Yet these apparently orchestrated attacks on China did not reflect the views of everybody within the administration. Townsend Hoopes, Under-Secretary of the Air Force from October 1967 to February 1969, believed that such rhetoric amounted to a 'dangerous rhetorical escalation.' East Asia specialists within the State Department believed that China was a backward country, too consumed with its own internal problems to pose any real threat. They realized that the Cultural Revolution was primarily a domestic matter. Its regime was prone to 'hysterical propaganda,' claimed Hoopes, 'but the corollary fact was an operational policy of extreme caution. Mao combined polemical ferocity with actionary prudence.'[12]

Secretary of Defense Robert McNamara appeared to be reaching the same conclusion. In October 1966 he had recommended to the President that a ceiling should be placed on the number of troops in Vietnam. The war could not be won quickly, he counselled, and certainly not before the 1968 elections. So sights had to be lowered. Privately, Johnson recognized that a military victory was not feasible and that the American involvement had to be limited. The acceptance of such limits suggests that the administration was beginning to reach a conclusion of far-ranging importance. If there was to be a lid on the level of American participation in the Vietnam war, that ceiling would have to be justified by reference to the apparent limits of the Chinese threat. At a news conference on 19 December 1967 Lyndon Johnson said he would like China to know that 'we have no desire to be enemies of any nation ... We think there are some very important things taking place in China today that will contribute to, we hope, a better understanding and a more moderate approach to their neighbours in the world.' The administration realized that changes in its Indo-China policy would have to be accompanied by changes in its representation of China. On 3 May 1968 United States Information Agency (USIA) Director Leonard Marks invited Chinese Communist journalists to come to the United States to cover the 1968 election campaign, and promised to make prime listening time on the Voice of America available for broadcasts back to their homeland. On 21 May Under-Secretary of State Nicholas Katzenbach repeated the hopes for 'better relations' and said that 'we are realistic enough to expect changes to come slowly.' But he did believe that changes would come.[13]

There were two particular events in 1968 that enabled the United States to back away from its position identifying Communist China as the principal foe in Vietnam. The first was set in motion on January 30 when a team of Vietcong sappers attacked and managed to penetrate the courtyard of the American embassy in Saigon. This attack was part of the massive synchronized Vietcong assault on nearly all major urban centres, the Tet offensive. Communist forces hoped that the Tet offensive would mark the beginning of a general uprising in the cities against the Republic of Vietnam and its American protectors. While the Vietcong were spectacularly successful in launching the surprise attacks, they failed to sustain momentum and to achieve the vaunted spontaneous uprising. Although the United States had been caught off guard, it recovered quickly and inflicted heavy casualties on Communist forces. Generals Earle Wheeler and William Westmoreland took the opportunity to try to get Washington to agree to the dispatch of a further 206,000 men; without these reinforcements, they argued, another offensive could be launched. But Clark Clifford, who had just replaced Robert McNamara as Secretary of Defense, rejected the new request and reiterated the view that the United States should lower its sights. It should strive, he said, to make the population of South Vietnam secure, not to defeat the Vietcong. America's war aims had to be more local in purpose and less ambitious in their overall design.

The new policy meant that the Chinese dimension was to be given less prominence. Mao himself provided corroborating signals. He had stressed that the Tet offensive underlined the inherent effectiveness of people's war, and that international socialist intervention was an un-necessary requisite for victory. Newspaper articles emphasized that the offensive was a special triumph because it was carried out by the Vietnamese alone: its success confirmed the wisdom of inaction by other parties. Washington concluded that its military policy had been ineffective in overcoming the insurgents and had done nothing to weaken China. Above all, the growing public discontent with the war, with its embarrassing demonstrations and expressions of general disaffection, made further escalation politically damaging. Policy-makers became convinced that the war could not be won on the battlefield. They believed that the time had come to tone down America's involvement, and to undertake a thorough review of Southeast Asia policy.[14]

The second event of 1968 that prompted a re-examination of the nature of China's challenge to the security of the United States was the Soviet invasion of Czechoslovakia in August. The Brezhnev doctrine, which the Russians enunciated to justify the attack, proclaimed that intervention was necessary as the political systems of neighbouring states directly affected the security of the Soviet Union. Mao feared that China could become the next victim of the Brezhnev doctrine. He condemned the invasion, and accused Brezhnev of behaving like a Russian czar. He portrayed the countries of Eastern Europe less as havens of revisionism than as nations struggling for independence from their tyrannical Soviet masters. China and the United States now found themselves portraying similar pictures of the Kremlin. The lesson was not lost on Mao. Denunciations of the United States started to diminish, and Chinese foreign policy began its remarkable change of course.[15]

While the Tet offensive and the Soviet invasion of Czechoslovakia were major contributory factors in persuading the Chinese leadership that the Americans were not such a threat to China as the Soviets, there was one other development that gave the Chinese a temporary confidence that the tide of revolution was on their side. The demonstrations and strikes in May 1968 throughout many western capitals and particularly in Paris provided fuel to the ideologues of the Cultural Revolution. The images of striking factory workers, angry anti-Vietnam war demonstrators and students occupying university administration buildings carrying placards with Mao's portrait, hoisting Chinese flags, and waving the 'Little Red Book' was used to portray the idea that the Cultural Revolution might develop into an international movement. A *People's Daily* editorial noted 'that a tremendous mass struggle has broken out in the heartland of the capitalist world.' It attributed the disturbances to the 'extensive dissemination of Mao Tse-tung's thought throughout the world.' The West was portrayed as decaying and moribund. While such decay gave little reason to reach any kind of accommodation, it did reinforce the image of the 'paper tiger' that could not really threaten the well-being of China and socialist revolution.[16]

There was no parallel portrayal of Soviet decay. If there was one single reason for China's reassessment of its external relations, it was China's fear of growing Soviet power. Its ambitions in Asia appeared to be increasing. In 1968 Moscow signed a major agreement that provided for a $133 million loan from Japanese banks for the development of Siberian timber production. Moscow also tried to involve Japan in the creation of a new Asian security system aimed at the containment of China. The growth in the Soviets' naval strength also alarmed Beijing. In 1965 the displacement of the Soviet Far Eastern fleet was 700,000 tons; by 1970 it had risen to one million tons. In the late 1960s the Soviets increased their arms exports to India. China feared that the Soviet Union was concentrating its defence build-up in Asia. The flow of arms to North Vietnam also continued to grow. At the same time the United States was beginning to retrench in Asia. The newly elected administration of Richard Nixon was committed to disengagement from Vietnam. The balance was swinging in Moscow's favour, and it seemed that the United States might attempt to deaden the impact by joining forces with the Soviets to create a new international order based on the joint containment of China. The age-old fear of encirclement began to loom in the thinking of Chinese policy-makers.[17]

In early 1969 matters seemed to come to a head. The USSR had increased its troop deployments along the Chinese border by ten divisions, an increase of some 60 per cent over a five-year period. This Russian challenge turned into an urgent crisis when an old boundary dispute flared up in fighting that broke out between Soviet and Chinese troops along the frozen Ussuri River, which separated Manchuria from the Soviets' Maritime Provinces. On 2 March 1969 a skirmish left over thirty Soviet soldiers dead – Chinese casualties were not reported. Two weeks later another battle occurred, with even higher casualties. Subsequent Soviet raids into Xinjiang province made the region highly volatile and unstable. The rival claims were not resolved, but a stand-off eventually ensued. Yet China's worst fears had now materialized. The war of words with the Soviet Union had escalated into an exchange of fire. China now had confirmation that the Soviet Union posed a greater threat to its security than the United States.[18]

At the same time, developments within the United States appeared to bode well for the future of Sino-American relations. America was divided over its Asian policy. The anti-war movement, which climaxed with scenes of public disorder in Chicago in August 1968 during the Democratic national convention, highlighted the bitter divisions that the war had created within the United States. A further escalation of America's involvement was politically unsustainable. The administration seeemed determined to negotiate an end to the war, and it sometimes seemed that it was the intransigence of the South Vietnamese leaders that presented the greatest obstacle to the peace negotiations. Johnson had realized that he was in a poor position to extricate the United States from the war, and had decided not to run again for the White House. At the end of October he tried to ease matters for his successor by announcing a bombing halt without the agreement of the South. When Richard Nixon was elected President in November, an opportunity arose to review policy for all Asia. During the campaign Nixon had pledged that he would wind down the war in Vietnam and look for new solutions. He had also indicated that he would not feel bound by his predecessors' policies towards the People's Republic of China. In October 1967 he had written in an article in *Foreign Affairs* that 'we simply cannot afford to leave China forever outside the family of nations.' He believed that the United States could play a leading role in reassimilating China 'as a great and progressing nation.' At the Republican national convention in Miami he expressed the hope that he might visit Beijing 'if they would give me a visa.' When he was warned by one conservative journalist against a switch in policy, he replied: 'I used to share your opinion, but I've changed.'[19]

In the early days of the Nixon presidency, Beijing remained publicly hostile towards the new administration. It repeated the familiar indictments meted out to all American leaders. The *People's Daily*, for example, dismissed Nixon's calls for national unity and peace as a subterfuge for the preservation of monopoly power. It pointed to the demonstrations that plagued American life as evidence of America's decline into a revolutionary situation. Articles repeatedly stressed that the United States was overextended, and that it had insufficient resources to meet its commitments. But they also implied that because the United States was overstretched, it was no longer a threat to Chinese security. China's foreign policy vacillated. It considered the United States an imperialist nation that sought to dominate international affairs through the United Nations. It was still not prepared to ease communications with Washington as long as it continued to guarantee the defence of Taiwan. However, the Chinese leadership was also divided from within. Zhou Enlai believed that deteriorating relations with the Soviet Union necessitated an alignment with the United States: China could not afford to be pressed on two fronts. The radicals, on the other hand, led by Mao's wife, Jiang Qing, still wanted no compromises. They believed that Chinese foreign policy required ideological purity; accommodation was unacceptable. On 18 February 1969, Jiang Qing was instrumental in getting the scheduled meeting of Chinese and American ambassadors in Warsaw cancelled. The Cultural Revolution group hoped it could slow down the retreat from radicalism by maintaining an uncompromising stand on foreign policy. However, the radical group did not enjoy ascendancy for long. Zhou was convinced that a more strategic foreign policy was necessary, and that the issue of Taiwan did not have to be an inflexible sticking point in China's relations with the United States. He realized that the United States and China had certain common strategic aims. Both wanted to see a reduction of tensions in Southeast Asia; both feared the growth of Soviet naval power in the Pacific. China wanted to diminish its role as midwife to international revolution and the United States wanted to curb its involvement in counter-revolution.[20]

The new President, Richard Nixon, and his enterprising National Security Adviser, Henry Kissinger, were in a position to reassess assumptions about the communist world that had governed American policy for over twenty years. Johnson's imposition of troop ceilings in Vietnam, the Sino-Soviet dispute, and the strong position of the Soviets in strategic missiles presented policy-makers with a set of circumstances that called for fresh approaches. Nixon himself also wanted the management of international affairs to be conducted with greater ease and efficiency. He strongly believed that international stability could best be achieved through the personal direction of policy. Close superintendence meant that he would need to cut a swathe through bureaucratic structures in both Washington and, if possible, foreign ministries abroad. But such an approach would only work if leaders of other nations acknowledged a community of interests and followed suit. The President also showed a remarkable confidence in his own judgement and ability to control events. His extraordinary comeback after repeated political defeat had, in his view, been due to his own relentless determination and acute political sense. He was well aware that his electoral support was based on admiration for his intelligence and determination, not for any instinctive empathy he displayed for the voter. Nixon wanted to establish himself as a pragmatist. He did not wish to be seen to be caught in the web of the past or to be ensnared by his earlier reputation for intransigence.[21]

Nixon believed that he was in a position to break with a number of inherited policies and that such change would enhance both his personal reputation and the standing of the United States in the world. He also knew that his ability to end the hostilities in Vietnam would be the measure of his success and reputation. An inability to resolve the issue would not only diminish America's standing, but would also fuel the domestic disorders and the growing sense of national crisis that had enveloped the country during the election campaign. He did not want to end up like LBJ. Accordingly, he indicated that the United States intended to disengage from the conflict, but not at any price. The war would have to be ended 'honourably,' a condition that would come to haunt him in the years ahead. An honourable settlement meant that there would have to be a negotiated agreement that would preserve South Vietnam as a separate entity and give it a reasonable chance of survival. An agreement of this kind would ensure that America's withdrawal would not look like a defeat.

Nixon planned to secure his peace with honour by two means. First, he intended to link America's relations with the Soviet Union and, possibly, China, to a settlement in Vietnam. He recognized that the changing balance in the communist world could be harnessed to the peace process in Indo-China. He believed that the Soviets wanted *détente* and that they did not want the war in Vietnam to impede it. They could use their influence on the North Vietnamese to help America extricate itself. Second, Nixon wanted to keep the North Vietnamese guessing about the strategy he would employ. He did not want to repeat his predecessor's mistakes. Johnson's repeated bombing halts and his public rejection of further escalation had convinced the North Vietnamese that they had him on the run and that he would not apply more military pressure. Nixon wanted to send out tougher signals. He would use every means at his disposal to secure an 'honourable' withdrawal from Vietnam. If negotiations stalled, then pressure would be increased until the Vietnamese communists were convinced that there was no upper limit to Washington's determination. As Nixon explained to H.R. Haldeman in late 1968: 'I call it the madman theory, Bob. I want the North Vietnamese to believe I've reached the point where I might do *anything* to stop the war. We'll just slip the word to them that, "for God's sake, you know Nixon is obsessed about Communism. We can't constrain him when he's angry – and he has his hand on the nuclear button".'[22]

Nixon did not believe that Hanoi acted in collusion with Beijing. He was determined to separate America's relationship with China from the tactical problems of disengagement from Vietnam. Despite continuing public support of the North in the Chinese press, the administration was aware of the historical tension between Beijing and its southern neighbour, and of the debate within China on the efficacy of military assistance to wars of national liberation. At no time did Washington make statements suggesting that military operations against Vietnam were directed at the Chinese. As Kissinger commented, 'we needed no additional enemies.'[23] The administration's policies in Southeast Asia were carefully designed to coerce Hanoi; they were not devised to apply corresponding pressure on Beijing. It believed that it could compel Hanoi to accept peace terms by showing that the United States meant business and that support for the North's cause in Moscow and Beijing did not extend to propping it up. The President began to step up the pressure. In March 1969, without consulting William P. Rogers, his Secretary of State, Nixon ordered intensive bombing assaults on North Vietnamese sanctuaries in neutral Cambodia. During the next fourteen months over 100,000 tons of bombs were dropped on Cambodia in an operation with the macabre codename of MENU. The bombing was kept secret from the American public for fear of arousing new protests. The secrecy was not intended to be as obsessive as it eventually became. But as the bombing continued, the deceptions became more elaborate and soon secrecy became more important to Nixon than the bombing itself. The administration went to extraordinary lengths to keep it from public knowledge. Secrecy became the distinguishing hallmark of Nixon's inner circle, and would eventually lead to its downfall. However, their clandestine manoeuvrings prepared them well for one acclaimed achievement, the surprising *démarche* towards Mao's China.[24]

Nixon was not quite sure how he would go about effecting a change in policy towards China, but he set in motion a series of steps that opened up the possibility of a bolder initiative at a later stage. He asked Kissinger to plant the idea of a Sino-American *rapprochement* among Eastern European leaders, if only to unnerve Moscow. Kissinger used the opportunity to initiate a broad policy review on all aspects of Sino-American relations, including the trade embargo. The administration continued to hint at the possibility of change in various public statements. In March Nixon met President Charles de Gaulle in Paris and told him that he intended to keep his options open on China. He also made more specific probes through Presidents Yahya Khan of Pakistan and Nicolae Ceauşescu of Romania. He asked them to serve as conduits and publicly opposed any attempt to isolate China through a Soviet-sponsored Asian collective security organization. Secretary of State Rogers broadly concurred with the new goals. However, Rogers wanted to move more cautiously as the State Department, accustomed to years of Rusk's hostility, was rather hesitant. Kissinger felt strongly that involvement by the State Department would create unnecessary obstacles – its views were too entrenched after years of animosity. He regarded bureaucracies as cumbersome; desk officers often believed they were sovereign in their domain, and anyway it was more difficult to get a large number of people to agree on anything. Also official contacts through the meetings of the nations' ambassadors in Warsaw had not produced one single notable accomplishment in the 134 sessions that had been held since 1954. Both Nixon and Kissinger believed that any progress on contacts with China would have to be undertaken surreptitiously. That would be more efficient, and it suited the temperaments of the two men.[25]

The manoeuvrings on China were inextricable from the general developments in the Vietnam war. Nixon did not believe that American policy had to be based on a Chinese calculus. He perceived that Beijing had diminishing interests and influence in Hanoi. Despite its attacks on American interference in Southeast Asia, China continued to cool to the North Vietnamese. It warned that the Russians would exact a high price for their support of the North's war effort. North Vietnamese aircraft were barred from Chinese bases, and China's news coverage of the war declined. When Ho Chi Minh died in 1969, Zhou Enlai hurried to Hanoi, but the death only got slender press coverage and his funeral was attended only by an alternate member of the Politburo. It seemed increasingly clear that while Beijing still regarded the presence of American troops near its borders as a threat, it did not want to see an American withdrawal only to be replaced by a corresponding Soviet presence. China felt pressure from the Soviets from the north and the south. The United States hoped that Beijing could be detached from Hanoi, thus forcing the latter to make peace. At the same time China hoped that the United States could step in and provide a counterbalance to the Soviets in Asia. In the administration's opinion a new relationship with Beijing would serve two purposes: it would force the Soviets to reconsider their commitment to confrontation on so many fronts, and it would broaden the prospects for the United States in its attempt to withdraw honourably from Vietnam. Rivalry within the communist world might force the hand of Hanoi in the peace process. As Kissinger commented in his memoirs:

> We did not consider our opening to China as inherently anti-Soviet. Our objective was to purge our foreign policy of all sentimentality ... We moved toward China not to expiate liberal guilt over our China policy of the late 1940s but to shape a global equilibrium. It was not to collude against the Soviet Union but to give us a balancing position to use for constructive ends – to give each Communist power a stake in better relations with us.[26]

Rather ironically, the manoeuvres of the Nixon administration received a fillip from what came to be one of the major foreign policy traumas of Nixon's presidency. In March 1970 Nixon announced with great personal reluctance the phased withrawal of 150,000 troops over the next year. He did not want the announcement to be misinterpreted in Hanoi. He was still committed to the survival of the Saigon regime, and was not prepared to sacrifice the Thieu government as the price of successful peace talks. He believed that a show of force would demonstrate that commitment. That opportunity came in March, when Prince Sihanouk of Cambodia was overthrown by the pro-American Lon Nol. The change of government in Cambodia gave Nixon the opprtunity to attack communist sanctuaries and so deliver a crippling blow to North Vietnamese power. He was persuaded that the dispatch of American forces into Cambodia would flush out communist forces that were disrupting the process of Vietnamization. At the same time, the operation would sustain the vulnerable but friendly government of Lon Nol. On 30 April 1970 in a televised speech he explained his decision to send troops into Cambodia. He concealed the existence of America's bombing campaign in Cambodia, and insisted that the operation was new and necessary. In fact, the incursion enlarged rather than diminished America's involvement in the region and unleashed a furious and widespread domestic reaction to the administration. Demonstrations erupted throughout the country. At Kent State University four young students were killed in confrontations with the National Guard. Congress voted to rescind the Gulf of Tonkin Resolution of 1964, and an amendment was put forward to cut off all funds relating to the military operations in Cambodia. Even though marginal military gains were made in Cambodia, the invasion deepened the divisions within the

United States and destroyed whatever domestic consensus Nixon had managed to hold together.[27]

The invasion of Cambodia affected China policy in two ways. First, Nixon had underestimated the extent and intensity of the domestic reaction. Support for his foreign policy was badly damaged – traditional Republican supporters, as well as liberals, began to question his judgement. Nixon had to recover his reputation and persuade the public that the extension of the war in Asia was temporary and a means of facilitating Vietnamization. If he could demonstrate in other spheres that he was not bound by old commitments, he might recover his position. Second, China's own reaction inadvertently speeded up the process of contact. It reacted to the Cambodian invasion by cancelling the ambassadorial talks scheduled to take place on 20 May. But the cancellation provided an opportunity for the White House to end the State Department's involvement in the tortuous negotiation process and to create instead a 'back channel' which could be closely controlled and monitored. The storm of fury convinced Nixon that he needed a spectacular triumph. If there were to be major changes, it would pay to plan for them quietly and out of the public eye.

The search for an effective triangular relationship appeared to take place in China too. There is insufficient evidence to show that it was pursued with the same kind of deliberation and determination as shown in the White House. However, an analysis of the signals coming from the Chinese leadership suggests that thinking within the ruling hierarchy was in the process of substantial change. Through the press the Chinese remained as critical of American policy as ever. Despite China's misgivings about the links between Hanoi and Moscow, Chinese leaders continued to condemn American policy in Asia. One typical editorial of February 1970 said that 'US imperialism ... rots with every passing day. Its aggression abroad suffered disastrous defeats.' The Vietnamese had beaten US imperialism 'black and blue.' After the United States had directed the South Vietnamese invasion of Laos in 1971 one commentator excoriated Nixon for 'reeking with gunpowder ... Now he has finally stepped forward to make frenzied war-cries, revealing his ugly warmonger's features in broad daylight.' But despite the chastisements of communist news analysis there was a small indication that the changes enveloping America could provide the foundations for future understanding. The press gloated over the growing protest movement in the United States. The gap that was presumed to exist between the leadership and the masses would be the catalyst for a new initiative. US imperialism, in China's opinion, was approaching exhaustion. Every time 'it started an aggression, every time it added a new rope that throttled it, and every time it started a war of aggression, every time it aroused stronger opposition from the revolutionary people.'[28]

By 1971 Mao had performed another of his famous about-turns. The Cultural Revolution had not strengthened the authority of the CCP, and had brought in its wake economic chaos and disruption in the educational system. Meanwhile, other Asian nations, including the 'province' of Taiwan, had forged ahead in economic growth. China had been weakened. It felt threatened by the Soviets on a number of fronts. The outbreak of war between India and Pakistan in early December 1971 and the open support of the Soviets for India heightened Mao's fears of encirclement. He therefore embarked on a programme to rebuild the CCP and to improve China's security, and dropped the pursuit of revolutionary zeal and ideological purity. A concern for increased production re-emerged, and even a small element of private economic activity was permitted in the communes. The People's Liberation Army, which had been responsible for the restoration of order and the dispersion of the Red Guards, was now itself the object of a new campaign that sought to strip it of its almost autonomous power. Senior army officers were required to make public self-criticisms and key personnel, particularly supporters of Lin Biao, were removed.

The climax to these developments came in September 1971, when Lin was allegedly foiled in an attempt to overthrow Mao and fled China. His military jet, apparently bound for the USSR, crashed in Mongolia, killing all on board. Lin's death accelerated the drive for internal stability and international rehabilitation. Lin had been the most ardent opponent of any opening to the United States; that opposition was almost discredited by his death. Mao encouraged Zhou to take new initiatives. Diplomatic relations with various nations were resumed, and in October 1970 Canada announced that it would recognize Communist China. More American scholars and journalists travelled to China. These visits of 'friendly personages' from the United States were enthusiastically reported in the Chinese press. Mao clarified the ideological basis for the sea-change by resurrecting in August 1971 an essay, 'On Policy,' originally written in 1940. This essay had justified collaboration with the Guomindang in the war against Japan. It proclaimed that cooperation with a less dangerous enemy was a legitimate tactic against a more dangerous 'principal enemy.' The essay was published in several papers and was broadcast by Radio Beijing. Its publication was designed to provide a rationale for the developing *rapprochement* with the United States.[29]

These changes in perspective in both China and the United States were picked up by one another and served to reinforce the proponents of change. At this stage deliberations were still cautious and undertaken without expectation. Indeed, in the case of China these reassessments were faltering and hardly apparent to the inexpert eye. Henry Kissinger has dubbed the various smoke signals as an 'intricate minuet ... so delicately arranged that both sides could always maintain they were not in contact, so stylized that neither side needed to bear the onus of an initiative.' The messages that came from Washington seemed more convincing than previous gestures, as they were part of a wider movement calling for improved relations with China and a more discriminating policy towards the communist world as a whole. Support for increased and extended contacts with China was gaining momentum among leading opinion-makers. They believed that China's recent turbulent experiences had forced it to re-examine some of its old prejudices. There was opportunity, they said, for bold moves, including a review of the country's unswerving support of Taiwan.[30]

America's commitment to the integrity of Taiwan had always been the major stumbling block to an accord with Beijing. Several opinion leaders believed that the time had come for the United States to accommodate China on the Taiwan issue in the broader interest of peace, and also to invigorate the United Nations by admitting to its membership the most populous nation on earth. Many of the proponents of a new policy were young scholars who had graduated in the growing number of degree programmes in Chinese studies. The Ford Foundation had contributed $22 million in the late 1960s to the development of Chinese language, and a further sum of $15 million had been put up through the National Defense Education Act. Leading scholars and Sinologists called for a China policy that came to terms with the Communist regime and argued that China's insularity, xenophobia and disregard for some of the norms of international life were due in part to the enforced isolation of the People's Republic. Many 'revisionist' scholars were rewriting and reinterpreting the origins and nature of the Cold War. They argued that America's economic and military muscle at the end of the Second World War had encouraged the adversarial tendencies of communist parties in poorer areas of the world. They believed that American foreign policy had to make adjustments in the light of that historical revision. These academics provided the Nixon administration with a ready-made image of a new China, stamped with the scholars' seal of approval.[31]

In 1971 the Foreign Relations Committee of the United States Senate held extensive public hearings on various Senate resolutions calling for the establishment of diplomatic relations with the People's Republic, and for its admission to the United Nations as the sole representative of China. The Senate resolutions were enthusiastically supported by American Sinologists. James Thomson of Harvard University provided the Senate with an articulate analysis of how out-dated US policy was towards China. He told Senator William Fulbright of Arkansas that American policy-makers had developed their policy to the Far East in the context of the immediate post-war crises in Europe. Americans, he warned, were too firmly entrenched in the belief that toughness was the only appropriate response to regimes that rejected American protection. Americans had become obsessed with power *per se*. 'Every book they write,' he said, 'is called The Obligations of Power, or the Needs of Power, or the Responsibilities of Power, or the Power of Power and so forth.' Containment had been ill-advised in the case of China, pushing it 'into a sense of threat, a sense of fear, pushing us away from vital knowledge of the Chinese, pushing all parties away from the vital learning processes.' Jerome Cohen, also of Harvard, told the Senate Committee that the United States could not expect China to waive its claim to jurisdiction in Taiwan, territory it regarded as its own. Another historian, Barbara Tuchman, the distinguished biographer of Joseph Stilwell, argued that the policy of non-recognition had not advanced the effectiveness of containment.[32]

Political leaders from both parties began to condemn a policy that was rooted in the events of 1949 and 1950. Senator Fulbright, the Senate's most vocal critic of the war in Vietnam, argued that the United States was simply wrong in believing that China was aggressive and dangerous. Washington had been mistaken in believing that Chinese power would be contained through involvement in Vietnam. Senator Edward Kennedy of Massachusetts was unequivocal in his advocacy of admitting only one China to the United Nations, the People's Republic. 'Our policy cannot be based on wishes and hopes. It must cope with reality,' he insisted. As Communist China and Taiwan would never agree on dual representation, the United States should make an independent decision on the matter. He pointed out that despite its possession of nuclear weapons, China was not a strong military power and carried little weight in the Third World. He urged the United States to show good faith while China remained weak. In the lengthy Senate hearings, witnesses repeatedly said that increased contacts with China would be a means of expunging the experience of McCarthyism from the national conscience. China policy had, in James Thomson's words, 'poisoned our domestic political bloodstream.' In some ways opening the door to China was a means of making amends for the past. There were also a number of new 'China Hands' serving in government departments or advising them. Most of them had undertaken one of the courses in Chinese Studies that had begun to burgeon in the universities. They included Marshall Green, Assistant Secretary of State for East Asia and Pacific Affairs, and John Holdridge, who read Chinese Studies at Cornell and was Kissinger's aide. They believed it was only a matter of time before full contacts with China were restored. John Stewart Service, one of the most notorious victims of McCarthy's purges, was invited to testify before the Foreign Relations Committee. He served as a poignant reminder of how prejudice in political attitudes could destroy the ability to think strategically. The reconsideration of America's China policy was not confined to the White House. In short, it was an integral part of the wider reassessment undertaken by the United States in the early 1970s of inherited assumptions about China and the very nature of the communist threat.[33]

The debate on relations with China did not just revolve around the mechanics of recognition and its complicated link to America's long-standing support of Taiwan. Inevitably, the very nature of the Communist regime in the People's Republic came under close scrutiny. Americans who had actually travelled to China were largely satisfied that the worst excesses of the Cultural Revolution were a thing of the past and that trade, scholarly exchanges and other forms of intercourse would benefit both societies. Arthur Galston, Professor of Biology at Yale, described how on a recent trip he had noticed the desire of Chinese to buy American goods and exchange information. Tillman Durdin of the *New York Times* reported that xenophobia in China was in decline and that current Chinese thinking placed material interests above ideological ones. The opportunities for trade were vast, but most experts agreed that trade would not increase to any substantial extent until the United States and China sorted out their political differences. Few believed in a large and infinite 'China Market.' Economic opportunity was viewed as a distant horizon, not an immediate incentive. Most were realistic in their assessments; they recognized that China lacked the income base for extensive trade and that the long embargo on trade had locked China into other markets. Certainly in the short term the Taiwan market was a better bet. Similarly, the opponents of normalization did not profess to be interested in economic opportunity. They maintained that Washington's links with Taiwan served its Asian interests and its moral obligations. They wanted no truck with the People's Republic, which still had a totalitarian regime with an appalling record on human rights. Senator Peter Dominick of Colorado, one of Taiwan's most persistent advocates and a spokesman for the Committee of One Million, argued that the Beijing government was tyrannical and contemptuous of international law. 'Which is the real communist China?' he asked. 'The "winsome" China which wines and dines visiting athletes and journalists? Or the brutal China of the Cultural Revolution which tortures its citizens and lets their bodies float down the rivers to the South China Sea?' According to Franz Michael of the Sino-Soviet Institute of George Washington University, Chinese leaders, especially Zhou Enlai, were as adept at deceiving Americans about their pragmatism as Stalin was during the Second World War.[34]

Despite the vigour of Taiwan's defenders, the changing climate of opinion at home and abroad convinced Nixon and Kissinger that the isolation of China no longer served America's interests. They wanted power to devolve to their Asian allies and to see more local responsibility for military defence. However, they did not want the devolution of military power to be confused with a general retreat from the responsibilities of power. They wanted more 'bargaining chips' with their rivals in the Kremlin, and believed that the fissures in the communist world presented them with a unique opportunity. A restructuring of America's global strategy could not be effected without a reconsideration of China policy. A two-front war was unthinkable, as it was to the Chinese. Both nations needed new friends.

There was one other motive for the move towards normalization, a motive that was probably shared by Nixon and Mao. Both men had inflated senses of their own political grandeur and were convinced of the uniqueness of their contributions to the unfolding of history. The memoirs of Nixon and Kissinger dwell at length on the significance of their China policy and brim with references to the enormity of the achievement of breaking the ice with their meeting in February 1972. Nixon himself may well have envied Mao's standing in Chinese politics. Mao had perfected the cult of personality. At home Nixon was almost a figure of derision, particularly with the press. As Stephen Ambrose has commented: 'All that power. Nixon could snap his fingers as he did thousands of times on his News Summaries and in his meetings with his aides, and nothing happened. Mao could snap his fingers, and tens of thousands died.' Nixon envied the ability of China's leaders to determine news images. 'I'd like to rearrange a front page now and then,' he muttered enviously after he had seen Zhou rearrange the galleys of a newspaper. Mao, too, was aware that his Cultural Revolution had devastated China and that Lin Biao, its most enthusiastic lieutenant, was disgraced. Rejoining the world would be an exercise in retrieval and provide an opportunity to regain national dignity.[35]

The diplomacy that led up to the meeting of the two leaders in Beijing also reflected the relish shown by Nixon and Kissinger for clandestine intrigue. The trip was preceded by a plethora of elliptical diplomatic smoke signals. Mysterious messages were conveyed by unlikely intermediaries. Restrictions on trade in certain non-strategic items were removed. Travel restrictions were relaxed and tourists were permitted greater duty-free allowances. American prisoners in China were freed, and the State Department issued statements endorsing the readmission of China to the United Nations. The most publicized gesture was the unexpected invitation in the spring of 1971 to the American table tennis team to visit Beijing after the world championships in Japan. The table tennis tournament that followed must have been the most highly profiled ping-pong game ever. It was 'the ping heard around the world,' as admirers called it, or 'the ping that ponged' as its detractors coined it.[36]

A week later, on 21 April, a new message came from Zhou Enlai through the offices of Pakistan's Ambassador, Agha Hilaly. Zhou Enlai had invited an emissary to come to China for discussions on outstanding issues. Nixon was thrilled. At first he wanted to go ahead himself without a preliminary visit from somebody else, but Kissinger dissuaded him. Nixon was intoxicated by the significance of the occasion. Kissinger felt that a new historical threshold had been reached. Nixon relished the invitation, and had it read out loud to Haldeman. 'It was not that Nixon did not understand it,' Kissinger remembered. 'It was rather that he wanted to savor the moment of accomplishment by hearing it described to an old associate from the lonely days of exile. It was a kind of vindication, proof that the solitude and travail of those years had not been in vain.'[37]

The preparations and subterfuges for the planned trip to Beijing are almost folklore. Henry Kissinger clearly relished the prospect of preparing the way, and made elaborate smokescreens for his first secret visit to China. He arranged a cover, a fact-finding trip to Southern Asia, in order to get to Pakistan, from where he would slip away to get to Beijing. Secretary of State Rogers was kept in the dark, as were most of Nixon's closest advisers. In Pakistan Kissinger developed a prearranged stomach ache. This enabled him to disappear before dawn over the border on his historic trip to the Chinese capital. It was clear, certainly from his memoirs, that Kissinger was in thrall to Zhou Enlai and was constantly charmed by his presence. He felt utterly relaxed – invigorated, no doubt, by the novelty of it all. 'We sat around a table in easy conversation, as if there had never been a day's interruption in contacts between our nations,' he wrote. Kissinger and Zhou seemed determined to hit it off. The conversations covered such sensitive issues as Vietnam and Taiwan, but always steered towards the promise of the future. In a second visit Kissinger even showed Zhou Enlai satellite photographs of Soviet military forces. Kissinger was determined to be seen as a serious partner. He was almost flushed by the occasion, throwing caution to the winds. On his return he transferred the sense of excitement to the President. Nixon had no doubt that the trip was momentous. Just before he left for Beijing he invited the French writer André Malraux to the White House. He hoped that the author of the famous La Condition Humaine (1933), based on his personal experiences in Shanghai during the civil war, could provide some last-minute insights. In their conversation Malraux dwelt upon a favourite theme, the phenomenon of historical destiny. He compared the forthcoming trip to the 'sixteenth century explorers, who set out for a specific objective but often arrived at an entirely different discovery.' Referring to Mao, Malraux told Nixon: 'Mr. President, you will meet a man who has had a fantastic destiny and who believes that he is acting out the last act of his lifetime. You may think he is talking to you, but he will in truth be addressing Death.'[38]

Nixon took Malraux's words seriously. 'History has brought us together,' he told Mao when they finally met in Beijing on 17 February

1972. They talked for about an hour, and most of their remarks consisted of mutual ingratiation. They praised each other for their successful rise from early poverty. Stretching credulity somewhat, Nixon told Mao that 'the Chairman's writings moved a nation and have changed the world.' The President's meetings with Zhou were more substantial, but they covered old ground and said nothing to change each other's minds. They knew they could not resolve the long-standing issue of Taiwan. Both had taken a gamble in meeting face to face and they did not want to take any more risks. The conferees knew they would have to set their differences aside if they were going to talk at all. Their objective was not to give up claims they had defended for nearly a quarter of a century, but to maintain their interests in the shifting realignments taking place in the world's balance of power. They could not expect to close a gulf that had lasted for over two decades. The Shanghai Communiqué issued at the end of the trip highlighted the nations' disagreements over Taiwan, but looked guardedly forward to future agreement. The United States acknowledged the position on both sides of the Taiwan Strait that there was but one China. It also affirmed that it would 'progressively reduce its forces and military installations on Taiwan as the tension in the area diminishes.' In these words the United States gave the Chinese a stake in helping it to bring peace to Asia and in defusing tensions across the Strait.[39]

Despite the outcry from Taiwan's supporters that inevitably followed the Shanghai Communiqué, Nixon believed that a monumental historical threshold had been crossed. In his farewell toast at the end of the week he proclaimed: 'This was the week that changed the world.' He probably believed himself. Certainly the two leaders' own sense of history and destiny had brought them together, but the world did not change as a result. The security interests of both nations were served by commencing a dialogue and recognizing common concerns. The historic meeting began the process of normalization, but it was a process that came about slowly. Years of hostility and suspicion would not evaporate as the result of one visit.[40]

Like all summit meetings, this particular one was greeted with a mixture of admiration and outrage. Most commentators sighed with relief that two decades of obstinate deadlock had been broken. Nixon's critics, however, echoed fears that transcended the immediate issue of Taiwan or the assessment of Mao's role in the excesses of the Cultural Revolution. They seized upon the problem that generally accrues from all personal diplomacy. Men are mortal; they change; leadership is not permanent. Structures are often needed to protect the durability of agreements and the wider national interest. There was no guarantee that the breakthrough would last. The visit and subsequent communiqué had been planned in utter secrecy. America's Asian allies had received no advance warning of the meeting and were scarcely consulted after the event. Japan resented the fact that it had given in to the United States by eschewing contact with the People's Republic in support of its Taiwan policy. A proven partner in Taipei was exchanged for a problematic tie with a nation that the United States scarcely understood. To the Japanese it now seemed that years of sacrifice had been in vain. The visit weakened the confidence of other Asian countries. President Thieu of South Vietnam commented sourly: 'America has been looking for a better mistress, and now Nixon has discovered China. He does not want to have the old mistress hanging around. Vietnam has become old and ugly.' Professor Edwin Reischauer of Harvard thought the visit 'so entirely unpredictable as to be quixotic.' He believed that the United States had shed its reputation for reliability. George Ball, former Under-Secretary of State, wrote in the *New York Times* that summitry was dangerous as it was subject to caprice. Chamberlain's face-to-face encounter with Hitler at Munich had cast a malign spell. 'Few myths,' Ball wrote, 'have done more harm than the sentimental conceit that men of different countries can understand one another better through direct conversation than when their exchange of views and ideas is filtered through experts sensitive to the nuances that derive from different cultures.' Little is known about disquiet within China, but there is evidence from at least one source that has been made available in the West that there were still residual doubts, even after the fall of Lin Biao. A document written by the army political department in Yunnan lumped the Soviet Union and the United States together as 'arch enemies' and warned the Chinese leadership that Nixon was still 'a man of transition.'[41]

Whatever the disquiet occasioned by the meetings in China, the visit meant things would never be quite the same again. President Nixon had broken the ice that had governed Sino-American relations since Mao had come to power. While conditions had been improving for some time, Nixon, Kissinger and Zhou deserve the credit for hastening the process. The visit captured the imagination of the Americans. It opened up a country that had always seemed remote and baffling. It was a magnificent public relations exercise. The media colluded with the White House, and for a short time Nixon enjoyed a rare honeymoon with the press. Americans were exhilarated by the occasion. Appearances governed the day. The sight of an American president on the Great Wall in the company of some of the most elusive leaders in the twentieth century was captivating – but that captivation disabled many Americans from digesting the fact that Mao had presided over some of the most devastating and bloody social experiments in the recent past. Many of America's top newspaper correspondents chose to turn a blind eye to the despotism that had survived unshaken by the Great Leap Forward or the Cultural Revolution. As one critic, Steven Mosher, has said, dozens of journalists, 'so sure-footed on their own turf, had fallen over themselves praising one of the most despotic regimes ever known to man.' Nixon led this indulgence. He ingratiated himself in Beijing by praising the political message of a revolutionary ballet, while at home he dismissed student protesters as 'campus bums.' What had been excoriated in the past as shortcomings were now extravagantly defended as legitimate and courageous programmes of social betterment.[42]

The excessive euphoria about all matters Chinese gave the makers of American foreign policy a much-needed fillip. The disaffection and pessimism of ordinary Americans that had arisen as a result of the Vietnam war was put aside, at least for the time being. The meeting with Chinese leaders demonstrated that the United States was not manacled by the commitments and assumptions of the past. It showed that the United States now was involved not in a Cold War confrontation but in a complex and permutating series of relationships with rival powers. The national interest would be protected through the traditional diplomatic exercise of the balance of power, rather than through military reinforcement of ideological proclamations.

The most problematic vestige of the old policy, the war in Vietnam, could now be resolved. The new diplomacy promised to make the process of withdrawal from Vietnam that much easier. The fighting in Indo-China could no longer be justified as the means of containing an expansionist and hostile China. China was no longer billed as an aggressive nation. Similarly, the Beijing government felt more assured that America's involvement in Vietnam was not simply based on its wish to encircle China and stamp out its revolution. It anticipated that as the United States gradually withdrew from the Far East, China would emerge as the dominant power in Asia. Moscow, too, now had a greater interest in *détente* with the United States. It wanted to make agreements with the United States in order to counterbalance China. Its interest in tying down American troops in Southeast Asia was diminishing. Nixon perceived that an opening with Beijing would not only put diplomacy on a new footing; it would also enable him to end the war with the 'honour' he had so persistently pursued. He did not want to be seen as the president who had sold out his allies. So he believed it was a safe gamble to order the new air offensive against Hanoi and the mining of Haiphong later in the spring of 1972 in order to put pressure on North Vietnam in the peace negotiations. He calculated correctly that while the temporary escalations would be publicly condemned in Moscow and Beijing, they would not push back the process of *détente*. China wanted a negotiated settlement. Chinese leaders also recognized that, if they were accommodating with the United States in its pursuit of an orderly withdrawal from Vietnam, then America's defence arrangements with Taiwan would be seen in Washington as increasingly dispensable. Although Nixon had made it clear that he would not abandon Taiwan, it seemed that American policy in Asia was now a moveable feast. If the week of Nixon's visit to China was, in the President's words, 'the week that changed the world,' then the troubled relationship might well become a thing of the past.[43]

NOTES

1. Stanley Karnow, *Mao and China: Inside China's Cultural Revolution* (Harmondsworth, 1984 edn.), pp.140–46; Tang Tsou, *The Cultural Revolution and the Post-Mao Reforms: A Historical Perspective* (Chicago, IL, 1986), pp. 64–79; Bill Brugger, *China: Radicalism to Revisionism, 1962–1979* (London, 1981), pp. 23–35; William F. Dorrill, 'Power, Policy and Ideology in the Making of the Chinese Cultural Revolution,' in Thomas W. Robinson, ed., *The Cultural Revolution in China* (Berkeley and Los Angeles, CA), pp. 52–79; Lowell Dittmer, *Liu Shao-ch'i and the Chinese Cultural Revolution: The Politics of Mass Criticism* (Berkeley and Los Angeles, CA, 1974), pp.43–51.

2. Mao speech, 18 November 1957, in *Quotations from Chairman Mao Tse-tung* (Beijing, 1967), pp. 80–81; 'South Vietnam Liberation Army is Fighting Brilliantly,' *Peking Review*, 7 April 1967.

3. Janos Radvanyi, 'Vietnam War Diplomacy: Reflections of a Former Iron Curtain Official' in Lloyd J. Matthews and Dale E. Brown, *Assessing the Vietnam War: A Collection from the Journal of the U.S. Army War College* (Washington, DC, and London, 1987), pp. 60–63.

4. Andrew Walder, 'Cultural Revolution Radicalism: Variations on a Stalinist Theme' in William A. Joseph, Christine P.W. Wong and David Zweig, *New Perspectives on the Cultural Revolution* (Cambridge, MA. and London, 1991), pp. 43–46.

5. Stanley Karnow, *Mao and China: Inside China's Cultural Revolution* (New York, 1972), pp. 157–93; A.S. Chang, 'The Proletarian Cultural Revolution,' *China Mainland Review, 2* (1967), pp.91–102; Philip Bridgham, 'Mao's Cultural Revolution in 1967: The Struggle to Seize Power, *China Quarterly 34* (April–June, 1968), pp. 6–37; Walder, 'Cultural Revolution Radicalism' in Joseph, Wong and Zweig, *New Perspectives on the Cultural Revolution*, pp. 43–6; Kikuzo Ito and Minoru Shibata, 'The Dilemma of Mao Tse-tung, *China Quarterly 35* (July–September 1968), pp.58–77.

6. Quoted in Hong Yung Lee, *The Politics of the Cultural Revolution: A Case Study* (Berkeley and Los Angeles, CA, 1978), p. 31.

7. Lynn T. White III, *Policies of Chaos: The Organizational Causes of Violence in China's Cultural Revolution* (Princeton, NJ, 1989), pp. 13–18, 221–305. See also Stanley Rosen, *Red Guard Factionalism and the Cultural Revolution in Guangzhou (Canton)* (Boulder, CO, 1982); Anne F. Thurston, *Enemies of the People: The Ordeal of the Intellectuals in China's Great Cultural Revolution* (New York, 1987). A particularly moving account is Jung Chang, *Wild Swans: Three Daughters of China* (London, 1991), pp. 256–405.

8. Stefan T. Possony, 'The Chinese Communist Cauldron,' *Orbis* (1969), 13, pp. 783–821; Lee, *The Politics of the Chinese Cultural Revolution*, pp. 204–52; Ezra F. Vogel, *One Step Ahead in China: Guangdong under Reform* (Cambridge, MA, 1989), 18–27; also, Yuan Gao, *Born Red: A Chronicle of the Cultural Revolution* (Stanford, CA, 1987).

9. William Hinton, *Hundred Day War* (New York, 1972); Parris H. Chang, *Power and Policy in China* (University Park, PA, 1978), pp. 198–9.

10. Clare Hollingworth, *Mao and the Men Against Him* (London, 1985), pp. 172–4; Melvin Gurtov, 'The Foreign Ministry and Foreign Affairs during the Cultural Revolution,' *China Quarterly* (October–December 1969), 40, pp. 65–102; David Mozingo, *China's Foreign Policy and the Cultural Revolution* (Ithaca, NY, 1970); Ronald C. Keith, *The Diplomacy of Zhou Enlai* (London, 1989), pp. 161–74; Brugger, *China: Radicalism to Revisionism, 1962–1979* , pp. 85–6; Uri Ra'anan, 'Peking's Foreign Policy 'Debate', 1965–1966 in Tang Tsou ed., *China in Crisis, II: China's Policies in Asia and America's Alternatives* (Chicago, IL, 1968), pp. 23–71; Michael Yahuda, *China's Role in World Affairs* (London, 1978), pp. 190–98; Chen Yi, Self-Criticism, 6 March 1968, in Harold C. Hinton ed., *The People's Republic of China, 1949–1979: A Documentary Survey, IV: 1967–1970, The Cultural Revolution, part II* (Wilmington, DE, 1980), p. 2089.

11. Lucian Pye, 'China in Context,' *Foreign Affairs 45* (January 1967), pp. 229–45; Leonard A. Kusnitz, *Public Opinion and Foreign Policy: America's China policy, 1949–1979* (Westport, 1984), pp. 116–20; Michael B. Yahuda, 'Chinese Foreign Policy after 1963: The Maoist Phases,' *China Quarterly* (October–December 1968), 36, p. 110.

12. Townsend Hoopes, *The Limits of Intervention (an inside account of how the Johnson policy of escalation in Vietnam was reversed)* (New York and London, 1987 edn), pp. 93–7; also, Clark Clifford (with Richard Holbrooke), *Counsel to the President: A Memoir* (New York, 1991), p. 452.

13. *Public Papers of the Presidents: Lyndon B. Johnson, 1967, II* (Washington, DC,

1968), pp. 1171–2; F. Charles Parker IV, *Vietnam: Strategy for a Stalemate* (New York, 1989), pp. 160–63; Bunker to the President, 13 January 1968, in Douglas Pike ed., *The Bunker Papers: Reports to the President from Vietnam, 1967–1973* (3 vols, Berkeley, CA, 1990), p. 287.

14. 'Victory Certainly Belongs to the Heroic Vietnamese People Persevering in the Struggle,' *Peking Review*, 16 February 1968; message, Zhou Enlai to President Huu Tho, SVNLF, in *Peking Review*, 9 February 1968; Larry Cable, *Unholy Grail: the US and the Wars in Vietnam, 1965–8* (London, 1991), pp. 217–20; Frances Fitzgerald, *Fire in the Lake: The Vietnamese and the Americans in Vietnam* (New York, 1972), pp. 518–34; Harry McPherson, *A Political Education* (Boston, MA, 1972), pp. 433–34; Lyndon B. Johnson, *The Vantage Point: Perspectives of the Presidency* (New York, 1971), pp. 365–424, 493–531; John Dumbrell ed., *Vietnam and the Antiwar Movement* (Aldershot, 1989).

15. Yahuda, *China's Role in World Affairs*, pp. 206–8.

16. *People's Daily* editorial; 'Spearhead of Struggle Directed Against US Imperialism,' *Peking Review*, 31 May 1968.

17. 'Soviet Revisionist Clique Cannot Escape the Punishment of History,' *Peking Review*, 8 March 1968.

18. The most comprehensive analysis of the border conflict is Richard Wich, *Sino-Soviet Crisis Politics: A Study of Political Change and Communication* (Cambridge, MA, 1980); also, John W. Garner, *China's Decision for Rapprochement with the United States, 1968–1971* (Boulder, CO, 1982), pp. 21–37, 55–70; William E. Griffith, *Peking, Moscow and Beyond* (Washington, DC, 1973), p. 11; Robert G. Sutter, *China-Watch: Toward Sino-American Reconciliation* (Baltimore, MD, and London, 1978), pp. 68–82; John R. Dewenter, 'China Afloat,' *Foreign Affairs*, 50 (July 1972), pp. 738–51.

19. Richard M. Nixon, 'Asia after Vietnam,' *Foreign Affairs* (October 1967), 46, pp. 111–25; Karnow, *Mao and China*, p. 493.

20. *People's Daily*, 27 January 1969, in Hinton ed., *The People's Republic of China, IV*, pp. 2204–6; Sutter, *China-Watch*, pp. 98–108; Kenneth T. Young, *Negotiating with the Chinese Communists: The United States Experience, 1953–1967* (New York and London, 1968), pp. 290–97; Ishwer C. Ohja, 'New Perspectives on Sino-American Relations,' in John Chay, ed., *The Problems and Prospects of American East-Asian Relations* (Boulder, CO, 1977), pp. 27–47.

21. Useful discussions of the Nixon presidency include: Stephen E. Ambrose, *Nixon: II, The Triumph of a Politician, 1962–1972* (New York, 1989); Robert S. Litwak, *Detente and the Nixon Doctrine: American Foreign policy and the Pursuit of Stability, 1969–1976* (Cambridge, 1984); Walter Isaacson, *Kissinger: A Biography* (New York and London, 1992); also, Robert A. Garson, 'A Rendezvous with History: Nixon, Mao, and the Politics of Normalization,' in Priscilla Roberts ed., *Sino-American Relations Since 1900* (Hong Kong, 1991), pp. 497–517.

22. H.R. Haldeman and Joseph DiMona, *The Ends of Power* (New York, 1978), p. 83; Henry Kissinger, *White House Years* (Boston, MA, 1970), pp. 160–61.

23. Kissinger, *White House Years*, p. 168.

24. Isaacson, *Kissinger*, p. 165–79; William Shawcross, *Sideshow: Kissinger, Nixon, and the Destruction of Cambodia* (London, 1979), pp. 19–35; Tad Szulc, *The Illusion of Peace: Foreign Policy in the Nixon Years* (New York, 1978), pp. 4–10.

25. Kissinger, *White House Years*, pp. 167–71; Henry Kissinger, *American Foreign Policy: Three Essays* (New York, 1969), pp. 17–43; Szulc, *The Illusion of Peace*, pp. 346–50.

26. Kissinger, *White House Years*, pp. 191–2; also, Arnold R. Isaacs, *Without Honor: Defeat in Vietnam and Cambodia* (Baltimore, MD, 1983), pp. 18–19; *China News Analysis*, No. 780, 31 October 1969.

27. Allan E. Goodman, *The Lost Peace: America's Search for a Negotiated Settlement of the Vietnam War* (Stanford, CA, 1978), pp. 104–11; William Safire, *Before the Fall* (New York, 1975), pp. 102–3; also, Richard A. Falk, 'The Cambodian Operation and International Law,' *American Journal of International Law*, 65 (January 1971), pp. 1–25.

28. New China News Agency, 15 February 1970; *People's Daily*, 20 February, 11 March 1971 in *Survey of China Mainland Press* (American Consulate-General, Hong Kong), Nos. 4603, 4605 (hereafter cited as *SCMP*).

29. Wich, *Sino-Soviet Crisis Politics*, pp. 256–60; Raymond L. Garthoff, *Détente and Confrontation: American-Soviet Relations from Nixon to Reagan* (Washington, DC, 1985), p. 235; *SCMP*, Nos. 4882, 4890; Robert A. Scalapino, 'China and the Balance of Power,' *Foreign Affairs* 52 (January 1974), pp. 372–4; Jaap van Ginneken, *The Rise and Fall of Lin Piao* (Harmondsworth, 1976), pp. 249–52, 263–74; Keith, *The Diplomacy of Zhou Enlai*, pp. 181–93; Griffith, *Peking, Moscow and Beyond*, p. 36.

30. Kissinger, *White House Years*, p. 187.

31. See, for example, Noam Chomsky, *At War with Asia* (London edn, 1971); Joyce and Gabriel Kolko, *The Limits of Power: The World and US Foreign Policy, 1945–1954* (New York, 1972); Diane S. Clemens, *Yalta* (New York, 1970); Walter LaFeber, *America, Russia and the Cold War, 1945–1966* (New York, 1980); Barton J. Bernstein, ed., *Politics and Policies of the Truman Administration* (Chicago, IL, 1972). A damning criticism of the emerging scholarly consensus can be found in Steven Mosher, *China Misperceived: American Illusions and Chinese Reality* (New York, 1990), pp. 120–32.

32. US Senate, *Hearings before the Committee on Foreign Relations: United States Relations with the People's Republic of China* (Washington, DC, 1972), pp. 90–93, 133–7, 225–38.

33. Senate, *Hearings: United States Relations with the People's Republic of China*, pp. 59, 179; US Senate, *Hearings before the Committee on Foreign Relations: China and the United States: Today and Yesterday* (Washington, DC, 1972), pp. 5–7, 47–50; A. Doak Barnett and Edwin O. Reischauer eds., *The United States and China: The Next Decade* (London, 1970), pp. 26–7, 35.

34. Senate, *Hearings: United States Relations with the People's Republic of China*, pp. 156–63; Mosher, *China Misperceived*, p. 138.

35. Ambrose, *Nixon, II*, p. 513.

36. New China News Agency report, 11 April 1971 in *SCMP*, No. 4882; *China News Analysis*, 7 May 1971.

37. Kissinger, *White House Years*, p. 717; Isaacson, *Kissinger*, pp. 338–40; Marvin and Bernard Kalb, *Kissinger* (Boston, MA, 1974), pp. 240–41.

38. Kissinger, *White House Years*, p. 742; Hersh, *The Price of Power*, pp. 375–6; Richard Nixon, *The Memoirs of Richard Nixon* (London, 1979), pp. 557–8.

39. Nixon, *Memoirs*, pp. 577–80; Kissinger, *White House Years*, pp. 1049–96; Ambrose, *Nixon II*, pp. 515–17; Garson, 'A Rendezvous with History,' pp. 509–14.

40. Nixon, *Memoirs*, pp. 577–80; Peter Van Ness, 'Co-opting China: The Realization of the American Dream?' in Yu-ming Shaw, *Mainland China: Politics, Economics and Reform* (Boulder, CO, 1986), pp. 609–15.

41. 'The New China Policy: Its Impact on the United States and Asia' in US House of Representatives, *Hearings before the Subcommittee on Asian and Pacific Affairs of the Committee on Foreign Affairs* (Washington DC, 1972), pp. 6–7, 12; Harold C. Hinton, *Peking-Washington: Chinese Foreign Policy and the United States* (Washington, DC, 1976), pp. 41–8; Thieu's quotation in Isaacson, *Kissinger*, p. 353; George W. Ball, 'Nixon's Appointment in Peking: Is This Trip Necessary? *New York Times Magazine*, 13 February 1972; Garthoff, *Détente and Confrontation*, pp. 239–40.

42. Mosher, *China Misperceived*, pp. vii, 5–8; Stanley Karnow, 'American News Media and China,' in Gene T. Hsiao, *Sino-American Détente and its Policy Implications* (New York and London, 1974), pp. 80–83.

43. Isaacs, *Without Honor*, pp. 18–19, 28; Earl C. Ravenal, 'Approaching China, Defending Taiwan,' *Foreign Affairs*, 50 (October 1971), pp. 52–4; Chiao Chiao Hsieh, *Strategy for Survival: The Foreign Policy and External Relations of the Republic of China on Taiwan, 1949–79* (London, 1985), pp. 143–5.

CHAPTER 6

HESITANT INTERLUDE: TOWARDS NORMALIZATION, 1972-79

President Nixon's visit to China broke the ice of a quarter of a century. It marked the turning point in Sino-American relations, and was probably the high point of Nixon's foreign policy. However, the momentum and euphoria generated by the visit were not sustained. It was not followed by formal recognition for nearly seven more years. In some ways the diplomatic energy that had been expended on trying to build bridges had burned itself out – but there were other factors which made further progress more difficult and more faltering. The mutual suspicion that had been generated since 1949, particularly as a result of America's defence treaty with Taiwan, was not going to evaporate as a result of one dramatic meeting between two heads of state. The economic and international considerations that had led the United States and China to review their long antagonism remained, and continued to inform the Sino-American relationship. America and China did not share the same political culture and were not natural partners. Both nations were inclined to hedge their bets. They believed that there was more to be gained through the guesswork and uncertainty of triangular diplomacy than through running headlong into immediate recognition.

As is often the case, greater contact exposes new fault lines. Isolation requires less effort and less diplomatic imagination. As communications improved, the sources of friction became more apparent and frequent. Above all, the state of Sino-American relations depended on the flux of international and domestic developments. The United States had played the 'China card' in order to show the Soviets that the United States was not locked into one single strategy. However, the overriding aim of policy-makers in Washington was still to provide coherent structures for the resolution of conflict and arms control with the Soviet Union. The apparent indivisibility of that strategy was galling to the Chinese. They did not want to be in a line of resort in the dealings of the superpowers;

they wanted to see a realignment in the balance of power. As successive administrations in Washington pursued *détente* with the Soviet Union, the Chinese felt that the rug had been swept from under them. The Soviet threat had brought the United States and China together. Whenever it seemed that that threat might recede through successful negotiations, China was put on the back burner. The Chinese believed that they still played second fiddle. To compound their problems, the governments in both Washington and Beijing experienced profound domestic difficulties that dissipated their diplomatic energies. A bold initiative on the issue of recognition was a risky undertaking.

After Richard Nixon won his resounding electoral victory in the election of November 1972 – he won more than 60 per cent of the total votes cast – it seemed that there were no obstacles to the continuation of his policies. National divisions over the war in Indo-China and the disaffection of so many of the nation's intellectuals had almost become a source of political strength for the President. The only cloud on the horizon that November was the fact that peace in Vietnam was still not at hand. Nixon believed that his mandate cleared the way for a rapid resolution. Although a peace proposal had been hammered out in Paris between the United States and North Vietnam, the South Vietnamese were digging in their heels. They were not prepared to accept a peace that permitted the North Vietnamese to hold on to some of their gains in the south.

Nixon, buoyed up by his landslide electoral victory and an assumption of Chinese tolerance, was sympathetic and wanted some revisions to the Paris agreements that would patch up some of the shortcomings in the draft treaty. The North Vietnamese were furious with the change of mind, and peace talks broke down on 13 December. By then, the US had little muscle on the ground. Fewer than 25,000 troops remained in Vietnam and there was no prospect of escalating the ground war. Nixon wanted to show Le Duc Tho, leader of the North Vietnamese delegation at the Paris peace talks, that his hands were not tied by the doves in Congress and that he could still harm the North. Well over one billion dollars worth of military hardware had been delivered to the South in a matter of weeks, in part to forestall a possible resupply effort by the Soviets and Chinese. Nixon decided to launch a major new bombing assault on North Vietnam. He was determined to wreak massive damage on the North Vietnamese. B-52s were ordered to bomb the urban areas of the North, including Hanoi. Over a period of twelve days the US unleashed one of the most devastating attacks of the entire war, dropping more than 36,000 tons of bombs. Nixon probably hoped to reduce the North's capacity to overrun the South after the peace and so increase the duration of the 'decent interval' that would ensue before the conflict was finally resolved. The pummelling of Hanoi aroused furious condemnation throughout the world. Pope Paul VI broke the Vatican's usual silence. China condemned it. The bombing continued until 30 December, when Hanoi agreed to return to the bargaining table. In early January Le Duc Tho relented and accepted revisions to the peace agreements. On 22 January Thieu also caved in and finally consented. A few days later the formal signing ceremonies took place in Paris, and America's agonizing participation in the Vietnam war came to an end. Ironically, the major issue over which the war had been fought – the political future of South Vietnam – was not resolved and was ultimately left to the warring Vietnamese parties. South Vietnamese independence was probably less secure then than it had been at the beginning of America's involvement. The face of communism had not changed, and America's insistence that it would always stand by its clients rang hollow.[1]

The administration was confident that the ending of America's role in Vietnam would provide one major dividend. Its involvement in Vietnam had always been cited publicly by the communist powers as evidence of America's hegemonic designs in Asia. It was hoped that the ending of the war would remove one of the principal obstacles to a working *rapprochement* with the Soviet Union and China. Although the Soviets and Chinese were likely to continue their assistance to the North Vietnamese, Washington recognized that this competition was likely to lead to a new regional rivalry among the communist nations. Kissinger and Nixon hoped that their meetings with Chinese leaders in 1972, together with the ending of America's participation in the Vietnam war, had cleared the way for a full working relationship with Beijing. They contended that many outstanding issues, such as trade and cultural exchanges, were matters of detail that could be worked out by careful diplomacy. Full recognition was still problematic because of America's ties with Taiwan, but the administration hoped that the two nations could agree to disagree on Taiwan and so assign the issue to the back burner. What it did not realize is that the United States and China had different expectations of *détente*. America still saw its relations as inextricably linked to its Soviet policies. The notion of 'triangular diplomacy' had become something of an *idée fixe*. The United States believed that closer relations with Beijing would push the Soviets into seeking *détente* with greater urgency. China, on the other hand, wanted closer ties with the United States in order to strengthen a realignment against the Soviet Union. The Americans believed that careful engagement of a policy of triangular diplomacy would enable them to act as broker in a new kind of great power consortium. The Chinese were more pessimistic. They thought the Soviets were intent on aggression and that they should be contained through a Sino-American front.

In mid-February 1973, one month after Nixon's second inauguration, Kissinger went back to China. He hoped to maintain the diplomatic momentum and to use the occasion to keep up pressure on the Soviets to build on the arms control agreements of 1972. Kissinger was acutely aware that the Chinese regarded their new *rapprochement* as an anti-Soviet instrument, and admitted in his memoirs that the Chinese expected more of their new ties. The Chinese, he wrote, were 'scientists of equilibrium, artists of relativity.' There was one thing they would not tolerate: 'no nation could be permitted to be preeminent, however fleetingly, over the combination of forces that could be arrayed against it.' He realized that the Soviets were less of a threat to the United States than to China, because the USA could match any increase in arms and thwart Soviet adventurism. China 'did not enjoy this luxury; it was far more easily threatened.' Ironically, having called for an American disengagement from Indo-China for over a decade, China felt even more exposed when it finally happened. The withdrawal was destabilizing for China, as there was now no significant check on the expansion of Soviet power on its southern periphery. Zhou Enlai wanted America to take the lead in an anti-Soviet coalition; he urged a strong NATO defence and close ties between Japan and the United States. Kissinger did not want to appear too brazen or too hurried. However, he recognized the need to maintain momentum and increase the range of contact. He and Zhou agreed to establish liaison offices in Washington and Beijing which would serve as the official channels of their governments. The liaison offices amounted to *de facto* recognition; no *de jure* recognition was possible until the Taiwan issue was resolved. Personnel were to be given diplomatic immunity and secure communications. The first liaison officers to be appointed were men of high rank. David Bruce represented the United States and Huang Zhen, former Ambassador to Paris and a member of the Central Committee of the CCP, represented China.[2]

The momentum was difficult to sustain. The Chinese leadership regarded with suspicion the continuing process of *détente* in Europe, especially the Vladivostok summit of 1974. China felt marginalized and saw itself as losing out. It regarded the United States as an appeaser, unwilling to adopt a more aggressive stance towards the Soviet Union. Nixon's visit in 1972 had raised its expectations. It had inevitably glossed over fundamental areas of disageement that could not be eradicated by a few conversations or photo opportunities. China had assumed that the Shanghai communiqué was the first step in an inevitable and eventual American withdrawal from Taiwan. It was insistent that full diplomatic relations with the United States would not be possible as long as Washington maintained its official tie with Taipei. Similarly, the favourable image of China projected by a number of Americans did not stick. Americans had not forgotten the excesses of the Cultural Revolution. In addition, they could not dissociate insurrectionary activity in all parts of the world from China's general enunciations on foreign policy. It was sometimes taken for granted that the cells of revolutionaries, irrespective of location or cause, were supported or financed by Beijing. Also, the promise of more contacts proved greater than the realization. China proved reluctant to open its doors in any substantial way. For example, after a spectacular surge in the increase in the volume of imports and exports, which began from a low base, trade began to slow down. In 1971 it had amounted to just five million dollars. This increased to $921 million in 1974, but fell back to $336 million, less than half that amount, in 1976. However, the greatest brake on this momentum lay in Nixon's personal difficulties. The ability of the Nixon administration to carry on with its China initiative became severely hampered as the Watergate scandal loomed larger and slowly crippled the process of government.

Although the radical factions in China had been usurped by 1973, particularly after the Tenth Party Congress held in August 1973, China still viewed the United States as an imperialist country that posed a serious threat to international socialism. According to the party line, the political struggle at home was a continuing process. The ambitions of the superpowers made it imperative that the leadership remain vigilant. According to Maoist thought, there is continued struggle even under proletarian dictatorship. The process of that struggle served to awaken people to the imperialist ambitions of the superpowers. Deng Xiaoping, who had begun to take authority for Chinese foreign policy as Zhou's health declined, echoed this theme in his first major international appearance before the UN General Assembly in April 1974. He informed the UN that the Third World as a whole was engaged in a massive struggle against exploitation of its own resources. 'History,' he told his predominantly Afro-Asian audience, 'develops in struggle, and the world advances amid turbulence. The imperialists, and the superpowers in particular, are beset with troubles and are on the decline.' While the new arrangements with the United States provided for more contacts and exchanges these were actually pursued guardedly. When foreign scholars came to China their visits were usually given a low profile in the press. China still pursued a policy of self-reliance and lacked the requisite foreign exchange to increase trade exponentially. It did not make any requests to the United States for development aid, nor did the Nixon administration proffer any.[3]

Until Mao's death in 1976, most Chinese comments on American society and politics were seen through the prism of Maoist thought. Individuals who observed and commented on American affairs were located primarily in the central government bureaucracy, research institutes and the universities. They were required to adhere strictly to the party line. The community of Chinese commentators reflected and sustained the framework on which policy was based. They provide an interesting clue to the shifting assumptions about the nature of American society. For example, university textbooks on political science echoed the basics of Stalinism. A political science text used as late as 1983 stated that bourgeois political parties in the Western world existed to perpetuate class rule, and that the major leaders were under the control of monopoly financial groups. However, as the reform process began to take root, Marxist categories of analysis became more refined. Polemicists pointed to the resilience of the economy and political system of the United States, and argued that impoverishment was not intrinsic to the economic structure. They even began to discern that political power in the United States was diffuse and that no single person or group exercised control over the political process. Marxist theorists were soon arguing that normalization with the United States was consistent with China's own national objectives. They contended that since imperialism was still in robust health and the state had some independence from monopoly bourgeoisie, diplomatic relations with the USA did not constitute a sellout.[4]

China's America-watchers still believed that the American polity was governed by the interests of large financial groups. They did not believe, however, that they were a homogeneous force. They competed with one another, usually along regional lines, for dominance. Zhang Jialin of the Shanghai Institute of International Studies thought that the Watergate scandal had been provoked by the media organs of the eastern establishment in protest against Nixon's sympathy for southern and western financial interests. By and large the President was seen either as a tool or as a victim of those interests. Such an analysis explains in part why individual presidents were warmly received in China. If they were mere agents, their individual policies should be tolerated. China's criticisms of America's leaders became more muted. The Chinese were often bewildered by the extent of partisanship in the American political system. As Mao is reputed to have told an American official: 'Watergate! What reason is that to get rid of a president?'[5]

President Nixon would have surely agreed with that sentiment. For the last year of his presidency the machinery of government became hamstrung by the series of revelations, plots and manoeuvrings which were collectively grouped as Watergate. The scandal emerged from the excessive zeal of Nixon and his entourage in the election campaign of 1972. A special committee, the Committeee to Re-elect the President, or CREEP, was formed to raise the public's esteem for Richard Nixon, largely by discrediting the Democrats. CREEP paid for a break-in at the headquarters of the Democratic National Committee in the Watergate building in Washington in order to tap the telephones there. The police intercepted the attempt on 17 June 1972, and the burglars were soon traced back to CREEP. Nixon chose to see the incident as a simple case of political bugging. He joined a White House cover-up to obstruct further investigation. For a short while perjury and false trails kept the scandal away from the White House. But the investigative reporting of two ambitious reporters on the *Washington Post*, and the trial of the indicted Watergate burglars, blew the lid off the White House cover-up. It was the cover-up, not the original break-in, that now proceeded to cripple the presidency. Gradually, many of the participants either cracked or ended their silence in an attempt to save their own necks. Within a period of weeks, John Mitchell, the Attorney-General, John Ehrlichman and H.R. Haldeman, two of Nixon's closest advisers, and finally the Vice-President, Spiro Agnew, were forced to resign. The White House command began to tumble like a house of cards. When it became known that Nixon had used a tape recorder to record conversations in the White House, both the President and his inquisitors were provided with the opportunity to vindicate themselves. The President at first refused to hand the tapes over on the grounds that the request for them violated the principle of executive privilege. When he realized that he had to obey a subpoena, he handed over doctored versions of the tapes. On 24 July 1974 the Supreme Court unanimously ruled that presidential immunity was not absolute, and required Nixon to deliver all the subpoenaed tapes. The game was up. The tapes showed that Nixon had tried to stop the FBI from investigating the Watergate break-in. Senior Republicans indicated that they would vote to impeach Nixon and on 8 August 1974, Nixon announced on television that he would resign.[6]

The storm generated by the Watergate case hampered the conduct of presidential business across the broad spectrum. Foreign policy leaders overseas wondered whether the administration would last. Important decisions were put on hold. The President himself may have allowed his judgement in foreign affairs to become clouded by his domestic troubles. His meeting with Brezhnev in June 1973 produced no results and deprived Nixon of the oppportunity to paper over the cracks of the continuing Watergate revelations. On 24 October 1973 Nixon ordered a nuclear alert when neither Israel nor Egypt accepted a ceasefire proposal during the Yom Kippur War. According to Kissinger, the President's attention was absorbed at the time by the crisis over the White House tapes. The alert, therefore, may well have been the consequence of panic within the White House. In the Soviet view, that was the most likely explanation. The process of *détente* was stalled as the two sides haggled over strategic arms limitation. Leading Soviet analysts blamed the lack of further progress on the White House's preoccupation with Watergate. Whatever the case, the creativity displayed by Nixon and Kissinger in the first administration seemed to have drained away.[7]

Relations between the United States and China just chugged along as Watergate cast its growing shadow. Even after the resignation of Nixon and the succession of Gerald Ford to the White House, progress towards normalization was held up as the United States concentrated its efforts on talks with the Soviets on strategic arms limitation. The Vladivostok summit conference held in November 1974 and the Conference on Security and Cooperation in Europe, held in Helsinki in July 1975, dominated the agenda. Ford kept Kissinger on as Secretary of State and as National Security Adviser, but the negotiations with the Soviets, the lack of progress on Taiwan, and divisions within the Chinese leadership held progress on normalization back. Kissinger admitted in his memoirs that his visits to China 'either were downright chilly or were holding actions.'[8]

Neither Washington nor Beijing were confident enough to transcend such holding actions. The Ford administration rested on a brittle legitimacy and did not want to risk further political rupture. It also realized that in China the leadership was also going through a period of transition and was unable to provide that sense of certainty. As Zhou Enlai's health continued to fail, authority over Chinese foreign policy passed to Deng Xiaoping, who had been rehabilitated from his disgrace in the Cultural Revolution. Deng endorsed Mao's recent pronouncements on unity and stability and believed that the introduction of advanced technology and machinery from foreign countries would help China's development. He opposed the absolute egalitarianism of the radical faction. But Deng had to move carefully and watch over his shoulder for the inquisitorial radicals headed by Mao's wife, Jiang Qing, who had accused Zhou and his appointed advisers of betraying the principles of the Cultural Revolution and accommodating China's enemy, the United States. Deng had to assimilate some of the radicals' criticisms. He insisted that little progress could be made while the United States recognized Taiwan and had troops stationed on the island. He also continued to attack the United States for its pursuit of accommodation with the Soviets without regard for China's interests.

The Ford administration was equally defensive. After Watergate and the collapse of the anti-communist regimes in both Cambodia and South Vietnam in April 1975, it was not going to risk a domestic backlash by abandoning Taiwan. Ronald Reagan, who was making a formidable challenge to Ford for the 1976 nomination, accused his fellow Republican of undue softness towards the communist world. Ford could not take any chances. He was happy to see relations with China stagnate for a while. In his view there would be no serious consequences if he just let matters ride for a time, particularly as China still felt more threatened by the Soviet Union than by the United States.[9]

If Ford did not want China policy to play into the hands of Ronald Reagan, the Chinese leadership, especially with the growing frailty of Mao, did not want policy to play into the hands of the radicals. The radicals still occupied powerful positions in the cultural and educational spheres. They still believed that access to Western culture would result in spiritual contamination. They did not want China to be exposed to the West, and made several attempts to cut off the flow of visits and exchanges. Western musical works were condemned as bourgeois. A delegation from Harvard University was cancelled because of an unfavourable book review written by John Fairbank, Harvard's dean of Chinese studies. Other scholarly delegations from the USA were cancelled because some of the visitors were considered unsympathetic to China. Foreign trade was condemned by the anti-Deng faction on the grounds that it would increase China's entanglement in the economic uncertainties of the world market. The volume of trade fell. Total bilateral trade had reached $921 million in 1974, but declined to $462 million in 1975 and $336 million in 1976. The decline was due in part to China's growing deficit and to inadequate banking facilities arising from claims on assets frozen in the United States. The main reason, however, was that commerce was affected by the political constraints and problems of the two nations. The absence of trade agreements meant that China had to pay high tariffs. In China the radicals argued against an increase in trade, as it would lead to unnecessary dependence on Western capital and goods and a corrosion of Chinese values.[10]

In the United States the euphoria that had emanated from some quarters after Richard Nixon's visit in 1972 had begun to die away. One-time sympathetic commentators began to take a more sober view. The Cultural Revolution was understood as a devastating and evil experiment undertaken to prop up an ailing megalomaniac. Few writers suggested that it had been just another mass movement in search of a vision. The activities of the Red Guards were no longer mistaken for youthful innocence. Liberal intellectuals were beginning to be less predisposed to compare America's struggle for racial and economic justice with China's pursuit of egalitarianism.

The novelty of China was also beginning to wear off for the American press. Reports were more critical. Newsmen resented the restrictions placed on them during Gerald Ford's visit in December 1975, and their reports of the occasion were muted. The business community realized that restrictions on trade and the poor quality and unfashionable design of many Chinese goods pushed back the prospect of a bountiful China market. China-watchers who testified before a special committee of the House of Representatives on US–China relations, which held hearings around the time of President Ford's visit, were somewhat hesitant about the process of normalization. Witnesses told the committee that tourism and scholarly exchanges tended to be a one-way street, and that they were usually hampered by secrecy and the slowness of the revival of university and cultural life. Douglas Murray, Vice-Chairman of the Board of the National Committee on US–China Relations, pointed out that around 12,000 Americans had visited China in five years while only 700 or so Chinese citizens had come to the USA. Nearly all of the testifying witnesses were concerned with cultivating positive images of China through sports and the performing arts. Allen Whiting, the historian, warned that the United States should not make all the calls. He criticized the Chinese for continuing to insist that they could not reciprocate while the USA maintained its ties to Taiwan. Ford's trip, he warned, 'does not add to our self-confidence and the confidence of our allies.' Philip Habib, Assistant Secretary of State for East Asian and Pacific Affairs, pointed out that not much had changed since Nixon's visit. In short, while there was still strong support for eventual normalization, its advocates were not in a hurry.[11]

The entire political landscape changed at the end of 1976. On 9 September 1976, Mao Zedong, the only leader Communist China had known, died. His passing marked the end of an era and opened up a political struggle between claimants for the succession and for the future of China. Less than two months later the United States elected the Democrat Jimmy Carter president. Carter was an unknown figure and owed few political debts in matters of foreign policy. The new President was eager to make his own mark on foreign policy and sought to provide coherent direction. In order to distance himself from the Republicans Carter pledged in his campaign to give priority to the revival of the process of *détente* with Moscow.

His initial instinct to improve Soviet–American relations was shaped in part by the political uncertainty in China. Within a month of Mao's death Hua Guofeng, who had succeeded Mao as Chairman of the Party, ordered the arrest of Mao's widow, Jiang Qing, the ringleader of the so-called Gang of Four, who advocated continued revolution and struggle in order to achieve the kind of egalitarianism envisaged in the Cultural Revolution. Hua Guofeng offered instead a programme of stability and national unity. He and his supporters condemned the disorder generated by the Cultural Revolution and denounced the radicals for betraying China's interests. They called for economic policies that would raise living standards. Reconstruction, not political education, was to be the main goal of Hua's government. Hua did not have any particular vision. He believed simply that it was possible to promote economic modernization without rejecting Mao's political legacy. He wanted a period of political equilibrium. Hua and his allies were prepared to look to the West for technology and equipment, but they did not want long-term credits or an expansion in student exchanges. They shared Mao's fear that too much exposure to the West would lead to dependence and ultimate erosion of China's political values.[12]

The new President, Jimmy Carter, came to the White House with a strong sense of moral purpose. He wanted peace and cooperation to be the hallmark of his administration. He also sought, in the aftermath of the Nixon scandals, to reconcile conservatives and liberals. He believed that the promotion of human rights should be a primary consideration in the making of America's foreign policy. He assumed that the use of human rights as a yardstick would serve to win over his erstwhile foes and would make the world a better place to live in. He set himself a difficult task. There was no necessary link between America's security interests and the protection of human rights: the reverse was often the case. Authoritarian regimes which disregarded liberties often aligned with the United States. He tried to convince his critics that the two were inextricable. However, he often exposed the contradiction and ended up with the opposite result. The more he insisted that other nations conformed to his understanding of human rights, the more those nations repudiated his leadership and purpose.

It soon became apparent that *détente* with the communist world could only work if it was combined with a high degree of realism. This meant that he would have to turn a blind eye to violations of human rights in the Soviet Union and other communist countries. Such *realpolitik* posed its own political risks. Carter had calculated that vigorous affirmation of Wilsonian ideals would attract a coalition of neo-conservatives and liberals. Conservatives would welcome the policy as an instrument of the Cold War. Liberals would applaud it as a means of disciplining America's authoritarian allies and clients. Realism would mean loss of face. It became clear within weeks of his accession to the presidency that the Soviets would not concede the new President some kind of moral superiority. They were not going to extend trust to an administration that appeared to challenge their very legitimacy. They rejected Carter's strictures as interference in their internal affairs. Soon relations were on a worse footing than they had been for some years. If anything, the Cold War had intensified.[13]

When Carter realized that his policies had driven an extra wedge between the United States and the Soviet Union, he was persuaded to examine the state of relations with the People's Republic of China. He did not believe that its record on human rights was any more commendable than that of the Soviets. But as China had a lower public profile in the United States and, at least within scholarly circles, a more favourable public image, he was less bound by his own moral strictures. He wanted to demonstrate that his policies enhanced the cause of peace and that he had the capacity to bury old enmities. In addition, there were a number of officials in Washington who began to push hard for progress on normalization with China. The most important was his National Security Adviser, Zbigniew Brzezinski. Brzezinski believed that if negotiations with the Soviet Union stalled, the United States should move openly and rapidly towards developing new accords with the Chinese. He even hoped that an accord could be reached on matters of military security as well. He believed that the world had entered a new post-Eurocentric era. The stand-off with the Soviets was no longer sufficient to assure peace and global justice. He was convinced that a new Sino-American axis was a more effective way of guaranteeing the prevalence of America's interests. His personal assistant on Chinese affairs, Michel Oksenberg, shared his view and pushed the case for China vigorously. He did not want full-blown public debate on the issue, as he was afraid that the Taiwan lobby would rally and kill off any initiative. Brzezinski and Oksenberg found willing allies in Richard Holbrooke and Roger Sullivan in the State Department. However, the Secretary of State, Cyrus Vance, did not want to endanger progress on agreements with the Russians and something of a rift soon developed within the administration.[14]

Carter himself was prepared to risk a new *démarche* towards the Chinese. He managed to swallow the inconsistencies arising from China's record on human rights. He believed he could appease the Taiwan lobby by insisting himself that there was only one China, and that it was indivisible. In his memoirs Carter castigated the persistence of the Taiwanese and their heavy-handed tactics of financial inducements. Carter managed to convince himself that progress towards normalization was compatible with his human rights policies and that the pro-Taiwan lobby would see sense. In May 1977 Carter told an audience at Notre Dame University that 'we see the American-Chinese relationship as a central element of our global policy, and China as a key force for global peace.' But he realized that if he met China's demands on Taiwan fully, he would be stigmatized with having betrayed America's old allies in Taipei. He told Brzezinski that the administration 'should not ass-kiss the way Nixon and Kissinger did, and also be careful not to antagonize domestic constituencies.' Shortly after his inauguration, Carter ordered an internal review of China policy. That review, in a memorandum with the code PRM-24, called for progress towards normalization. Carter resigned himself to the fact that the United States would have to accept the three conditions from which Beijing had never wavered: the ending of official relations with Taiwan, the abrogation of the mutual defence treaty, and the withdrawal of all American troops from the island. But he hoped that he could persuade the Chinese to accept some concessions, particularly on unofficial American representation in Taipei and on a renunciation of the use of force by the Beijing government.[15]

In his first year of office President Carter did not pursue the cause of normalization with China with the vigour and energy devoted to *détente* with the Soviet Union. However, relations with the Soviets worsened as the Russians became more involved in the civil conflicts in Angola and Ethiopia and dug in on their refusal to agree to further arms cuts in the SALT agreements. As a result, the 'China Card' looked an increasingly attractive option. The administration also made it easier for itself to pursue a new accord with China by downgrading acceptable human rights practices as a condition of international cooperation. Brzezinski, who had never been sympathetic to the emphasis on human rights, put pressure on Carter to let him go to China to pave the way for a normalization agreement. He met frequently and regularly with Chai Zemin and Han Xu, the ranking officials of the Chinese liaison office in Washington. The secret negotiations gave him the same sense of elation that Kissinger had experienced a few years back. Brzezinski reflected in his memoirs that 'I knew that I had badgered the President enormously, but I felt that I was right in doing so. My own talks with the Chinese convinced me that I was the top official in the Carter Administration in whom they had a genuine confidence.' Accompanied by Michel Oksenberg, Brzezinski went to Beijing in May 1978 with the authority to tell the Chinese leadership that 'the United States has made up its mind.' In the conversations that followed, the United States insisted on retaining the right to continue to provide Taiwan with defensive military equipment and to maintain extensive unofficial relations with Taiwan after normalization. Brzezinski also emphasized the wider issue of China's security. He alerted the Chinese to the fact that the Soviets might soon achieve strategic superiority. They were, he warned, in a position to destabilize southern Asia and might eventually encircle China.[16]

The Chinese did not need much convincing – they wanted to proceed without any more delays. They realized that Washington had conceded on most substantive items relating to Taiwan and that they were unlikely to get any more concessions in the future. In addition, China's relations with Vietnam were close to breaking point. It was alarmed by the large volume of Soviet aid going to Vietnam, and had tried to persuade the Vietnamese to turn down assistance from Moscow. It believed that Vietnam was becoming a client of the USSR. It was also aware of Vietnam's own ambitions for hegemony in Indo-China. In late 1977 Vietnamese forces had thrust deep into Kampuchea (Cambodia), then under the tyrannical and genocidal rule of Pol Pot. As a result of China's overt support for the Khmer Rouge, ethnic Chinese in Vietnam were victimized and forced to leave – over 150,000 refugees fled to China. In June 1978 Vietnam formalized its ties with the Soviets by joining the Soviet-sponsored Council on Mutual Economic Assistance. The Chinese retaliated by closing down Vietnamese consulates in China and closing its border.[17]

The threat to regional stability, together with the overtures on military security arrangements from Brzezinski, had a deep impact on political authority in China. These developments strengthened Deng Xiaoping in his bid to wrest power from Hua Guofeng and the Maoist faction within the Chinese leadership. As the principal negotiator in Beijing he realized that he could create a political programme of his own by drawing together his advocacy of modernization on the domestic front, the challenge to America's former foes in Vietnam, and normalization of relations with the United States.

Deng Xiaoping had been reinstated to active political life in 1977. In July he was appointed Vice-Premier and Vice-Chairman of the party. Deng had become convinced that China needed to break away from its past and undertake fundamental political and economic reforms. His conviction was boosted by his own ambition. By aligning himself with the cause of liberalization he made it easier for his followers to throw off the shackles of Maoist radicalism. He also believed that a sustained interaction with the West was crucial in the modernization process.

This meant that class struggle would have to be ditched in favour of policies that concentrated on investment and the development of technology. By December 1978 his allies in the Politburo had won support for his general programme. They advocated joint venture laws, devaluation of the currency to make exports more competitive, the opening up of China to tourism, and the creation of special economic zones (SEZs) in order to encourage foreign investment in export projects. The SEZs also served as bridges linking China to Hong Kong and the rest of the world. Above all, they served as laboratories for testing reforms that were considered too radical for the rest of China. Deng believed that China had to risk change. It had not recovered from the damage caused by the Cultural Revolution, and the party's flagging prestige needed bolstering. It also felt threatened by its communist neighbours to the north and south. Deng concluded that a treaty of peace and friendship with Japan and normalization of relations with the United States were vital instruments in the strengthening process.[18]

The Chinese put no more obstacles in the way of an agreement with the United States to normalize relations. The Carter administration insisted that the right to sell defensive arms to Taiwan would continue and that the defence treaty with Taiwan would remain in effect for one year after the signing of an agreement with the PRC. It attempted to appease Deng by inviting him to visit the United States as soon as diplomatic relations were established. The way was clear. Accordingly, on 15 December Washington announced that full diplomatic relations with China would be established from 1 January 1979. It acknowledged that Taiwan was a part of China and that the United States was withdrawing diplomatic recognition from Taiwan. China, in a separate statement, insisted that the 'way of bringing Taiwan back to the embrace of the motherland' was its own internal affair and was of no concern to other nations. The Chinese statement hailed the ending of a 'prolonged abnormal relationship' with the United States and acclaimed that 'this is a historic event in Sino-American relations.' Thirty years after its establishment, the United States formally recognized the communist regime on the mainland of China.[19]

One month later Deng Xiaoping was received in Washington with full triumphal honours. He met Congressional leaders and attended sports events, a rodeo and a barbecue. He met up with Richard Nixon, who attended the State dinner. In his discussions he made it quite clear that Sino-American cooperation was a vital tool against Soviet influence in the Middle East, Cuba and southern Asia. He admonished the Americans for not doing enough to curb the Soviets. He gave Carter notice that China would take military action against the Vietnamese. Brzezinski and Harold Brown, the Defense Secretary, were determined to push the advantage and enlarge the scope of the new relationship. They were prepared to discuss security arrangements and the sale of advanced technology and arms to China. Secretary Vance was more cautious and wanted an even-handed approach. Brzezinski believed that since China was so much weaker than the Soviets, 'greater consideration' for China was necessary. He wanted to strike while the iron was hot. He thought the prospect of new security arrangements with China would compel the Soviets to reassess their policies. Carter too wanted to give China a fillip by granting it most favoured nation (MFN) status. The President managed to delude himself into thinking that China's human rights record was better than that of the Soviet Union, since it placed no equivalent restrictions on emigration. Carter seemed as intoxicated by the Chinese as Nixon had been seven years earlier. He reminisced: 'Everything went beautifully. Both before and after normalization, the Chinese exhibited a fine sensitivity about my other duties, also about our domestic political realities.'[20]

Although Carter was delighted with the ease with which recognition came, the same could not be said for Congress. Many members of Congress objected to the secrecy with which the negotiations with China had been conducted. Carter had deliberately kept the discussions a secret as he wished 'to avoid building up excessive expectations.' Capitol Hill does not like surprises; it felt particularly irked as Carter had so often condemned the secrecy of Nixon's foreign policy. Most important, however, was the sense that the White House had not protected Taiwan's security. The Taiwan Enabling Act, which had been submitted by the administration, simply provided for an American Institute in Taiwan which would represent US interests on the island and a vague expression of concern that the issue of reunification should be resolved peacefully. Senator Barry Goldwater of Arizona filed a legal suit challenging the administration's right to terminate the mutual defence treaty without the express approval of the Senate. In the event he was unsuccessful, but Congress undertook major revisions of the administration bill and passed a final version by large margins that bore little resemblance to the original. The new bill, renamed the Taiwan Relations Act, was something of a slap in the face for the administration.

While it seemed that Congress wanted normalization with Communist China, it was profoundly disturbed by Carter's seeming abandonment of its old allies on Taiwan.[21]

Congress did not want to turn the clock back. It knew that the United States could have the greatest impact on the international order if it had a working arrangement with the People's Republic of China. The time for recognition had come – but not at any price. The storm of criticism that broke out had less to do with Communist China than with the consequences for Taiwan that flowed from the new policies.

Most members of the Senate accepted Carter's decision to end the formal security relationship with Taiwan, but they were not prepared to put Taiwan's social and economic system at risk. They insisted that dealings with Taiwan needed a proper legal framework in order to instil confidence among America's Asian allies. They also believed that it was important to signal to Beijing that it could not expect to call the shots on the matter of America's relations with the Nationalist regime. Republican leaders in the Senate were disturbed that no specific mechanism existed for continued arms sales to Taiwan. Republican Senators Dan Quayle of Indiana and Charles Percy of Illinois proposed clauses that equated any threat to the security of Taiwan with a threat to the security of the United States. They also wanted to upgrade America's representation in Taipei. They argued that the US should be permitted to retain the same number of offices in Taiwan as they had before the recognition of the PRC, and that the new American Institute in Taiwan, which would unofficially represent the USA's interests, should perform consular functions. The final version of the Taiwan Relations bill, passed in April 1979, tried to guarantee that the Nationalists would receive enough 'defensive arms' to furnish them with a sufficient defence capability. It also provided that Taiwan would not be denied eligibility for programmes that legally required the maintenance of diplomatic relations. The bill passed both houses by huge margins. President Carter had no choice; with great reluctance he signed the bill. He did, however, reassure Deng privately that he would use his discretion in the interpretation of the new law. Deng was not consoled. As far as China was concerned the Taiwan Relations Act provided for the sale of arms to the local authorities in a Chinese province. Thus soon after the normalization agreement Congress had created a new thorn in the flesh that was to dog Sino-American relations in the years ahead. And far from dampening the matter, the President provided his Republican opponents with an effective issue in their forthcoming electoral challenge.[22]

Notwithstanding the passage of the Taiwan Relations Act, Washington and Beijing enjoyed something of a honeymoon for the remainder of the Carter presidency. By the end of 1979 a Gallup poll showed that 65 per cent of Americans looked on China favourably, while only 25 per cent had an unfavourable impression. The business community anticipated new opportunities and growing commercial ties. Tourists looked forward to easier and cheaper access to China. Chinese news coverage of matters American was less hostile. The Chinese journalists who accompanied Deng on his visit to the United States commented on the efficiency of its service, the sophistication of its technology and the visible prosperity of its people. Other Chinese visitors were struck by the wide ownership of motor vehicles and consequent mobility of the population. They marvelled at the abundance of goods and foods available and the facilities in the nation's universities. The new horizons made Chinese feel more confident. China's importance was now universally acknowledged. On the day normalization was announced the *People's Daily* published an extra edition printed entirely in red, the traditional colour of happiness. While the resumption of full diplomatic relations was hailed as the beginning of a new era, it did not result in the disappearance of the familiar criticisms of American society. Chinese commentators repeatedly drew attention to the disparities in wealth, the impoverishment of America's underclass and the environmental damage caused by factories and exhaust fumes. They looked forward to acquiring the benefits of closer ties, but were wary of their consequences. As one journalist commented: 'For us it is a matter of acquiring the best of the developed capitalist countries while rejecting that which is decadent. A society which is materially affluent can be spiritually poor.'[23]

Unsurprisingly, the honeymoon was qualified. Impressions do not die overnight. China remained a closed society with a poor record on human rights. The repression of Tibet continued; dissidence was not tolerated. The United States was still hostile to communism. And the Taiwan Relations Act served as a reminder that the most thorny issue, the reunification of China, had not yet been resolved. However, Brzezinski and Harold Brown, Secretary of Defense, were determined to push the advantage. They confirmed that an effective Sino-American understanding would be the most effective deterrent to Soviet expansion.

Brzezinski argued that as China was so much weaker than the Soviet Union 'greater consideration for China' was necessary. They also believed that an alignment with China would raise America's standing in the underdeveloped world. Brzezinski tried to keep the ball rolling by setting up special committees within the NSC on Economics, Science and Technology and Culture. He wanted China to be declared a friendly nation and to be granted MFN status as rapidly as possible. And he believed that the most effective way of maintaining momentum was to send a number of top-ranking officials to China to pave the way for agreements on strategic exchange, technological transfer and trade. The Secretary of State, Cyrus Vance, opposed this policy of 'tilt.' He wanted a more even-handed approach towards China in order to prevent the Soviets from feeling threatened. If they were forced into a corner, he averred, they would show even less restraint. So when the Soviet Union invaded Aghanistan in December 1979, Vance believed that he had been vindicated. He maintained that America's vigour in pursuing a new understanding with China had prompted the Russians to look for tighter security along their borders. Brzezinski, on the other hand, held that the invasion confirmed his view that the only way to restrain the Soviets was to loosen up controls applying to China on exports and technology transfer.[24]

Thus when Defense Secretary Harold Brown arrived in Beijing in January 1980, just two weeks after the Soviet invasion of Afghanistan, to discuss defence arrangements and military ties, there was a sense of urgency. On 31 December the Chinese had stated that the Soviets' military intervention posed a direct threat to China's security. Brown's trip was timely. He began to pave the way for a further relaxation of controls. As a result of his discussions in Beijing a regular exchange of Chinese and American military personnel was arranged. Brown also agreed that the United States would authorize the sale of technology and equipment that had military use. During the visit the Chinese were briefed by the Americans on Soviet deployments in the Far East and were provided with satellite photographs of Soviet positions along the Sino-Soviet border. They even discussed the possibility of providing assistance to the anti-Soviet resistance movement in Aghanistan. The Chinese intimated that they might provide covert aid to the Afghan rebels. While the Chinese were wary of establishing too close a relationship, they did little to apply the brakes. In 1980 alone over one thousand Chinese delegations visited the United States, while over four thousand students went to the US to study. Bilateral trade, helped by the granting of MFN status in January 1980, was worth nearly five billion dollars in 1980; it had been worth virtually nothing a decade earlier.[25]

There were limits on the new strategic relationship. China was still barred from purchasing lethal military equipment. American policy-makers realized that arms sales were politically unpalatable to the friends of Taiwan and that the balance in the Far East might swing too far in favour of China. A better-armed China would not serve the interests of non-communist nations of the Pacific rim. The willingness of the United States to sell technology with military potential did not have any identifiable impact on the policies of the Soviet Union. It occupied Afghanistan, established a base at Cam Ranh Bay in Vietnam, and enhanced its military forces off the coasts of Japan, Thailand and the Philippines. The growth of Soviet forces in Asia, together with the enhancement of the PRC's military capabilities, actually made Asia more threatened. The non-communist nations did not necessarily welcome the new *rapprochement*. They feared that the hand extended to China was a sign that American power in the Far East was diminishing. And above all, Ronald Reagan, now the major challenger to the Democrats, argued that the tilt to China had confirmed that American power was in decline.[26]

Reagan based his bid for power in the 1980 election on Carter's seeming inability to assert American authority. He argued that Carter's preoccupation with principle hit a blind spot when it came to dealing with the communist world. Carter's vigorous pursuit of *détente*, argued the Reagan camp, had resulted directly in the largest build-up of Soviet power since the Second World War. The Soviets had become confident that they would not face a decisive response if they embarked on new military ventures. The Kremlin leadership believed that it could nurture Marxist governments on their periphery without regard to the consequences on the domestic economy or the Soviet Union's relations with the West generally.

Carter was an easy target for the plain-speaking Reagan. The Republican challenger repeatedly flayed the President for reducing America's standing in the world to an all-time low. Reagan pointed out that the Soviets had increased the size and firepower of their armed forces and had succeeded in occupying Afghanistan without serious repercussions. The Americans were powerless in their quest to secure the release of the embassy hostages held in Iran. Reagan successfully and probably justifiably succeeded in persuading the electorate that his opponent was weak, vacillating and misguided in his optimism. Reagan ran on a platform which opposed the SALT II treaty, advocated a large increase in defence spending that would restore America's military superiority and prescribed a general return to a policy of containment and con-frontation as a means of checking Soviet power.

In his election campaign Reagan also attacked Carter's policies to-wards the People's Republic of China. He realized that normalization had been necessitated by the failure of *détente* with the Soviets and the apparent increase of Soviet power. Reagan did agree with Carter that the Soviets posed the greatest challenge to world peace, and that China served as an important counterweight. But he was aware that closer association with Communist China was an expedient, and an unpalatable one. In his view the disciplined and closed Communist system, together with abuses of human rights in China, was not a formula for success in consolidating the relationship. Reagan believed that the historical tide was running against Marxism. America could hasten its demise by building up its military strength and providing strong support for anti-communist governments around the world. Thus he believed that the United States had sacrificed its old ally in Taiwan for an expedient relationship with Beijing that anyway had dubious and ephemeral value. In the election campaign he indicated that America's relations with Taipei would be upgraded and that some kind of official status would be granted. He even referred to Taiwan as the 'Republic of China', deliberately annoying the mainland Chinese. He did send George Bush, the vice-presidential candidate and former head of the US liaison office in Beijing, to China at the end of August to try to soothe Chinese anxieties. But the mission was not successful, as Reagan's unconcealed sympathy for Taiwan on the campaign trail and Bush's reassurances in Beijing simply did not square with one another.[27]

Reagan won the November election comfortably. His victory was not so much an endorsement of his conservatism as a popular re-pudiation of Carter. Two-thirds of Americans polled after the election said they had voted for Reagan because they wanted to see somebody who was strong in the White House. If there had been euphoria in the nations' capitals after the normalization agreement of December 1978, the mood was now more cautious and sober. While Reagan had trim-med some of his utterances about China during the campaign, it was clear that he was an enthusiastic supporter of the Taiwan Relations Act and did not want to see arms sales to Taiwan curbed. Reagan wanted to create the impression that he would champion American interests and that the United States would honour its long-standing obligations. He was less likely to sacrifice America's remaining ties with Taiwan for the uncertain prospect of a *rapprochement* with Communist China. Reagan believed that as leader of his nation, it was his job to highlight the strengths and qualities that he perceived within the American polity. As more Americans visited China and as trade between the two nations increased, the differences between the societies were there for all to see. He did not wish to project an image of China that did not square with what people could see with their own eyes.

Reagan's election campaign was closely watched in China. The Chinese press expressed dismay at Reagan's open sympathy for Taiwan. Commentators argued that the Republican candidate's challenge to the normalization process went against America's best interests. He was going against the grain of popular opinion and was providing help to the Soviets in their quest for hegemony. 'Reagan has placed himself in a tight corner,' said one critic. 'Whoever turns back the wheel of history will always run into a stone wall.' The Chinese believed that there was a distinction between public law and the policy-making process. The Taiwan Relations Act, in their view, was a separate and discrete policy. They had the impression that presidents were not bound by acts of Congress and could ignore, at least in spirit, the laws. Reagan, they argued, owed his nomination to the Republican right. Some of his advisers, they claimed, had in the past even been on Taiwan's payroll.

But all was not despair. They believed that once elected Reagan would fall into line. They noted that there was evidence of trying to backtrack. He had sent George Bush to Beijing and made fewer references to the issue as the campaign wore on. Above all, they believed that normalization had been the product of historical forces rather than the diplomacy of individuals. Normalization, according to one writer, was 'inevitable. History and international developments made it so.'[28] Reagan would soon realize that nothing had changed and would revert to policies that would keep the Soviets in check. But that might take time. It seemed that after nearly a decade of growing accord, the Sino-American relationship would revert to a period of strain and uncertainty.

NOTES

1. Frank Snepp, *Decent Interval: The American Debacle in Vietnam and the Fall of Saigon* (Harmondsworth, 1980), pp. 42–63; Stephen E. Ambrose, *Nixon: III, Ruin and Recovery, 1973–1990* (New York, 1991), pp. 38–46, 53–8; Allan E. Goodman, *The Lost Peace: America's Search for a Negotiated Settlement of the Vietnam War* (Stanford, CA, 1978), pp. 143–64.

2. Henry Kissinger, *Years of Upheaval* (Boston, MA, 1982), pp. 44–62, 687–96; Tad Szulc, *The Illusion of Peace: Foreign Policy in the Nixon Years* (New York, 1978), p. 687; Harold C. Hinton, *Peking–Washington: Chinese Foreign Policy and the United States* (Washington, DC, 1976), pp. 53–9.

3. *China News Analysis*, No. 891, 18 August 1972; Deng Xiaoping Speech, 10 April 1974 in Harold C. Hinton, ed., *The People's Republic of China, 1949–1979, A Documentary Survey, V: 1971–1979, After the Cultural Revolution* (Wilmington, DE, 1980), p. 2434; Harry Harding, 'The Domestic Politics of China's Global Posture, 1973–78,' in Thomas Fingar and the Stanford Journal of International Studies, eds, *China's Quest for Independence: Policy Evolution in the 1970s* (Boulder, CO, 1980), pp. 96–110; Parris H. Chang, *Power and Policy in China* (University Park, PA, 1978), p. 199.

4. David Shambaugh, *Beautiful Imperialist: China Perceives America, 1972–1990* (Princeton, NJ, 1991), pp. 53–69, 278–82; see also Merle Goldman, 'China's Anti-Confucian Campaign, 1973–76,' *China Quarterly*, 63 (September 1975), p. 435.

5. Shambaugh, *Beautiful Imperialist*, p. 177.

6. On Watergate, see: Stanley I. Kutler, *The Wars of Watergate: The Last Crisis of Richard Nixon* (New York, 1990); Bob Woodward and Carl Bernstein, *The Final Days* (New York, 1976); Gladys Engle Lang and Kurt Lang, *The Battle for Public Opinion: The President, the Press and the Polls During Watergate* (New York, 1983).

7. Kissinger, *Years of Upheaval*, pp. 481–7, 519; Raymond L. Garthoff, *Détente and Confrontation: American–Soviet Relations from Nixon to Reagan* (Washington, DC, 1985), pp. 381n., 434–45.

8. Kissinger, *Years of Upheaval*, p. 698.

9. Gerald R. Ford, *A Time to Heal: The Autobiography of Gerald R. Ford* (New York, 1979), pp. 335–7; Tang Tsou, *The Cultural Revolution and the Post-Mao Reforms: A Historical Perspective* (Chicago, IL, 1986), pp. 131, 150–51.

10. Harry Harding, *A Fragile Relationship: The United States and China since 1972* (Washington, DC, 1992), pp. 54–60, 364; Ann Fenwick, 'Chinese Foreign Trade Policy and the Campaign Against Deng Xiaoping' in Fingar et al., *China's Quest for Independence*, pp. 200–10. I would like to acknowledge my considerable debt in this section to Harry Harding's outstanding work.

11. U.S. House of Representatives, 'United States – China Relations: The Process of Normalization of Relations', House of Representatives, *Hearings before the Special Subcommittee on Investigations of the Committee on International Relations* (Washington, DC, 1976), pp. 107–8, 135–6, 162–5; *China Year Book, 1975* (Taipei, 1975), p. 361; Robert G. Sutter, *The China Quandary: Domestic Determinants of US China Policy,*

168   THE UNITED STATES AND CHINA

1972–1982 (Boulder, CO, 1982), pp. 48–9; Donald S. Zagoria, 'China by Daylight,' *Dissent*, 22 (Spring 1975), pp. 135–47.

12. Harry Harding, *China's Second Revolution: Reform after Mao* (Washington, DC, 1987), pp. 40–57; Chang, *Power and Policy in China*, pp. 218–28; Michael Yahuda, *Towards the End of Isolationism: China's Foreign Policy After Mao* (London, 1983), pp. 127–30; Report to the second Tachai Conference, 20 December 1976 in Hinton, ed., *The People's Republic of China: A Documentary Survey, V*, pp. 2619–26.

13. Joshua Muravchik, *The Uncertain Crusade: Jimmy Carter and the Dilemmas of Human Rights Policy* (Washington, DC, 1988); Donald S. Spencer, *The Carter Implosion: Jimmy Carter and the Amateur Style of Diplomacy* (New York, 1988); Stanley Hoffmann, 'Requiem', *Foreign Policy*, 42 (Spring 1981), pp. 3–26.

14. Cyrus Vance, *Hard Choices: Critical Years in American Foreign Policy* (New York, 1983), pp. 75–9; Michel Oksenberg, 'A Decade of Sino-American Relations,' *Foreign Affairs*, 61 (Fall 1982), pp. 181–3.

15. Zbigniew Brzezinski, *Power and Principle: Memoirs of the National Security Adviser, 1977–1981* (New York, 1981), pp. 199–200; Jimmy Carter, *Keeping Faith: Memoirs of a President* (New York, 1982), pp. 187, 190.

16. Brzezinski, *Power and Principle*, pp. 206, 209–12, 551–5; Carter, *Keeping Faith*, pp. 190–91; for a critical view see Stephen B. Gilbert, *Northeast Asia in US Foreign Policy* (Washington, DC, 1979), pp. 56–7.

17. The best study of the conflict between China and Vietnam is Robert S. Ross, *The Indochina Tangle: China's Vietnam Policy, 1975–1979* (New York, 1988); William T. Tow and William R. Feeney, *US Foreign Policy and Asian-Pacific Security: A Transregional Approach* (Boulder, CO, 1982), pp. 20–21.

18. Harding, *China's Second Revolution*, pp. 53–66, 155–70; A. Doak Barnett, *The Making of Foreign Policy in China: Structure and Process* (London, 1985), pp. 20–21; Nina P. Halpern, 'Economic Reform, Social Mobilization, and Democratization in Post-Mao China,' in Richard Baum, ed., *Reform and Reaction in Post-Mao China: The Road to Tiananmen* (New York and London, 1991), pp. 43–5; Lowell Dittmer, 'Learning From Trauma: the Cultural Revolution in Post-Mao Politics' in William A. Joseph, Christine P.W. Wong and David Zweig, *New Perspectives on the Cultural Revolution* (Cambridge, MA, and London, 1991), pp. 22–30; Robert Kleinberg, *China's 'Opening' to the Outside World: The Experiment with Foreign Capitalism* (Boulder, CO, 1990), pp. 19–40; Kuang-Sheng Liao, *Antiforeignism and Modernization in China* (Hong Kong, 1990), pp. 227–37; communiqué of Third Plenary Session of Eleventh Central Committee, 22 December 1978 in Hinton, ed., *The People's Republic of China: A Documentary Survey, V*, pp. 2722–7.

19. Deng Xiaoping speech, 30 January 1979 in Hinton, ed., *The People's Republic of China: A Documentary Survey, V*, pp. 2951–3.

20. Carter, *Keeping Faith*, pp. 202, 211; Brzezinski, *Power and Principle*, pp. 403–6, 415; Vance, *Hard Choices*, pp. 114–19; *Beijing Review*, 12 January 1979.

21. Harding, *A Fragile Relationship*, pp. 84–7; Sutter, *The China Quandary*, pp. 74–7, 96; Lester L. Wolff and David L. Simon, eds, *A Legislative History of the Taiwan Relations Act* (New York, 1982); Charles T. Cross, 'Taipei's Identity Crisis,' *Foreign Policy*, 51 (Summer 1983), pp. 51–2.

22. Jacob K. Javits, 'Congress and Foreign Relations: The Taiwan Relations Act,'

Foreign Affairs, 60 (Fall 1981) pp. 54–62; Louis W. Koenig, James C. Hsiung and King-yuh Chang, eds, *Congress, the Presidency, and the Taiwan Relations Act* (New York, 1985); Sutter, *The China Quandary,* pp. 74–7.

23. 'Impressions of the United States,' *Beijing Review,* 26 January 1979, pp. 16–19; Liao, *Antiforeignism and Modernization in China,* pp. 227–30, 239–44; Harding, *A Fragile Relationship,* pp. 100–6; Shambaugh, *Beautiful Imperialist,* pp. 158–9.

24. Brzezinski, *Power and Principle,* p. 415.

25. Garthoff, *Détente and Confrontation,* pp. 983–8; Harding, *A Fragile Relationship,* pp. 364, 367; A. James Gregor, *Arming the Dragon: U.S. Security Ties with the People's Republic of China* (Washington, DC, 1987), pp. 15–18.

26. Gregor, *Arming the Dragon,* pp. 24–38.

27. An Ding, 'No Compromise on the Question of Principle,' *Beijing Review,* 1 September 1980; Ronald Reagan, *An American Life* (London, 1990), pp. 360–61; Robert Dallek, *Ronald Reagan: The Politics of Symbolism* (Cambridge, MA, 1984), p. 140; 'The November Vote for President: What Did it Mean?' in Austin Rannry, ed., *The American Elections of 1980* (Washington, DC, 1981), pp. 240–49; Richard H. Solomon, 'East Asia and the Great Power Coalitions,' *Foreign Affairs,* 60 (1982), pp. 695–6.

28. Zhuang Zong, 'Reagan's "Erroneous" Views on "Two Chinas" Scorned,' *China Report: Political, Sociological and Military Affairs,* 21 November 1980; Ding, 'No Compromise on Question of Principle;' Wang Fei, 'Why Reagan Won,' *Beijing Review,* 17 November 1980.

CHAPTER 7

A NERVOUS OPEN DOOR: THE ROAD TO TIANANMEN SQUARE, 1980–89

The Chinese leadership was in two minds about the new President, Ronald Reagan. It was very concerned about Reagan's well-known personal views on China. The new President had lambasted Carter in his election campaign for selling out Taiwan. He had intimated that he would look again at the normalization agreements with China and that he would not let Taiwan down. On the other hand, China could only approve of the aggressive anti-Soviet rhetoric that was coming from Reagan and his coterie of new advisers. Reagan had called for a return to the containment of the Soviets in its most militant form. In his very first press conference he told reporters that *détente* had been a 'one-way street' and that the Soviets still promoted 'world revolution and a one-world Socialist or Communist state' by reserving to themselves 'the right to commit any crime, to lie, to cheat, in order to attain that.' He pledged that the United States would use all the resources at its disposal to redress the balance. There would be a massive arms buildup, which would be the centrepiece of his foreign policy. Despite China's ambivalence there was a consistency between the two stances. Reagan believed that an aggressive posture towards the communist world would serve to undermine it. The Chinese chose to ignore that consistency, and hoped that the new President would concentrate on his declared policy of rearming the United States in response to the growing Soviet threat.[1]

Reagan's appointments gave China some encouragement. Alexander M. Haig, the new Secretary of State, displayed a combative style from early on. He combined a tough anti-Sovietism with a pragmatic view towards the rest of the world. In his confirmation hearings he accused the Carter administration of allowing the Soviet Union to replace the United States as the major military power on earth. He pledged that the new administration would reverse this process. However, he affirmed that his department would continue to pursue the normalization process with China. He believed that China's modernization policies would undermine Maoism and that the country would never return to the Marxist orthodoxies of the late 1960s. 'I see a compatibility and convergence between ourselves and the PRC,' he told Senators. He foresaw an increase in trade and labelled joint ventures 'constructive.' He later reflected: 'Our relationship with China is, therefore, a great opportunity for human progress. China is the bridge on which the First World and the Third World may meet.' China's initial reaction was hopefully upbeat. The Xinhua news agency reported Haig's optimism approvingly. Zhao Ziyang sent Reagan the customary congratulatory telegram, and China was pleased to note that at the inauguration ceremony people from Taiwan attended only as private individuals and not in any official capacity.[2]

However, it soon became apparent that Alexander Haig's insistent pragmatism did not reflect the private views of the President. Reagan wanted to restore the association with Taipei. He had not disowned his campaign promise to consider upgrading relations with Taiwan. He never contemplated recognizing Taiwan as the sole government of China. But he expected to elevate the nominally nongovernmental American Institute in Taiwan to the same official status that the liaison office in Beijing had enjoyed before normalization. He wanted Taiwan to be given as much encouragement as possible since it had enjoyed close links with the United States for so long. He believed that Taiwan symbolized the hope that the most populous nation on earth would free itself of communism, and wished to keep that hope intact. To Reagan the abandonment of Taiwan equated with the abandonment of that hope. He was encouraged in his views by a vocal right-wing bloc of Republican Senators, led by Barry Goldwater of Arizona and Jesse Helms of North Carolina. They realized that the clock could not be turned back, but they anticipated that they could tilt the balance in Taipei's direction by selling them more sophisticated weapons and encouraging the island regime generally.[3]

Reagan realized that he would have to give in to Haig: it did not make sense to sacrifice the goodwill of China for the uncertain benefit of a few symbolic gestures towards Taiwan. But he agreed with Senate Republicans that the supply of arms to Taiwan should not be suspended. In June 1980 the Carter administration had authorized American aircraft manufacturers to negotiate the sale of the FX fighter aircraft to Taiwan.

The Taipei government anticipated that it would place the order. Contrary to expectations, the flow of arms to Taiwan had increased after normalization and Reagan was instinctively sympathetic to the continued supply of defensive weapons in accordance with the provisos of the Taiwan Relations Act. Beijing viewed these sales with alarm. In its view they contravened the normalization agreement and worked against the prospect of national reunification. The Chinese proposed that the United States should undertake to reduce the supply of arms gradually and to set a firm date for the termination of all arms sales. In return China produced a new plan for the peaceful reunification of China with the mainland.[4]

Reagan was swayed by Secretary of State Haig and Congressman Stephen Solarz, chairman of the House Foreign Affairs Subcommittee on Asian and Pacific Affairs. They did not want to endanger good relations for the sake of the sale of an aircraft that was not crucial to Taiwan's defences. Haig told the President that if he faltered in his relations with China the result would be 'the most significant diplomatic disaster since the "loss of China" in 1949.' Reagan relented and agreed to discuss the matter. When a Pentagon study showed that the FX was not vital to the defence of Taiwan, the administration ordered the suspension of the sale of the aircraft. Haig suggested that the United States should agree on levels of arms supplies, and proposed that the flow to Taiwan could be reduced gradually. But Washington was not prepared to tie its hands by agreeing on a specfic date for the termination of arms sales. The United States asked China to renounce the use of force against Taiwan but, as had been the case for three decades, China was not prepared to surrender sovereignty over what it considered to be its own territory. The negotiations stalled while each side insisted on its own right to determine policy towards Taipei. The stalemate was finally ended when the United States agreed that it did not intend to sell arms to the Taiwanese in the long term. Both sides wanted to see the deadlock broken, and eventually an agreement was drawn up.[5]

The final agreement, which was publicized in the form of a Joint Communiqué on 17 August 1982, included concessions by both sides. America agreed not to exceed current levels of arms exports and to 'reduce gradually' the sale of arms to Taiwan. China reaffirmed its support for peaceful reunification, though it would not be drawn on the issue of the use of force. The communiqué served its purpose. It defused the crisis over arms sales and put an end to the worry in

Beijing that Reagan was a doctrinaire leader who was prepared to repudiate all dealings with communist governments. But while the Joint Communiqué assuaged the distrust that had grown in Sino-American relations since Reagan's accession to power, it did not in any way resolve or even move towards resolution of the Taiwan dispute.

Both Taiwan and the PRC still insisted that there was only one China, even though both had stable and functioning governments. The provision of arms to their respective rival was seen by both sides as a military interference in a domestic problem. The communiqué accepted the fudge; it did not advance either the issue or the Sino-American relationship. Senator Samuel Hayakawa (Republican, California) pointed out that even though the communiqué committed the United States not to exceed current levels of arms exports to Taiwan, the mainland Chinese 'do nothing more than make a big squawk and accept what is essentially an illogical situation ... It seems to me that this joint communiqué is just another one of the necessary ways of enduring this illogic.' Despite its contrary instincts, the administration wanted to foster closer ties with the PRC, particularly in the light of its worsening relations with the Soviet Union. John Holdridge, Assistant Secretary of State in the Bureau of East Asian and Pacific Affairs, assured Congress that the administration recognized obligations to old friends 'and we will not turn our backs on them.' However, it did not want to cause a further deterioration in its relationship with China and wished to nurture a stable regional order in the Far East. It calculated that a policy of restraint in the supply of arms to Taiwan would encourage the PRC to seek a peaceful solution of the dispute. It was aware that the economic importance of the Asian Pacific loomed ever larger. By 1980 the value of America's two-way trade with Asian and Pacific countries surpassed the value of trade with western Europe. The administration believed that if it could win the confidence of the Communist Chinese, then a wide array of areas for cooperation would open up. It even thought it possible that the Chinese might model their modernization programme on the United States.[6]

The rate of political change in China offered new challenges to the foreign policy of the United States. Policy-makers became increasingly convinced that the development of closer ties with the People's Republic of China would provide an opportunity for the United States to play a formative and influential role in its development. The President firmly believed that a combination of example and a tough military stance would expose the weaknesses in communist regimes throughout the world. The changes and reforms undertaken by the Chinese in the early years of the decade were signs that China was changing and that it would increasingly yield to economic and political penetration from the outside world. Caspar Weinberger, Secretary of Defense, was convinced that China was moving down the 'capitalist road' and that it ought to be placed in 'a different category' from other communist nations. He was convinced that the United States could play a part in the disentanglement of the Maoist order.[7]

The leadership of Hua Guofeng, who succeeded Mao as Party Chairman, was something of an interregnum. He aimed to provide China with stability rather than to initiate reform. By 1981 pressure against him had mounted. His critics realized that the political system they had so carefully built in the 1950s and early 1960s no longer served China's best interests. If China were to increase production and modernize its industry and agriculture, it would have to start afresh.[8] A gradual repudiation of Mao's legacy began. Hua Guofeng was chided for his uncritical acceptance and continuation of Mao's economic policies. A common adage, employed sarcastically, was that Hua had adopted the policy of 'the two whatevers'. According to his detractors, whatever Mao did or whatever Mao said had provided the overall framework for Hua's economic and cultural policies. His main rival, Deng Xiaoping, distanced himself from Hua. He claimed that he would not be bound by doctrine and would 'seek truth from facts.' He called for a radical rethink and adaptation of Marxism. Hu Yaobang, probably the most vocal of the reformers, in a speech celebrating the sixtieth anniversary of the founding of the Communist Party of China, said that Marxism 'does not embrace all the truths in the unending course of human history ... the theory of Marxism is the guide to action and by no means a rigid dogma to be followed unthinkingly.' He spoke of Mao's 'shortcomings and mistakes' and advised that China could learn from the experiences of others. The campaigns of Deng and Hu won the day, and by the middle of 1981 Hua was forced to step down and give way to the reformers under the chairmanship of Hu Yaobang.[9]

The post-1981 reforms covered all aspects of political and economic life. Centralized bureaucratic systems were replaced by a modified market system. Price mechanisms were introduced, and the profits of some enterprises could be kept and ploughed back. The leadership recognized that the relationship between the party and the masses had eroded.

Confidence had to be restored. Research institutes and universities were strengthened, writers were permitted to discuss past mistakes and scientists were once again given an important role in the decision-making process. The responsibility system in agriculture was introduced, permitting those engaged in farming to keep part of their produce and sell it privately. Private plots were encouraged. Even the political system became more pluralistic in the sense that a wider spectrum of opinion was tolerated within the Communist Party. Proposals in the process of policy formulation came from a wider array of sources and from lower down in the system. More cadres were elected, and more extensive debate was permitted in the farms and factories.[10]

The pace of reform boded well for the future of Sino-American relations. Until the signing of the August communiqué the Taiwan Relations Act and the sale of arms to Taiwan were something of a blot. For the first two years of the Reagan presidency there were what Harry Harding has called distinct 'growing pains' that affected the academic and commercial relations between the two countries. These 'growing pains' were perhaps inevitable. The two societies were very different, and the establishment of common ground rules for trade and educational exchanges reflected those divisions. The leaders of the two countries were hesitant and faltering in their respective attitudes to one another. Reagan's well-known antipathy towards communist regimes and his reluctant distancing from Taipei made Beijing guarded and suspicious. The changes in the leadership and its attendant policies in China pointed to policies that would be cautious. If China was going to open up, it would do so slowly in order to maintain political stability. For example, in the field of academic exchange, a number of frustrations emerged. Visiting American scholars demanded access to archives and libraries that were closed even to Chinese scholars. Two American graduate students were expelled from China for allegedly conducting research in areas that had not been authorized. As a result of these cases the Chinese Academy of Social Sciences, which sponsored many student visits, placed a three-year moratorium on further field research. The number of Chinese students visiting the United States fell slightly between 1981 and 1983.[11]

Although these 'growing pains' did not disappear, they did diminish towards the end of Reagan's first term in office. There were a number of reasons. Perhaps the most important was the signing of the 17 August communiqué, which sought to defuse the issue of arms sales to Taiwan. In addition, by then the State Department was headed by a new

Secretary, George Shultz. Shultz did not agree with Haig about the importance of China. He was confident that a combination of America's formidable military power and its growing economic ties with Japan and the newly emerging economies of Hong Kong, South Korea and Southeast Asia diminished the importance of the PRC. He believed that a good relationship with China should follow on from a resolution of specific differences and not be the driving force. He warned against 'too much emphasis on a relationship for its own sake.' He did not seek a confrontation with China, nor was he particularly concerned to shift the balance back to Taiwan. Quite simply, he exhibited the confidence of a man who thought that his country's star was rising and that he could play for time.[12]

If the United States felt a little more confident about itself, so then did China. The leadership of Deng Xiaoping, Hu Yaobang and Zhao Ziyang, a radical reformer who became Premier in 1980, was consolidated and faced no effective challenge from other aspirants. It was thus able to plan for a further programme of economic reform. After a short period of retrenchment, the initial reforms showed early signs of success as the Chinese economy began to grow rapidly. Investment had increased and the rewards were being reaped. For example, between 1981 and 1986 extra-budgetary investment in capital construction by state-owned units increased at an average rate of 30 per cent a year. By 1985 nearly one half of the increase in national retail sales was accounted for by the private sector of the economy. National output grew from 387 billion yuan in 1981 to 586 billion yuan in 1985, an average annual growth rate of nearly 11 per cent. The country's total world trade also increased spectacularly. In 1981 it had been $41 billion; it remained more or less static for the next two years and then climbed to $70 billion by 1985.[13]

China also felt more secure on the international front. It felt less threatened by Taiwan, and began to plan for negotiations with Britain for the handback of Hong Kong in 1997. Its management of these issues resulted in a relaxation of old tensions and produced fresh negotiations on the sale of weapons and technology to China. The renewed confidence of China was encapsulated by Zhao Ziyang, the Chinese Premier. When he visited Washington in January 1984, Zhao insisted that China should not be treated as a regional power but as a world power. This was a far cry from the days of Mao, who had always identified China as part of the Third World.[14]

The sense of confidence that permeated both Beijing and Washington served to embolden the relationship. Both sides believed that closer ties would provide positive benefits without loss of political identity. The Chinese leadership needed to trade with and receive investment from the West, and particularly the United States, in order to expedite its modernization programme. The Reagan administration wanted closer ties to demonstrate the vitality and efficiency of the capitalist system. Reagan abandoned his earlier reservations and argued that American penetration of China would serve to accelerate the rate of liberalization. He reflected in his memoirs that although China 'was still a decidedly Communist country,' recent developments there 'made me feel optimistic; they were an exciting glimmer on the horizon, the first public admission in the Communist world that Communism wasn't working.' So he dropped the tough line he had demonstrated around the time of his inauguration and authorized his staff to identify the areas on which cooperation could be safely undertaken.[15]

Reagan changed his mind about one other issue, which did trouble the Chinese. In the first term Reagan had begun to backtrack on his deliberate belittling of Carter's human rights policies. The administration recognized that an emphasis on human rights could serve to reinforce its overall foreign policy. If the weaknesses of communism were to be exposed, the strengths of Western liberalism had to be championed. By highlighting the deficiencies in the human rights record of other nations, the administration was able to provide an ideological coherence to its policies and so gain public support. The nomination of Elliott Abrams as Assistant Secretary of State for Human Rights marked the beginning of a new phase. Abrams believed that drawing attention to infringements of human rights served to highlight differences between East and West. In places like the Philippines, Haiti and Chile the Reagan administration perceived that the promotion of human rights coincided with America's strategic interests. At home it encouraged a programme of conferences and grants to human rights organizations, and funded the creation of the National Endowment for Democracy. The State Department raised individual violations of human rights with the Chinese government. The administration conspicuously withheld $25 million from the UN Fund for Population Activities because of China's policies of forced abortions and sterilization. China objected to the infusion of human rights issues, but believed that they could be contained as essentially cosmetic devices. If they could demonstrate that the liberalization process

was consistent with Washington's objectives, they could be the beneficiaries of the change of heart in the United States. They wanted to
pave the way for more American aid and investment. They recognized
that American involvement in the modernization programme was dependent on general approval from Washington.[16]

Reagan too wanted to improve relations between the two countries,
but realized his task would be made easier if China were to become
more accessible to the outside world and more hospitable to a liberal
order. He had no doubts about its geopolitical importance. If strong
ties with China could be maintained, the Soviet Union would continue
to amass its troops in the East (and so divert them from Europe), the
Chinese would restrain the North Koreans, and US warships would be
permitted to call at Chinese ports. American businesses would continue
to invest in Chinese projects. Above all he looked to the long term,
and recognized the importance of the prosperity of the Pacific region.
Although the USA no longer held the dominant economic position in
Asia, it was still a major player. Asian nations, particularly Japan, enjoyed
increasing trade with China, and the United States realized that it could
not lose this potentially lucrative market to one of its largest trade rivals.
It also appreciated that military modernization had a low priority in
China, and so American assistance in industrial modernization would
not be diverted for military purposes, at least for the time being. In
short, Reagan wanted China to play a constructive role in the Asia–
Pacific region. His impeccable conservative credentials enabled him to
side-track the pro-Taiwan lobby in his quest for broad Asian security.
He told a delegation of Republican candidates in October 1982 that if
China kept its word on the issue of peaceful resolution, 'yes, then there
would be no longer any need for us to provide defense weapons, and
there would be a decline and an end at that time.' He argued that if
China opened its door to Western goods the result would be a relaxation
of political controls. His administration would then become a midwife
for human rights in the communist world.[17]

Such a strategy was consistent with Reagan's general foreign policy.
Reagan was aware that since Nixon's presidency successive administrations had played the 'China card' in their dealings with the Soviet
bloc. He saw no reason to discontinue this practice, although he was
wary of its tendency to manoeuvre the United States back and forth
too much. His administration was also actively encouraging the retreat
from statism throughout the world, and if it could play a role in China's

move towards a market economy, it would do so. It believed that its economic revolution at home, with its rollback of state responsibility for welfare, would spread abroad. George Shultz, Secretary of State, wrote in *Foreign Affairs* in 1985 that rapid political change in the Pacific was altering American perceptions of the world, and remarked that 'the hopes for economic modernization have been invested – wisely – in a bold program of reform. China's long march to the market is a truly historic event.' The choice was clear to the Reagan administration. If it did not harness itself to China's modernization programme, others would.[18]

Both China and the United States began to de-link various issues that had hindered agreements in the past. The row over Taiwan was swept aside as agreements on double taxation for oil companies were made. PanAm was granted the right to fly to both Taipei and Beijing. Four new science and technology protocols were signed in 1983 by Jay Keyworth, the President's science adviser. In September 1983 Caspar W. Weinberger, Secretary of Defense, went to Beijing where he offered to add more weapons to the list that the United States was prepared to sell to China. He also agreed to resume military exchanges between high-ranking officers. In January 1984 Reagan welcomed Zhao Ziyang to Washington. Zhao, who had been Prime Minister since 1980, was the most prominent sponsor of radical reform in China. He had been attracted by pluralist political institutions in the United States, and was impressed by the speed of the industrialization process of the countries of East Asia. He was inspired by their blend of private enterprise and public ownership, and of market forces and government regulation. Reform, he foresaw, would eventually demonstrate the strength of the socialist road. He believed that an individual enterprise should be responsible for its own profit and loss. It should be granted sufficient autonomy to make its own decisions about investment, salaries and pricing. He believed in a reward system and was opposed to Maoist notions of equality. He wanted to encourage certain regions and enterprises to concentrate on growing wealthy, so that a ripple effect could be created. Thus when Zhao met with Reagan on 10 January, Zhao's views were grist to the mill. Zhao told a group of businessmen on his visit that China's opening to the world was 'an objective necessity ... The different social systems in China and the United States should not impede their economic cooperation.'[19]

Reagan kept up the momentum with an official visit to China in

April 1984. It was his first visit to any communist country. He made the compulsory trip to the Great Wall, and Nancy Reagan went to see the inevitable pandas at Beijing zoo. In the speeches he made he did not conceal the differences between the two countries. But he also insisted that there were common interests that overshadowed their dissimilarities. In his talks with Chinese leaders Reagan welcomed China's modernization plans, and reiterated that the United States sought to develop cooperative ventures and relax its export controls. He predicted that the changes enveloping China would bring the United States and China even closer together.[20]

There were strong domestic reasons for the new *rapprochement*, and the reasoning in both Washington and Beijing was similar. As already stated, Reagan firmly believed that American power would be enhanced if the United States led the world in rolling back the tide of central economic planning. Zhao and the radical reformers also realized that there was opposition within China to the new course of economic policy and, crucially, the extent to which China's modernization should be conducted with aid and investment from outside. Deng Xiaoping had sought to maintain a consensus within the higher echelons of the party. When the party leadership displayed nervousness about the extent of the reforms, Deng lent his weight to campaigns against 'bourgeois liberalism' and 'spiritual pollution.' He came out against student protests in 1986 and condemned the tide of anti-government criticism, the so-called Democracy Wall movement. But he also gave his blessing to some of the more radical reforms espoused by Zhao Ziyang. He supported opening up China to the outside world, and particularly approved of the special economic zones which were designed to en-courage foreign investment in export projects. The zones, all on the coastal areas, enjoyed preferential tax scales, could offer pay at favourable rates, and above all embarked on economic and social reforms that were not permitted elsewhere. The idea of the zones was transformed into a plan for creating a large number of open cities, which would attract more foreign investment and foreign technology. Between 1978 and 1986 China imported foreign technology valued at almost $10 billion, and attracted over $8 billion in foreign investment. The impact, at least in the cities, was enormous. New consumer goods and fashion items were available, new international hotels shot up, tourists began to arrive in large numbers, and many Chinese travelled abroad, particularly to universities and international financial centres.

The United States realized that by tying itself to American and foreign capital the reform movement in the People's Republic of China would strengthen. The reformers also recognized that as the authority of the Communist Party and the army weakened, social and political harmony would come to depend on the perceived success of the economic reforms. They also understood that their own influence could only survive if the reforms continued. They knew that the ideological restraints on economic activity and on public debate would have to be reduced further if success was to be assured and their own positions maintained. Abuses of power by party and state officials, they understood, were easier if the system did not provide alternative voices and mechanisms of policy-making. Ideological and structural pluralism would benefit their political careers.

The Chinese leadership therefore encouraged the proponents of political reform and academic freedom. In the mid-1980s the reformers, under the leadership of Premier Zhao Ziyang and Hu Yaobang, General Secretary of the party from 1982 to 1987, identified themselves with the calls for further political reform. Management committees of development zones were elected by ballot. The social hierarchy was restructured. Scholars and specialists, who had been almost outcasts under Mao, were rehabilitated and employed in advisory research centres. A number of senior officials in the party apparatus, whose careers had been advanced by the Cultural Revolution, were expelled in a new rectification programme between 1983 and 1987. Deng Xiaoping was sympathetic to economic liberalization and did not want entrenched officialdom to stand in the way. However, he feared that if an intellectual revolution rode on the tide of economic change, the authority of the senior leadership would be undermined. There were limits to democracy: anything that challenged the leadership of the party hierarchy was to be proscribed. Modernization would not be permitted to undermine the supremacy of the Communist Party. So when 'abstract democracy' and 'spiritual pollution' were denounced, the advocates of change recognized the smoke signals. In November and December 1986 thousands of students launched protests in the nation's streets, for fear that the tide of reform was being stopped. China's leaders realized that the demands for political change were becoming inseparable from the demands for economic modernization.[21]

The United States was all too keen to encourage and remain involved in political and economic liberalization. It saw what it believed was the writing on the wall. In other parts of East Asia the buds of pluralism were blossoming. The emergence of an opposition party in Taiwan, the moves towards constitutional change in South Korea, and the overthrow of Ferdinand Marcos in the Philippines suggested that a new tide of political liberalization was sweeping the Asian Pacific region. There was little illusion that Western-style liberal institutions would take a hold in Asia. The traditional ties to personality were too strong and deep-rooted. But the old order did seem to be crumbling, and this perception was reinforced by the changes in Poland and Hungary. China, through its open door policy, was trying to identify and associate itself with the emerging nations of East Asia. The United States had every interest in fostering that sense of association. If it could involve itself in those changes, particularly through structural and institutional mechanisms, it might make such changes more difficult to reverse. Joint venture companies, academic exchanges, tourism and direct investment provided some opportunity to influence the direction of reform. While that opportunity should not be exaggerated, American officials believed that the United States had a special role to play. If the United States backed off, it would not stop the flow of change: other nations would step in to fill the gap. Furthermore, continuing investment in China would demonstrate to the rest of Asia that the policies of the Reagan administration were based on realism, and not on blind loyalty to old friends. The President wanted to show that the United States was not locked in to the support of right-wing, authoritarian regimes. And in the unfolding moves towards *détente* with the Soviets, Reagan could demonstrate that America's tentative accommodation with the communist world was not confined to the Soviet bloc.[22]

The Chinese themselves were in two minds about the value of the American model. A large number of public statements and articles excoriated the United States for its continued support of Taiwan. During Reagan's first term, there was professed scepticism about the extent and nature of American power. Some commentators believed that the emperor had not changed his clothes. In a 1984 article, Zhuang Qubing, an America-watcher from the Institute of International Studies, labelled the administration 'the most conservative US Government since World War II' and pointed out that it was escalating the arms race. He dismissed Reagan's overtures of peace as mere election ploys. The United States, the author claimed, faced difficulties on a variety of fronts that disqualified its claim as the unrivalled leader of the Western world. Its

Western European allies were divided over nuclear policy, it had come unstuck in Lebanon, and it continued to support 'reactionary regimes' in Israel, South Korea, and South Africa. He also pointed out the mounting deficits in the trading account and the federal budget. Unlike Zhao, he identified China with the Third World and counselled limited support for the United States. Other writers disagreed. If China was to become a great power, it had to acquire the economic trappings of an international leader. In language more reminiscent of Adam Smith than of Mao or Marx, one commentator asked 'Why is China opening to the outside?' His answer was that China had to learn modern industrial and management techniques, particularly as it still lagged far behind. The reason for China's backwardness was 'the lack of competition and the closed economic system, which isolated China's domestic economy from the heated competition of the world market ... Competition brings out the social nature of modern production and consumption, it equalizes the value of products ... The coercive forces of competition, more than any administrative means or subjective desires, bring about economic development.' The United States seemed a natural partner in such an enterprise.[23]

Although an increasing number of commentators welcomed the economic reforms, there was still some wariness about tying China's fortunes too closely to those of the United States. Analysts in the research institutes and foreign policy-making circles tended to view American policy in the mid-1980s as 'offensive' rather than 'defensive.' Reagan, they claimed, was trying to establish the United States as the world's overlord. China had to be wary of this new invigorated hegemonism, but it was fairly confident that this natural drive towards hegemonism would be checked by recent changes in the international order. Western Europe, Japan and the emerging nations, they contended, had a fiercer sense of independence than in the 1950s and 1960s. The bipolar system was on the decline, and the exercise of military power would not produce the results it had once achieved. America, Chinese observers maintained, had not adjusted to the diversity of international life. Huan Xiang, one of Deng Xiaoping's senior foreign policy advisers, published a blistering attack on the United States in 1987, excoriating it for 'great-nation chauvinism' and for believing that 'it has all the truth and strength in the world at its disposal.' He singled out America's interference in such matters as China's birth control practices, its policies towards Tibet, and its attitudes towards intellectuals as evidence of its insensitivity to other societies. However, because the United States was regarded as less capable of dominance than it had once been, many Chinese reformers believed that they could absorb a greater volume of American investment, technological transfer, and scholarly exchange without endangering the socialist system.[24]

The changes in China reinforced the positive attitudes of public opinion in the United States. According to Gallup polls in the mid-1980s about 70 per cent of Americans had favourable impressions of China. American press coverage of the economic reforms was widespread and enthusiastic. The press frequently contrasted the booming and modernizing economy of the mid-1980s to the xenophobic, terror-struck state of Mao's Cultural Revolution. There were reports of Chinese beauty pageants, rock music and fashion, all of which fuelled the impression that China was becoming Westernized. *Time* magazine named Deng Xiaoping man of the year for 1985. There was even a sense that China was abandoning communism. *Business Week* spoke of the re-emergence of capitalism in a cover story on China. It was reported that Marx was being put on the back burner and that free markets were gradually replacing the planned economy. Indeed, the most glowing accounts of the developments in China tended to come from conservatives rather than academic specialists on China who tended to remain sceptical of the ability of the political system to absorb these changes. Harry Harding has demonstrated that conservatives viewed the developments in China as a vindication of their faith in the inevitable dissolution of the communist system.[25]

Although China's leaders warned that increased exposure to things foreign would increase the chances of 'spiritual pollution,' some Chinese commentators and spokesmen reinforced the buoyant optimism in the United States. They maintained that China had much to learn from the United States. Portrayals of American life highlighted its positive aspects as well as its downside. Han Xu, the Chinese Ambassador to the United States, spoke glowingly in April 1988 of the mutual benefit of the growing ties between the two nations. In 1987 300,000 Americans had travelled to China. Twenty-thousand Chinese students were studying in American universities. The United States was second only to Hong Kong in its level of direct investment in China. Trade between the two countries had grown by an impressive 28 per cent between 1987 and 1988. China was America's thirteenth largest trading partner, and was the leading overseas market for wheat. When some Chinese compared their economic achievements to those of the United States, they no longer backed away from attributing their shortcomings to themselves rather than to any trade restrictions or lack of investment on the part of the Americans. Li Guoyou of the Institute of the Chinese Academy of Social Sciences wrote that 'China is like a dragon. With its head, tail and body twisted together, in the past the dragon tossed about in the shallows. China should raise its dragon's head and enter the international market ... A dragon can soar to the sky by leaving its body, shaking its head, and wagging its tail.' Li Guoyou and other pro-reform critics argued that the United States still provided an impressive model for economic development. It was, Li claimed, less hierarchical, and still had a high rate of social and geographical mobility. He argued that if Japan and the 'four dragons' could take off, then so could China. China should take a leaf out of America's book. It should learn from other nations and could base its policies on experiences in the West. By competing in the American market, China would not only reap material rewards but also would acquire new managerial skills. This would pay political as well as economic dividends.[26]

Americans naturally welcomed this new role model. Winston Lord, US Ambassador to China, described the year 1988 as 'the most positive year ever' in the history of Sino-American relations. The State Department wanted to encourage this new buoyancy and tried to present China in a favourable light. It distanced itself from the various protests at China's suppression of the Tibetan independence movement, and said little about the PLA's desecration of local cultural sights in and around Lhasa. It also opposed attempts by the US Senate to make high-tech transfer conditional on the improvement of human rights in Tibet. In short, before the outbreak of the new protest movement that would climax in the bloody events of 4 June 1989 both nations sought to project positive images of each other and to convince themselves that the old divisions were gradually breaking down.[27]

Indeed, China's improved relations with the United States were paralleled by a thawing of its hostility to the Soviet Union. The reforms had forced the Chinese to re-examine many of their long-held suspicions and images of other nations. Their rivalry with the Soviets was due for reassessment. Mikhail Gorbachev made it evident that the Soviets did not intend to enforce obedience or conformity of political and economic practice from their neighbours. Diversity was to be tolerated. The opportunity for ideological *détente* was reinforced with military retrenchment by both sides. China pulled back many of its forces from the Sino-Soviet border and cut its armed forces by a million men between 1985 and 1987. The Soviet Union reduced its forces by 80,000 men, and in December 1988 Gorbachev announced that 200,000 Soviet troops would be removed from the Far Eastern theatre. The Soviets planned to reduce their overall military deployments in the Far East by a half. There were also important concessions on the long-standing border dispute. Visa restrictions on travel between the Soviet Union and China were lifted. Above all, Gorbachev ended the Soviet occupation of Afghanistan and put pressure on Vietnam to end its conflict with China.[28] The Chinese government also recognized that the Soviets' *détente* with the United States altered the old configurations. There was no need to unite with one power against the other, as, in China's eyes, the arms control agreements between the Soviets and Americans represented strategic parity. Equilibrium meant that the threat of war was receding, so Chinese diplomacy was geared to maintaining that equilibrium.[29]

The most compelling consideration for the Chinese leadership was the changes that were being unfolded in Eastern Europe. The reforms in Eastern Europe, followed by the virtual disintegration of Soviet control and the dominance of the communist parties in practically all its neighbouring countries, caused an uncomfortable dilemma for the Chinese. To begin with, the Chinese government looked favourably on the changes sweeping the Soviet satellites. For half a century the Soviets had been trying to assert absolute hegemony over other socialist nations and had tolerated no variations, however legitimate, in either ideology or policy. That policy was now in the process of abandonment. China applauded the Russians' agreement to reinvestigate the Katyn massacres, to apologize to the Yugoslavs for their expulsion in 1948 from the Cominform, and even to encourage liberalization of the political systems of the Eastern bloc. The economic reforms in Hungary and Poland were seen to mirror China's own reforms. The Soviets' relaxation of political controls was regarded as a good omen. The Chinese had long argued that there was no single socialist model, and the growing diversity within the Soviet orbit was a recognition of this point.[30] Clearly, if the Soviets were going to permit greater autonomy in Eastern Europe, then they would be equally less concerned about developments on their eastern frontiers.

However, the Chinese would shortly learn a lesson from the Soviet experience. They recognized that as the grip of the state apparatus declined, so did the authority of the government. Events in Poland and Czechoslavakia showed that the Communist Party did not command support, and that liberalization undermined the authority of the ruling party. So Deng and the leadership welcomed the Soviet model for its implications around the world, but they did not wish to see it applied at home. When Gorbachev came on his historic visit to China in May 1989, President Yang Shangkun warned the Soviet leader: 'We feel that our speed is too fast; it should be reduced a little.' The demonstrators outside in Tiananmen Square were well aware of the leadership's nervousness. The slogans on their banners read: 'democracy our common ideal' and 'In Moscow they have Gorbachev, who do we have in China?'[31]

The protest movement that culminated in the demonstrations in Beijing's Tiananmen Square and other cities in China in May and June 1989 had their immediate roots in the politics and economic problems of China. Much of the dissidence was the consequence of the liberalization that had been fostered over the previous four or five years. The political earthquake that struck China in 1989 grew directly out of the problems that had become closely identified with the reform effort. There were a number of contributory causes. In August 1988 it was announced that the Politburo had adopted a new five-year plan for price reform. The details of the plan were never released, but anticipation of massive inflation prompted a run on the banks, as people wished to buy consumer goods before price rises came into effect. In addition, the greater discretionary authority given to individual enterprises and local government brought about a diminution of state revenues. A new class emerged in the process of reform, consisting of people who were in a good position to exploit the new rules. High-level officials and their children were particularly well placed in this respect. The government encouraged a segment of the population to enrich itself. Small businessmen and farmers flourished, and disparities in wealth grew. Li Shuxian, wife of astrophysicist Fang Lizhi, pointed out that after teaching at university for thirty-one years, she was paid only 122 yuan a month, a salary 20 per cent lower than the average construction worker.[32]

Technicians and intellectuals had expected to play a large role in the planning of the reform programme. However, as they became more insistent on open debate, the Chinese leadership began to reverse itself.

General Secretary Hu Yaobang was dismissed in January 1987 and there followed a new campaign against 'bourgeois liberalization.' Government patronage of the arts and scholarship declined, and many intellectuals found themselves marginalized once again. Their sense of frustration and injustice grew. Chinese intellectuals began to challenge the supremacy of their rulers. The reforms undertaken to redeem the party's legitimacy contributed to the decline in the regime's authority and to a wave of questioning about the character and values of Chinese society. The party no longer seemed to have the ideological authority or the political will to enforce intellectual conformity.[33]

As has already been seen, the reforms had encouraged cultural diversity and had deliberately exposed China to a variety of Western cultural products. Classics, ranging from Beethoven to Shakespeare, were rehabilitated, overseas radio broadcasts were permitted, foreign films were licensed. Avant-garde Western art exhibitions were mounted, including a well-publicized and well-attended exhibition of nudes at the National Gallery in Beijing. In the words of one critic, 'this was a bold, unignorable assertion that modern Western art and modern Western cultural values had arrived in force.'[34] Even American foods had an impact. Coca-Cola and Pepsi-Cola had become popular soft drinks among China's young and thousands flocked to the largest Kentucky Fried Chicken outlet in the world, which had opened just off Tiananmen Square. Tourism and student exchanges exposed an increasingly large number of Chinese to Western tastes. Since 1987 alone 4,800 Chinese students had enrolled for tourism courses in the nation's colleges and universities. Exposure to the ideas and models of the Western world provided a new awareness of political and cultural alternatives. About one thousand students returned from abroad to China annually, many of them disenchanted. A special Chinese Returned Students Service Centre in Beijing was formed to help them readjust to the changes. The official press admitted that many students found their sojourn abroad disturbing and tantalizing, and that they returned to China dissatisfied with their lot.[35]

The news from abroad, especially the changes in Eastern Europe, the overthrow of the Marcos regime in the Philippines and the emergence of political pluralism in Taiwan, encouraged a greater sense of autonomy and independence within China. Because of the easing of restrictions and China's wider exposure to the world, dissidents believed that criticism of Deng's leadership did not carry significant risk. It was thought that the authorities would hesitate before clamping down. The critics of the system appreciated that the Chinese leadership was split between reformers and hard-liners. If the reform faction under Zhao Ziyang were to prevail, it had to be encouraged. Public pressure could promote its cause. Thus the Democracy Movement was encouraged by its sense that China was no longer immune to 'world opinion' and that pressure for further reform was likely to be applauded, and, consequently, fruitful.

The immediate spark for the series of demonstrations that culminated in the massacre of 4 June was the sudden death on 15 April 1989 of Hu Yaobang. It was Hu who had pushed China towards a market economy and a more open political system. Hu was immediately hailed as a champion of democracy, and large-scale demonstrations were held as a tribute to him. The demonstrators rapidly turned the exercise into a crusade that called for a reappraisal of Hu's disgrace, an apology for the anti 'spiritual pollution' campaign, democratic elections to the National People's Congress, and freedom of the press. Soon the demonstrators organized boycotts of lectures, and later, when joined by workers, deliberate absence from work. They demanded negotiations with the party elite. Deng ordered the *People's Daily* to write a forceful editorial condemning the demonstrations and warning that the reform programme was being undermined by the demonstrations. The editorial hinted strongly of the danger of a military crackdown: 'All comrades of the Party and people throughout the whole nation must understand clearly that if we do not resolutely check this turmoil, our State will have no calm days.' However, the Chinese leadership was not fully behind Deng. Secretary-General Zhao Ziyang took the opportunity of Gorbachev's visit to portray himself as China's counterpart to the Soviet leader. He directly contradicted Deng by saying in public on 4 May that there would be no 'great turmoil' and said that the demonstrators' 'reasonable demands' should be met by democratic means. The hard-liners refused to give in to the insistence on negotiations, and the demonstrators in Tiananmen Square dug in their heels. Zhao was isolated and Deng turned on him as soon as Gorbachev had departed from the summit. Zhao went to Tiananmen Square in person on 19 May and encouraged the crowds. He was immediately ousted from the top party position and attacked publicly.[36]

With Zhao ousted, the way was open for the military crackdown. Martial law was declared, tanks and water cannons were brought into the city, and troops arrived in droves at the railway station. At two o'clock in the morning of 4 June a convoy of trucks accompanied by armed infantry stormed through the crowded Tiananmen Square and randomly shot people on sight. They hunted in packs. Tanks moved across the city, firing rapidly. Blood was being shed indiscriminately. The morgues soon filled, the bodies laid out for the relatives to identify. The intention was clear. The opposition had to be cowed and the authority of the Party was to be unquestioned.

As the news of the Tiananmen massacre flashed around the world, it became clear at once that China's 'open door' policy had come full circle. The changing political landscape in so many parts of the world had influenced China's own political development. The military crackdown now placed China's domestic politics squarely on the agendas of those nations with whom it had the closest contacts. In Hong Kong stock indices plummeted as the colony's citizens reassessed their prospects for the hand-over in 1997. Political leaders throughout Western Europe condemned the crackdown. In the United States, President George Bush, Reagan's successor, was forced to call a temporary halt to the favourable treatment given to the Chinese in its trading policies. The reassessments throughout the world were made more urgent by the official reaction of the Chinese government, which blamed the Western involvement in its modernization policies on the dissident movement. On 9 June Deng Xiaoping praised the People's Liberation Army for creating 'a Great Wall of iron and steel' and for saving China from becoming 'a bourgeois republic.' The editorial of the *Beijing Review* excoriated the 'trouble-makers ... who have collaborated with hostile overseas forces.' The paper insisted that opening up to the outside world was still the best course for China, but it also warned that 'the practice of economic reform and opening up has also let in some bad things from the West. To this, the party leadership has always kept alert.' In short, China reaffirmed its ties with the West and at the same time it condemned the consequences of those ties.[37]

The bloodshed in Tiananmen Square inevitably led Americans to reappraise their entire position on China. The live pictures on television of tanks crushing unarmed civilians, the makeshift morgues, and the unforgettable image of one lonely protester trying to stop a tank in its tracks by standing in front of it resulted in a surge of revulsion against the Deng leadership. American opinion reacted swiftly against the gruesome events. Before the Tiananmen crisis only 13 per cent of

Americans had an unfavourable image of China. After 4 June the figure shot up to 58 per cent. The Chinese leadership, recently hailed for its reforming vision, was now dubbed a group of ageing butchers. The styrofoam statue of the *Goddess of Freedom and Democracy*, bearing a close resemblance to the Statue of Liberty, which the pro-democracy demonstrators had hoisted a week before the tanks moved in, was converted from a symbol of hope to one of despair. Human rights organizations, which had been strangely silent about China before 4 June, began to publish details of the repression that underpinned Chinese society. Organizations that had pushed for closer ties with China now fell silent. In just a matter of days years of carefully cultivated goodwill had evaporated.[38]

Although the Bush administration shared the sense of outrage, it was mindful of the fact that things change and that it would have to take the longer view. It had taken years to build up a working relationship with China; care had to be taken before bridges were burnt. Bush's initial reaction reflected the popular desire to take measures against China. He immediately offered humanitarian aid to the Red Cross and met with a small group of dissident students in the White House. He ordered the suspension of high-level contacts, Export-Import bank loans, and all sales of military equipment. Visa waivers were granted to Chinese students resident in the US and Fang Lizhi, the noted astrophysicist and human rights activist, was given asylum in the American Embassy in Beijing. On Capitol Hill the House of Representatives unanimously adopted fresh sanctions against the Beijing government, though Bush was given discretion over their implementation. The United States also put pressure on the World Bank, which on 8 June announced the suspension of $780 million in loans. Private companies reconsidered their future plans. American Telephone and Telegraph indefinitely delayed a joint venture that had been originally agreed in May for the manufacture of optical fibres. Individual tourists cancelled their plans to visit China, and the nation's hotels were suddenly emptied of life.

Despite the widespread revulsion to the crackdown, the United States did not close the door on China completely. Beijing tried to signal that nothing had changed. While China's leadership was unrepentant over its use of military force, it made it clear that it still wished the reforms to continue. It did not believe that the quashing of the democracy movement required a reversal of the policies that had been the basis of economic policy since 1979. People who had done much to solder the

Sino-American relationship warned against reacting precipitately. Winston Lord, former US Ambassador to China, urged Americans to look beyond what he called the 'big chill' and to 'sketch blueprints for a warmer climate.' The United States, he said, should not squander the influence it possessed on Chinese affairs. It had even managed to influence aspects of China's foreign policy. If the United States cut itself off from China, its influence would be replaced by another power. He reminded readers of *Foreign Affairs* that many Chinese officials had been instrumental in the democratization process. One day those officials would hold centre stage again: 'What we see in China today is not what we will see within a few years.' For these reasons, Lord urged the administration to tread cautiously and not to close the door: 'While we must not condone what has happened in China, we must not totally isolate the Chinese and rip out all the roots that we have so carefully nurtured.' Caspar Weinberger reflected in his memoirs that while the action in Tiananmen Square had been a setback, 'nothing has changed the vital necessity' for the two countries to re-establish their military relationship. Lord and Weinberger saw the massacre as an exceptional and unfortunate incident. A kind of dependency had been created since 1979 and that dependency had paid dividends. If the United States turned its back on developments, then that influence would dwindle.[39]

The Bush administration was caught on the horns of a dilemma. The events of 4 June showed that China was changing faster than the people who ruled it. The forces for liberalization had been scattered, but it was unlikely that they could be destroyed. There were still some moderates within the ranks of the Chinese leadership. Deng himself indicated that he did not want to turn the clock back. Reforms would proceed even though political liberalization was to be shelved. Bush did not want to 'lose China' again. The United States had interests there, and he wanted to give the forces of democracy encouragement. It was the old story. A policy of ostracism would satisfy the instinctive desire to punish and show the nation's distress, but it would also deprive the United States of a valuable lever of influence. Deng had, after all, blamed foreign influence for the catastrophe. If the West had been responsible for the pro-democracy movement, it was surely unwise to cast that influence aside. More contacts could well put China back on the road of reform. China itself would want international rehabilitation. It wanted tourists and investors to come back. It wanted the valuable British colony in Hong Kong to return to China with its skills and economic infrastrucure intact; it did not want to see the wealth of Hong Kong take flight. Equally, the United States (and Great Britain) did not want a repressive international pariah to take over the British colony after 1997. The Bush administration believed that it could still cajole the PRC into tolerating a degree of diversity within its polity. Bush also remembered how America's relations with China had caused serious partisan division in the past; he wanted to avoid a repetition. The action in Tiananmen Square, however, had changed the agenda again. A new and delicate balancing act was about to unfold.

NOTES

1. John Lewis Gaddis, *The United States and the End of the Cold War: Implications, Reconsiderations, Provocations* (New York and Oxford, 1992), pp. 120–21; also, Michael Schaller, *Reckoning With Reagan: America and its President in the 1980s* (New York and Oxford, 1992), pp. 119–35.

2. U.S. Department of State, *American Foreign Policy: Current Documents, 1981* (Washington, DC, 1984), p. 3; *Xinhua News Agency*, 11, 20, 21 January 1981; *Beijing Review*, 22 June 1981.

3. Alexander M. Haig Jr., *Caveat: Realism, Reagan, and Foreign Policy* (London, 1984), pp. 195–8; Ronald Reagan, *An American Life* (London, 1990), pp. 360–61; I.M. Destler, 'The Evolution of Reagan's Foreign Policy,' in Fred I. Greenstein, ed., *The Reagan Presidency: An Early Assessment* (Baltimore, MD, and London, 1983), pp. 131–3.

4. Zhuang Qubing, Zhang Honzeng and Pan Tongwen, 'The US "Taiwan Relations Act",' *Beijing Review*, 7 September 1981.

5. Jaw-ling Joanne Chang, 'Negotiation of the 17 August 1982 U.S.–PRC Arms Communiqué: Beijing's Negotiating Tactics,' *China Quarterly*, 125 (March 1991), pp. 33–54; Haig, *Caveat*, pp. 207–11, 214; Martin Lasater, *The Taiwan Issue in Sino-American Strategic Relations* (Boulder, CO, 1984), p. 182.

6. *Hearing Before the Committee on Foreign Relations*, U.S.Senate, 97 Cong. 2 Sess, 17 August 1982, pp. 6, 9–12; also, Robert A.Manning, 'China: Reagan's Chance Hit,' *Foreign Policy*, Spring 1984, No. 54, p. 93; Charles T. Cross, 'Taipei's Identity Crisis,' *Foreign Policy*, Summer 1983, No. 51, p. 55; Chang, 'Negotiation of the 17 August 1982 U.S.–PRC Arms Communiqué,' pp. 33–54; Akira Iriye, 'U.S.–Asian Relations in the 1980s,' in David E. Kyvig, *Reagan and the World* (New York and London, 1990), pp. 139–50. For a rather different view, see Bruce Cumings, 'The Political Economy of China's Turn Outward,' in Samuel S. Kim, *China and the World: New Directions in Chinese Foreign Relations*, (Boulder, CO, 1989), pp. 226–9.

7. Caspar Weinberger, *Fighting for Peace: Seven Critical Years at the Pentagon* (London, 1990), pp. 178–9.

8. Tang Tsou, *The Cultural Revolution and Post Mao Reforms: A Historical Perspective* (Chicago, 1986), pp. 150–52; Chang, *Power and Policy in China*, p. 199.

9. *Beijing Review*, 13 July 1981; *China Report*, 162, 5 February 1981.

10. Tsou, *The Cultural Revolution and Post Mao Reforms*, pp. 152–6; Donald S. Zagoria, 'China's Quiet Revolution,' *Foreign Affairs*, 62, Spring 1984, pp. 882–3; Harry Harding, *China's Second Revolution: Reform After Mao* (Washington, DC, 1987), pp. 70–130.

11. Harry Harding, *A Fragile Relationship: the United States and China Since 1972* (Washington, DC, 1992), pp. 125–7.

12. George P. Shultz, *Turmoil and Triumph: My Years as Secretary of State* (New York and Toronto, 1993), pp. 381–6.

13. Harding, *China's Second Revolution*, pp. 106, 116, 146–7; John C. Hsu, *China's Foreign Trade Reforms: Impact on Growth and Stability* (Cambridge, 1989), pp. 96–100.

14. Michel Oksenberg, 'China's Confident Nationalism,' *Foreign Affairs*, 65, 1987, pp. 501–23; Roy Medvedev, *China and the Superpowers* (Oxford, 1986), pp. 146–8; Gerald Segal, *The Fate of Hong Kong* (London, 1993), pp. 38–44.

15. Reagan, *An American Life*, p. 372.

16. Richard Holbrooke, 'East Asia: The Next Challenge'; Tamar Jacoby, 'The Reagan Turnaround on Human Rights,' both in *Foreign Affairs*, 64, 1986, pp. 737–45, 1075–85; Robert W. Tucker, 'Reagan's Foreign Policy,' *Foreign Affairs*, 68, 1988/89, pp. 19–22; Human Rights Watch and Lawyers Committee for Human Rights, *The Reagan Administration's Record on Human Rights* (New York, 1987), pp. 118–20; Andrew J. Nathan, *China's Crisis: Dilemmas of Reform and Prospects for Democracy* (New York, 1990), pp. 86–7.

17. Remarks at meeting with Republican Congressional candidates, 6 October 1982, *Public Papers: Reagan, 1982* (Washington, DC, 1982), p. 1274.

18. George P. Shultz, 'New Realities and New Ways of Thinking,' *Foreign Affairs*, 63, Spring 1985, pp. 706–21; Shultz, *Turmoil and Triumph*, p. 382; also, James Armstrong, 'US Military and Political Interests in East Asia,' in Philip West and Frans A.M. Alting von Gesau (eds), *The Pacific Rim and the Western World* (Boulder, CO, 1987), pp. 74–5.

19. Manning, 'China: Reagan's Chance Hit', pp. 83–101; *Beijing Review*, 9, 16, and 23 January 1984; Immanuel C.Y. Hsu, *China Without Mao: The Search for a New Order* (New York and Oxford, 1990), pp. 183–5; Weinberger, *Fighting for Peace*, pp. 184–96; Shultz, *Turmoil and Triumph*, pp. 394–8; see also Zhao Ziyang, Report of the Sixth Five-Year Plan, in *Beijing Review*, 20 December 1982.

20. Reagan, *An American Life*, pp. 368–9; *Beijing Review*, 7 May 1984.

21. Harding, *China's Second Revolution*, pp. 131–201; Robert Ross, 'From Lin Biao to Deng Xiaoping: Elite Instability and China's U.S. Policy,' *China Quarterly*, 119, June 1989, pp. 265–99; Perry Link, 'The Limits of Cultural Reform in Deng Xiaoping's China,' *Modern China*, 13, April 1987, pp. 115–76; Richard Madsen, 'The Spiritual Crisis of China's Intellectuals' in Deborah Davis and Ezra F. Vogel, *Chinese Society on the Eve of Tiananmen* (Cambridge, MA, and London, 1990), pp. 243–8; A. James Gregor, *The China Connection: U.S. Policy and the People's Republic of China* (Stanford, CA, 1986), pp. 166–82; Jonathan Mirsky, 'Broken China,' *Foreign Policy*, 66, Spring 1987, pp. 70–71.

22. Zagoria, 'China's Quiet Revolution', pp. 903–4; Robert A. Scalapino, 'Asia's Future,' *Foreign Affairs*, 66, Fall 1987, pp. 92–9.

23. Zhuang Qubing, 'US Foreign Policy Clarified,' *Beijing Review*, 27 February 1984; Chen Qiwei, 'Why is China Opening to the Outside?' *Beijing Review*, 1 April 1985; also, David Shambaugh, *Beautiful Imperialist: China Perceives America, 1972–1990* (Princeton, NJ, 1991), pp. 238–9.

24. Shambaugh, *Beautiful Imperialist,* pp. 266–7.

25. Harding, *A Fragile Relationship*, pp. 169–72.

26. *Renmin Ribao (People's Daily)*, 25 April 1988; *Beijing Guoji Maoyi (International Trade)*, October 1987, both in *Joint Publications Research Service Reports*, 11 February and 25 April 1988 (hereafter cited as *JPRS Reports*); Li Guoyou, 'U.S. Importance in World Markets Viewed,' *JPRS Reports*, 29 March 1988; interview, Liu Guoguang in *Beijing Review*, 27 March 1989.

27. Winston Lord, 'China and America: Beyond the Big Chill,' *Foreign Affairs*, 68 (Fall 1989), p. 20; 'U.S. Importance in World Markets Viewed'; *Beijing Review*, 23–29 January 1989.

28. Gerald Segal, *The Soviet Union and the Pacific* (London, 1990), pp. 50–53, 85–93.

29. Xie Yixian, 'China's Foreign Policy: A 1980s Tune-Up,' *Beijing Review*, 13–26 February 1989; Donald S. Zagoria, 'Soviet Policy in East Asia: A New Beginning?' *Foreign Affairs*, 1988/89, vol. 68, pp. 120–38.

30. Ruo Yu, 'The Soviet Union and East Europe Head to New Relations' in *JPRS Reports*, 7 September 1988, pp. 2–3.

31. Michael Fathers and Andrew Higgins, *Tiananmen: The Rape of Peking* (London, 1989), pp. 61–2.

32. Chu-Yuan Cheng, *Behind the Tiananmen Massacre: Social, Political, and Economic Ferment in China* (Boulder, CO, 1990), pp. 86–7; Jürgen Domes, 'China's Internal Dynamics in the 1990s: Political, Economic and Social Trends' in Jürgen Domes et al., *After Tiananmen Square: Challenges for the Chinese–American Relationship* (Washington, DC, 1990), pp. 1–7; Tony Saich, 'When Worlds Collide: The Beijing People's Movement of 1989,' in Tony Saich, ed., *The Chinese People's Movement: Perspectives on Spring 1989* (Armonk, NY, and London 1990), pp. 25–49.

33. Liu Binyan, *China's Crisis, China's Hope* (Cambridge, MA, and London, 1990), pp. 3–30; Nina P. Halpern, 'Economic Reform, Social Mobilization, and Democratization in Post-Mao China,' in Richard Baum, ed., *Reform and Reaction in Post-Mao China: The Road to Tiananmen* (New York and London, 1991), pp. 51–3.

34. Ralph Croizier, '"Going to the World": Art and Culture on the Cosmopolitan Tide' in Anthony J. Kane, *China Briefing, 1989* (Boulder, CO, 1989), p. 69; also, *Beijing Review*, 16–22 January 1989.

35. *Beijing Review*, 23–29 January, 13–19 March 1989.

36. Cheng, *Behind the Tiananmen Massacre*, pp. 122–33; Fathers and Higgins, *Tiananmen*, pp. 32–75; John Fincher, 'Zhao's Fall, China's Loss', *Foreign Policy* (Fall 1989), No. 76, pp. 3–25. For a broader perspective on Deng Xiaoping see Peter Nanshong Lee, 'Deng Xiaoping and the 1989 Tiananmen Square Incident' in Peter Li, Steven Mark and Marjorie H. Li, *Culture and Politics in China: An Anatomy of Tiananmen Square* (New Brunswick, NJ, 1990), pp. 173–96.

37. Fathers and Higgins, *Tiananmen*, p. 139; An Zhiguo, 'On the Events in Beijing,' *Beijing Review*, 26 June–2 July 1989.

38. Robert Garson, 'The Road to Tiananmen Square: the United States and China, 1979–1989,' *Journal of Oriental Studies* 30 (1992), pp.119–35; Harding, *A Fragile Relationship*, table A-1, p. 363.

39. Lord, 'China and America: Beyond the Big Chill,' pp. 1–26; Weinberger, *Fighting for Peace*, p. 203; Allen S. Whiting, 'China's Foreign Relations after 40 Years' in Anthony J. Kane, *China Briefing, 1990* (Boulder, CO, 1990), pp. 72–5; Cheng, *Behind the Tiananmen Massacre*, pp. 147–8.

CHAPTER 8

OLD PROBLEMS IN A NEW
WORLD ORDER

George Bush had been in the White House for less than five months when Chinese armour moved in to Tiananmen Square in the early hours of 4 June 1989. Although Bush had served as Reagan's Vice-President, he brought with him a different style to the White House. Where Reagan enjoyed the political scrum, Bush preferred the safety of company of people like himself. He felt most at ease with the country club set. He tried to appeal to the more fundamentalist Republicans, but his words never sounded right. His famous urging to the voters that they should 'read my lips' on the issue of tax increases reflected his general demeanour. Things should not have to be spelled out in understandings between gentlemen. Reagan promised change and a touch of soul. Bush offered stewardship. If the people could trust Reagan because he was one of them, then they could trust Bush because he had been there before. He was a man of wide experience and good judgement. He was well informed and could field questions on most subjects. He tried to exude energy as well as knowledge. He loved to be questioned by reporters while jogging in the early hours. He had benefited from the extraordinary changes that had occurred in the communist world and the once unimaginable agreements on arms control that had been made between the United States and the Soviet Union. It was neither in his temperament nor in his interests to rock the boat. Bush offered the United States stability and confidence in the 1988 election and it was that image that he would carry with him in his presidency.

So when Bush learned of the tragedy at Tiananmen Square his instincts were cautious. Having spent fourteen months as head of the US liaison office in Beijing in 1974–75, Bush believed that he had special insight. 'I know the Chinese,' he told his aides. 'I know how to deal with them, and it's not through pressure or sanctions.' A man of decency, he denounced the massacre, but he did not feel comfortable with his own denunciation. The democracy movement was an un-known. Even more important, his Republican predecessors in the White House had worked hard to foster Sino-American understanding and he did not want to see that evaporate as a result of the panic decisions that had led to the military confrontation in Beijing.[1]

While Bush therefore joined the public chorus of denunciations and imposed a number of restrictions on contact with China, he secretly worked to limit the damage to Sino-American relations. He was convinced that the crackdown of 4 June was a blip. In his view China would not depart from the economic reforms and the gradual liberalization that had begun in the early 1980s. He insisted also that America's contacts with China had produced the yeast of the pro-democracy movement. 'I happen to believe that commercial contacts have led, in essence, to this quest for more freedom,' he told reporters on 6 June. Only one month later, in July, the President sent his National Security Adviser, Brent Scrowcroft, and the Deputy Secretary of State, Lawrence Eagleburger, on a secret mission to Beijing to meet with the Chinese leadership. Although they later claimed that they had expressed their sense of horror, they were there to try to smooth matters over and to identify points of possible agreement. Bush wanted to keep lines of communication with Beijing open. He believed that memories were short and that China could be kept on the course of reform.[2]

Bush's restraint was not matched by Congress and public opinion as a whole. News coverage of the aftermath of the blood-letting was extensive, and the sense of revulsion did not go away. The arrest and executions of a number of people accused of participating in the demonstrations kept up the momentum of calls for more far-reaching sanctions. The pro-Taiwan right joined forces with liberals in Congress to demand tougher action. However, White House comment was muted. It was soon clear that the President would take no further initiatives on the isolation and punishment of China. Congress began to initiate its own measures. A comprehensive sanctions amendment was attached to the Foreign Relations Authorization Act. It endorsed the measures taken by Bush and stipulated that sanctions would not be lifted until the President certified that China had reformed itself by lifting martial law, ending the reprisals against the demonstrators and moving towards a wider protection of human rights. Congressional leaders insisted that it was inadequate to leave the sanctions programme to the discretion and whim of the President. It needed underpinning.

Executive orders can be rescinded as quickly as they are imposed; Congress wanted the sanctions to have the force of the law. China had to realize that it would not be sufficient to persuade the President or the Secretary of State in the comfortable haven of private discussion that relations could revert to a normal footing as soon as possible. China had to understand that if it did not reform itself further sanctions would be imposed. These would include the revocation of most-favoured-nation (MFN) status for purposes of trade. A bill was also introduced that gave Chinese students living in the United States a four-year extension to their stay and permitted them to apply for immigrant visas during that period. Bush vetoed the bill on the grounds that legislating on foreign policy deprived him of necessary flexibility. The antagonisms between executive and legislature that had characterized policy towards China in the late 1970s had returned.

The Chinese leadership believed that its main mistake in the run-up to the crackdown at Tiananmen Square had been its tolerance towards intellectual and cultural freedom. The reform programmes had created new interest groups that had begun to reject the authority of the ruling Communist Party. Beijing's leadership resolved to suppress these groups and to cut down on cultural contacts with the West, at least in the short term. However, it did not reverse the course of economic reform. It realized that the United States and the West were locked into China's economic destiny. There could be no reversion to isolating China from the world community. It took a few retaliatory measures against the United States, such as jamming some of the frequencies used by the Voice of America and suspending scholarly exchange programmes. But in the main it contented itself with condemning American interference in China's internal affairs and hoped that time would diminish the desire for retaliatory action and put Sino-American relations on an even footing again. It was confident that there were too many interests at stake – in trade, in strategic planning, in joint venture programmes, and in the future of Hong Kong, to name but a few – to prolong the marginalization of China.[3]

It was trade that provided the greatest confluence of interest between the United States and China. Both the President and Congress believed that the United States could make the greatest impact on developments in China through a judicious trade policy. However, they disagreed strongly on how that trade policy could be used to best effect. The key to the matter was the issue of granting China MFN status. MFN status provided for normal, non-discriminatory trade. It was extended to most countries of the world and simply meant that the US would accept a trading partner's exports at the lowest tariff rates that applied, the rates that each nation charged its 'most favoured nation.' Under an amendment passed in 1974 the President could only grant MFN status to a communist country if he could certify that the country permitted free emigration or, at least, was improving its emigration policies. Congress could reject the certification by joint resolution, which could only be overcome if the President could make a veto stick.

China first received MFN status in 1980 and had had it extended annually ever since. It was a crucial matter for China. Trade had become an economic lifeline. By 1990 China was the US's tenth largest trading partner; it had imported $12 billion worth of goods in 1989. In May 1990 the White House announced its decision to renew MFN status for China. The administration insisted that MFN status did not imply approval of the Chinese regime. Richard Solomon, Assistant Secretary of State for East Asian and Pacific Affairs, said on 24 May that most favoured 'does not mean that the country in question is our most favorite nation.' There were, it argued, sound economic reasons for renewing the terms. Bush contended that the 'people in China who trade with us are the engine of reform, an opening to the outside world.' If the US revoked favourable trading terms China would become more enclosed; the damage in places like Hong Kong, through which most of China's exports to the United States passed, would be enormous. The advocates of MFN renewal warned that the withdrawal of MFN would hurt the very groups the US sought to protect. In China the most Western-orientated sectors of the economy would suffer the most. In the United States, they claimed, prices would rise. The denial of MFN status could result in a tenfold increase in tariffs on imported Chinese products, perhaps doubling the domestic prices of some Chinese-made goods.[4]

The House of Representatives was partly swayed. In July 1990 the House Ways and Means Committee voted to continue normalized trade with the PRC on the condition that the President could report that China had made 'significant progress' towards achieving specific human rights goals. A bill passed by 384 votes to 30, although it never became law as the Senate failed to act on the measure. However, Congress had fired a warning shot. America's China policy would be subject to close legislative scrutiny as it touched upon fundamental political values.

Congress had stated that it could no longer be taken for granted that trade, investment and scholarly contacts were the most effective means of maintaining the momentum of reform in China. China was warned that trade on an equal footing could no longer be assumed. An issue that had almost disappeared from the political agenda was once again opened up.[5]

The Bush administration firmly believed that the continuance of trade on a normal basis would promote the cause of human rights in China and at the same time would serve the economic interests of the United States. Before the debate in the House on MFN Bush had sent Brent Scowcroft and Lawrence Eagleburger on a second mission to Beijing to explore the possibilities of improving relations. The mission backfired. The photographs in the press of the two emissaries toasting Deng Xiaoping may have enhanced China's self-image, but they harmed the President's cause. The administration found itself on the defensive. Critics accused the administration of callous appeasement. At the time they did not even know that the two men had visited China the previous July, just a few weeks after the Tiananmen bloodshed. Scarcely a news conference passed without searching questions from the press about the direction of Bush's China policy. Bush was convinced that diplomacy and continued economic ties would make the Chinese leadership more yielding. He told reporters at news conferences in January 1990 that the Scowcroft mission in December had produced positive results. He dwelt on China's progress in the area of liberalization rather than on its documented violations of human rights, pointing to the fact that China had lifted martial law and that 573 people had been released from prison in a general amnesty. He attributed these changes to the pressure that economic contact had generated. 'I think,' he claimed, 'if we let Congress have its head and do what is emotionally popular, these things would be changed.' He also argued that as the USA wanted to play a major role in the Pacific, it had to acknowledge the power of China with its population of over one billion people. 'We've got to work with them,' he insisted.[6]

Bush's insistence that it was not in America's interests to ostracize China acquired a new force with the crisis in the Persian Gulf and the collapse of communism in Eastern Europe and the Soviet Union. In August 1990 Iraq invaded Kuwait and faced a rapid ultimatum from the United States. Saddam Hussein was warned that if he did not withdraw his forces from Kuwait the full military power of the USA and the

United Nations would be brought to bear on Iraq. Bush recognized the importance of international solidarity on the issue; China's position would be critical.[7] When Bush sought to get the UN to impose sanctions on Iraq he realized that China could block collective action by use of its veto power. China had extensive political and military contacts in the region. It had sold arms to Iraq and frequently railed against superpower intervention in regional conflicts. Its pronouncements over the years pointed to the likelihood of strong oppostion to the introduction of US forces in to the region. In Bush's view, the Gulf crisis could provide the opportunity for China's international re-habilitation. He worked energetically to ensure China's cooperation. Bush sent Richard Solomon, Assistant Secretary of State, to Beijing to elicit support for the UN action. In his view, it made no sense to marginalize China and then expect it to cooperate on international policing operations.

The Gulf crisis also gave China a chance to disarm human rights activists and its critics on Capitol Hill. It could take the opportunity to demonstrate its commitment to peace and show that its assignment to the status of pariah was both undeserved and unwise. Hopefully the Western powers could put the Tiananmen incident behind them. How-ever, it did not approve of the use of force in the Gulf. Thus China voted for the first eleven UN resolutions condemning the Iraqi invasion, although it abstained on the twelfth, Resolution 678 of 29 November 1990, which authorized the UN to adopt the necessary measures to force an Iraqi withdrawal. China's principal objective throughout the Gulf crisis was to secure a settlement through the UN. It hoped to be rewarded for its cooperation with the creation of an external en-vironment that would enable it to pursue its programme of domestic reform. Since the beginning of 1990 Beijing had striven to participate actively in world affairs in order to extend the opportunities for trade and investment and to encourage the trend towards multipolarity. Beijing hoped that if it supported the UN resolutions on Iraq, the West would cease to marginalize it. It recognized that if it was going to influence the shape of the much-vaunted new world order it would have to be perceived as a cooperative partner.[8]

China's pragmatic approach to United Nations action in the Gulf was consistent with the campaign it had waged since the beginning of 1990 to counter the charges of human rights groups. It had reinstated the Fulbright and Peace Corps programmes, lifted martial law in Beijing and Tibet, and had allowed the dissident Fang Lizhi to leave the country. It had also launched a public campaign to defend its actions in 1989 and to promote the reform effort that was to be pursued even more vigorously. In early January Li Peng, China's hard-line prime minister, told the State Council that the PRC should maintain a firm belief in itself while attesting to its policy of opening up to the outside world. In the same month Qian Qichen, the Foreign Minister, said that China's 'door will remain open to the outside world' and expressed the hope that 'other countries do not close their doors on China.'[9] China went onto the offensive in the spring of 1990. It welcomed contacts with the outside world but warned against 'bourgeois liberalization' which threatened the very stability of the state. The Ministry of Foreign Affairs protested the US State Department's 1989 Country Reports on human rights practices. It claimed that it had meddled in the internal affairs of China and that it failed to understand the pressures that faced the Chinese government during the Tiananmen crisis. The *People's Daily* rejected America's criticisms of birth control policies and repeated that the quelling of riots in Lhasa, Tibet, in March 1989 was a legitimate response to a separatist movement that sought to split China. It pointed out that the United States would not brook separatism in its own country. On 11 June 1990 General Secretary Jiang Zemin wrote a long open letter to nine students at California State Polytechnic University who had initiated a public correspondence. Jiang defended the military action taken in June 1989 against the demonstrators, who, he claimed, 'would have put our country in a state of disintegration and ruined our nation-building endeavour overnight.' He reaffirmed China's desire to 'learn from and absorb' the technology, managerial expertise and 'fine cultural fruits created in the capitalist world.'[10]

The threat of war in the Gulf gave China the opportunity to apply pressure on the United States and to demonstrate its fundamental commitment to international law. Chinese Foreign Minister Qian Qichen warned Secretary of State James Baker that China might block the UN's international military action against Iraq if it received no rewards for cooperation. Baker reportedly told Qian that Beijing's support would not be forgotten by the United States. In the event China abstained on the resolution that authorized military force, and the way was cleared for the war against Saddam. In December Qian travelled from New York to Washington after the UN vote and met with Bush. It was the highest-level meeting since the June crackdown.

In the encounter Qian urged Bush to reopen the dialogue with China and to engage in high-level diplomacy again. Bush insisted that the ostracism of China would only end if China improved its human rights record and cut down on its exports of weapons. Although the conversations did little more than reaffirm old positions, China believed that it had achieved a breakthrough by getting the President to meet. However, Bush did not succeed in persuading China to lend its active support to the military effort. It backed the Security Council's call on Iraq to leave Kuwait, but it opposed the allied attack. It called, rather pointedly, on 'both belligerents' to exercise restraint and tried to pose as a constructive arbiter. It believed the coalition would not hold together as the various members would come to realize that America's principal reason for going to war was to gain control of the oil resources in the region. The Beijing government thought the United States would get bogged down, as it had in Korea and Vietnam. Thus when the UN coalition achieved its lightning victory in the desert, China's leaders recognized that the old Maoist doctrine of 'people's war,' in which human waves would triumph over technology, was an anachronism. The message of the smart bombs was that technology would triumph in modern warfare. If American hegemony was to be contained, the Chinese leadership concluded, the best way forward was to work with the United States. Deng had come to the same conclusion as Bush. Contact and cooperation was the most effective way of protecting the national interest.[11]

The united front against Iraq, together with the extraordinarily rapid collapse of communism in the Soviet Union and Eastern Europe, generated a belief in Washington that the post-war order, with its divisions between the superpowers, had finally come to an end. George Bush identified the emergence of a new world order in an address to a joint session of the US Congress on 11 September 1990. 'We stand today at a unique and extraordinary moment,' the president intoned. 'Out of these troubled times ... a New World Order may emerge: an era freer from the threat of terror, stronger in the pursuit of justice, and more secure in the quest for peace.' Bush was aware that this new world order would be underpinned by the almost unchallenged power of the United States. Its leadership of the coalition war against Iraq showed that America could once again project its military might abroad. It had cast aside the shadow of the Vietnam experience and could finally lay to rest the memory of Jimmy Carter's impotence in the face of

Iranian blackmail. The United States had successfully led an alliance on a course of action that it had believed to be right. In the confident aftermath of the Gulf war, the Bush administration was sure that the new world order would be collectively policed and that the very activity of policing would nurture the spread of a liberal ideology. Bush was confident that the rejection of communism and the very broad consensus for the Gulf War would make the twenty-first century, like the twentieth, 'the American century.'[12]

China's leaders were wary of Bush's pronouncements. They had miscalculated on the outcome of the Gulf crisis and realized that an adjustment was necessary in the light of American triumphalism. Chinese critics of American policy reiterated their old fears of American hegemonism. They argued that the world order was nothing more than the sum of its parts. Each nation had different interests and differing ideas about government. The emerging world order had to take cognizance of that variety. They recognized that strong nations would have special responsibilities in the areas of peacekeeping, arms reduction and environmental protection. But responsibilities did not mean that special privileges would be conferred on the great powers. In a speech to the United Nations in October 1991 Qian Qichen endorsed the idea of a new order, but reiterated China's opposition to an order based on a uniform conception of human rights. He expressed concern that the human rights banner would provide a mask for 'power politics.' Pan Tongwen of the Foreign Ministry's Institute of International Studies, and a leading specialist on US domestic politics, wrote that Bush's proposal aims 'to create a structure and world order that can maintain US dominant position and promote US interests in the world.' He argued that the new order applied mainly to the already converted. It had little bearing on North–South problems. 'To impose US values on the whole world gets nowhere,' he warned.[13]

China's concern about the growth of American power was magnified by the events that followed the abortive coup against Mikhail Gorbachev in the Soviet Union in August 1991. Gorbachev's pursuit of *perestroika* over the years had resulted in the disintegration of communist control in Eastern Europe and the dismantling of the Berlin wall with its resultant moves towards the unification of Germany. The failure of the coup confirmed the irreversible dissolution of the Soviet Union. Gorbachev disbanded the Communist Party, the cement that had held the Soviet Union together for seventy years. Ukraine, the Baltic states and the three Transcaucasian republics declared their independence. The new nations formed a loose confederation, dominated by the largest member, Russia. The old Soviet empire was no more.

The disintegration of the Soviet Union had a profound impact on the People's Republic of China. The Soviet Communist Party had made the Soviet Union one of the two most powerful nations on earth. In just a matter of months the ruling party was disgraced and the very fabric of the state had been destroyed. China's leaders realized that there were crucial lessons to be learned from the Soviet experience. If they failed to learn, the same fate could await them.

The Chinese believed that the Soviets had made the vital error of putting political reform before economic reform. Soviet citizens had no stake in the changes, as no material comforts flowed from liberalization. China, on the other hand, had produced remarkable economic growth throughout the 1980s. As a result, the ruling Communist Party was seen as an organization that could deliver. This sense of legitimacy emboldened the Chinese government in its crackdown on dissidents in 1989. It did not fear serious domestic repercussions. China's ruling system worked; the Soviet Union's did not. Stability, in China's view, was a prerequisite of economic reform. The government had demonstrated that economic growth and political discipline were compatible. The extraordinary increase in prosperity in Southern China, the coastal arc stretching from Hainan island in the southwest through Guangdong province and on to Fujian, had arguably accentuated the gap between the rich and poor zones of China. The rulers in Beijing were and are aware that differentials generate resentments and disunity. But they also believe that they can serve as examples to the rest of China. If reform under a communist system can produce one of the fastest-growing regional economies in the world, then those sections of the population that are not yet touched by the boom may realize that they can emulate the experience of Guangdong and Fujian. Moreover, the spectacular growth of investment by Hong Kong and Taiwan in the development of southern China has improved the chances of peaceful national reunification through economic integration. Southern China is at the heart of an ethnic Chinese network that stretches across Southern Asia. Deng Xiaoping has acknowledged that the integration of the economies of the region encourages stability and renders the business interests in Taiwan and Hong Kong more amenable to discussions on unification. In Southern China the grip of the Communist Party is looser and the atmosphere is generally more relaxed. Deng presumes that as long as prosperity increases people will not want to kill the goose that laid the golden egg.[14]

The second implication of the disintegration of the Soviet Union lay in China's foreign policy. Since the late 1960s the Soviet Union had been identified by China as the principal threat to its security. The Soviet Union was now in tatters, and the threat practically evaporated. Russia was in no position to maintain the existing level of forces in the Far East and was concentrating its energies on securing economic aid from Europe and the United States.

The only remaining military superpower was the United States. China's America-watchers noted the sense of confidence that swept through the United States. Americans believed that the dissolution of the Soviet Union marked not only the passing of an empire but also the triumph of liberal ideology. Scholars were even predicting the 'end of history,' as Lockean liberalism appeared to have no serious rival in the Western world. Some Chinese observers believed that the United States regarded China as the last remaining obstacle to a universal capitalist order and that it was preparing for a final heave to undermine socialism through economic penetration, disguised under the coda of 'peaceful evolution.'

However, the majority of commentators in China disagreed with this ideological prism and insisted that the United States was pragmatic and driven by geopolitics. The disintegration of the Soviet Union and the triumph of the West's military power in the Gulf meant that Americans would concentrate on increasing their economic competitiveness with other developed nations. China's realist analysts maintained that the United States did not pose a threat to China. They advised that Chinese strategists would be unwise to base their policies on the contingency of American pressure. China was more likely to become a strategic partner of the USA against other major forces, including Islamic fundamentalism. Indeed, all the signs pointed to a gradual military withdrawal of the United States from East Asia. The defence burden seemed unduly heavy, especially when the United States was losing vital markets to the emerging economies of Asia. Americans were asking why Japan bore so little military responsibility for Asian security. American bases in the Philippines were shut down and troops were withdrawn from South Korea. China was also becoming more integrated with the regional economy. Japan had become the largest investor in East Asia, and Hong Kong held the key to much of the prosperity in Guangdong province. In Shenzhen, just across the border from Hong Kong, the Hong Kong dollar was almost universally used and, according to some estimates, about 20 per cent of Hong Kong's notes and coins were in circulation in Guangdong. Thus while the collapse of the Soviet Union gave the United States the military edge, in the short term China's security was not endangered by the collapse of the Soviet Union.[15]

Indeed, the Chinese leadership realized that it had to develop policies that ensured that China did not share the same fate as the Soviet Union. The tightening of political control after June 1989 was coupled with renewed calls for economic reform. Within days of the Tiananmen incident Deng Xiaoping had said that there should be no slowdown in the pace of economic change. Perhaps with an eye to attracting members of Zhao Ziyang's reformist coalition, the hard-line Prime Minister Li Peng also endorsed key elements of the reform programme, particularly coastal development. The leadership believed that its legitimacy rested on the ability to deliver higher standards of living. The Eighth Five Year Plan, approved in 1991, advocated continued movement towards a market economy and provided for the gradual withdrawal of price controls on most items. At the Fourteenth Party Congress held in October 1992 a reshuffle of the party leadership was undertaken to guarantee the continuation of the reforms. Deng's call for economic growth was enthusiastically endorsed. Leaders were convinced that prosperity could be achieved without damage to political security. Indeed, the more the reforms were seen to succeed the more confident the leadership felt about the validity of its programme of political retrenchment. Political pluralism not only endangered their own positions; it brought economic uncertainty in its wake. There was no benefit. The economy continued to boom. Gross national product in 1992 grew by 12 per cent, and in the coastal provinces the spurt was even higher. The contribution of the state sector continued to decline. Nearly one half of China's industrial output was now produced by the collective and private sectors.[16]

The reform programme was harnessed by a modified tightening of political discipline. The crackdown in June 1989 obviated the need for continuing police intimidation. The heavy-handed tactics of the government and the severe punishment that followed in the wake of the liquidation of the demonstrations meant that the subsequent repression could become more invisible. Memories of what befell the protesters were enough to make the population submissive. The defence budget rose after 1989 too, with a large proportion of the increase going to the People's Liberation Army. Although the increase was predicated in part on the uncertainty generated by the Gulf war, the leadership was mindful of the crucial role played by the PLA in saving the regime in 1989. The Soviet armed forces and the security services in Eastern Europe had failed to counter the challenge of the dissidents. The Chinese authorities were convinced that loyalty could only be commanded if the servants of the state believed that there was something worth rescuing. The leadership in Beijing was able to stabilize power and prevent further political disorder through the combined approach of discipline and economic growth.[17]

Despite the energy of China's programme of economic reforms and the return on the surface to normal political life, the United States Congress did not change its mind about the direction of China's development. When President Bush notified Congress in May 1991 that he intended to renew MFN status for China, the move was greeted by widespread bipartisan opposition from the nation's law-makers. Most members of Congress did not believe that China merited privileged trade conditions. In their view, repression had not lifted significantly. They were also vexed by China's sale of advanced military technology to unstable areas. China was the fourth largest arms trader in the world, taking 10 per cent of the world market share. Arms were being supplied to the Khmer Rouge, there were reported plans to sell medium range missiles to Syria and it was revealed that China was helping Algeria build a nuclear reactor. And that was not all. American manufacturers had long complained that China violated patent rights and was openly copying American products, including computer software. They also cited evidence that China was using convict labour to produce goods that were then exported to the United States. In the area of trade the American deficit with China had grown to over $12 billion and was projected to rise further. The indictment against China was extensive and long. Congress was not willing to continue to approve MFN unconditionally and so give China *carte blanche* to continue practices that ran contrary to the interests and beliefs of the United States.

It became clear that Congress would only grant China MFN status if it fulfilled a number of stringent requirements. It sought to impose strict guidelines on the President. The finally approved conference bill attached a number of conditions which China would have to meet before it could be granted MFN status in 1992. China was required to release prisoners incarcerated for their role in the protest movement that preceded the Tiananmen crackdown, to cease exporting products made by forced prison labour, to adhere to the Sino-British Joint Declaration on Hong Kong, to stop transferring M-9 and M-11 missiles to Iran and Syria, and to abide by multilateral non-proliferation agreements, including the Missile Technology Control Regime.[18]

Bush tried to use all his influence to defeat the measure. In a speech given at Yale University's Commencement Ceremony the President warned against the attempt to revoke MFN. 'You do not reform a world by ignoring it,' he told the students. He believed that China's experience in trade and in international organizations would expose it to the political practices of the West. China was more likely to change through participation than through isolation. MFN, he maintained, was 'a means to bring the influence of the outside world to bear on China.' On the eve of the Senate vote in July, Bush acknowledged the spirit of Congress's objections in a letter to Senator Max Baucus. He changed his tune, and undertook to tackle China directly. He promised tougher action on infringements of copyright and China's evasion of trade rules through its practice of relabelling. However, he did not want MFN to depend on Chinese compliance. Bush's letter did not stop the resolution passing the House of Representatives by 409 votes to 21. In the Senate, however, the vote passed by a narrower margin, 59 votes to 39. Bush vetoed the bill on 2 March 1992 on the grounds that measures were being taken anyway and that 'if we present China's leaders with an ultimatum on MFN, the result will be weakened ties to the West and further repression.' There were insufficient votes to override the veto in the Senate, and MFN received approval for another year. But the argument would not go away. Three months later, on 2 June 1992, the process started all over again.[19] Congress passed bills placing stiff conditions on the President's ability to extend MFN, although it favoured granting MFN status to goods produced by privately or collectively owned enterprises. Once again Bush vetoed, and the veto was sustained by the failure of the Senate to muster up enough votes. China was given a breathing space for yet another year.[20]

Throughout 1992 China actively sought to project a positive image of itself and to play a larger international role. It promised to end restrictive trade practices in order to secure membership of GATT. It established diplomatic relations with South Korea and received official visits from both the South Korean President and the Japanese Emperor. It even advised South Korea on how to apply pressure against North Korea's weapons programme. It campaigned to host the summer Olympics in the year 2000 in Beijing, and promised to include Hong Kong and Taiwan as Olympic sites. Although it was critical of America's open support of democratic reforms in Hong Kong and the Bush administration's decision to sell F-16 fighter planes to Taiwan, it continued to open up its economy to overseas investment, especially from Hong Kong and Taiwan. In 1992 between nine and ten billion dollars were invested by foreigners in China, almost the same amount that was lured by the United States, the world's biggest economy. China boasted of its phenomenal rate of growth and welcomed the international interest in the opening of stock exchanges in Shanghai and Shenzhen. A limited number of 'B' shares were made available to foreign investors, who stumbled over themselves in the scramble for the equities. The Chinese government gave permission for the establishment of foreign branch banks and many foreign financial institutions, including Citibank and Bank of America, opened up branches. Per capita income had almost quadrupled since the beginning of the reforms in the late 1970s. In 1992 the economy grew by nearly 13 per cent in real terms; it edged towards 20 per cent in 1993. Savings and disposable income were growing and the foreign debt was modest by any standard. China was openly cocky about the attractiveness of investment opportunities in the country. Time and again it reiterated the view that the economies of Russia and the other states that had once constituted the Soviet Union were in disarray as a result of hasty and premature political reform. The Chinese leadership remained convinced that Western democracies would not strive to destabilize the fastest-growing economy in the world and risk disruption and chaos.[21]

There was one area in particular where the economic interests of China converged with those of other nations, and that was Hong Kong. Although the negotiations on the transfer of the colony to Chinese sovereignty in July 1997 were a Sino-British matter, the ramifications are enormous. The fate of Hong Kong has provided a window on China's future political intentions. Hong Kong has become the pivot in the economy of southern China and Southeast Asia. Chinese institutions, to say nothing of the families of China's rulers, have invested in the territory to the tune of over US$12 billion. The traffic in venture funds has been two-way. Hong Kong businessmen have also invested heavily in the businesses of southern China. It is estimated that nine out of every ten Hong Kong manufacturers rely on factories in China for their output. The territory itself serves as the major entrepôt for trade in the region. Hong Kong has become crucial to China for two reasons: it has facilitated the reform process and the opening up of the economy in southern China and it serves as a showcase of Chinese intentions in the post-Cold War era. Deng has become increasingly aware that communism in China can only survive if economic development strengthens the apparatus of the state. That development is nurtured through accesss to the international economy, much of which circulates through Hong Kong and South China. If Hong Kong is strangled economically and the transition from British rule fails, then China's insistence that economic growth and prosperity is consistent with a centralized, authoritarian state will seem hollow. If Hong Kong is the key to China's strength, it can also be the key to China's collapse.[22]

Although the United States was essentially a bystander in the negotiations between Britain and China on the transfer of Hong Kong to Chinese authority, the Tiananmen killings generated special concern. While Washington has been glad to leave Hong Kong's future to Britain and China to sort out, the US recognizes a close convergence of interests. By 1990 Hong Kong was the US's fourth largest export market in Asia. The US had invested over $6 billion in the territory which was second only to Japan in the level of US investments. The colony's economy was open to foreign trade with few restrictions, and the Hong Kong dollar is tied to the US dollar. There are about 15,000 American residents in Hong Kong, more than there are from Britain. Also, Hong Kong's fate provides clues on what might befall Taiwan should reunification occur. China has insisted that the absorption of Hong Kong would not mean the destruction of its unique economy. If two systems can indeed survive in one country, as China insists they can, the prospects of reunification, or at least a new association with Taipei, are enhanced.

The convergence of the economies of southern China and Hong Kong informed the discussion in Washington on the granting of MFN status to China. A failure to grant MFN status to the PRC would have had a profound impact on Hong Kong. The Americans realized that they could not disentangle their policy on China from their position on Hong Kong. In May 1992 Congress passed the US–Hong Kong Policy Act, which confirmed America's support for the autonomy of the colony in the run-up to the hand-over. The legislation followed on the heels of the immigration act of 1990, which raised the limits on the number of visas which were to be issued to Hong Kong emigrants. The White House did not change its strategy. Bush continued to argue that sanctions against China should be lifted. Opening up trade and investment with China would facilitate that country's liberalization. It would also facilitate economic integration in East Asia. Bush claimed that a smooth hand-over without damage to the economic and financial infrastructure was consistent with his general strategy of creating a dynamic and prosperous East Asia. Such prosperity, he believed, would help to keep the region friendly to the United States and would make it more likely to welcome a continuing American military presence in the area.[23]

However, China's careful cultivation of international support did not have a significant impact on opinion in the United States. In the 1992 presidential campaign both candidates, President Bush and Bill Clinton, the Democratic challenger, acknowledged the groundswell of opinion in favour of a tougher approach to China. Both men indicated that international pressure was responsible for some of the concessions on human rights that had been made in China. Bush realized that in trade terms China, not the United States, was the main beneficiary of MFN. In 1991 China had run up a trade surplus with the United States of $15.6 billion. He got tougher. In August 1992 Carla Hills, the US trade representative, listed four billion dollars of China's exports to the United States that would face higher US tariffs unless China opened up its trade more.[24] The Chinese conceded, and agreed to clean up the restrictive regulations and quantitative barriers to American imports. In the campaign itself Governor Clinton vowed to work more closely with Congress and to review Bush's resistance to the imposition of conditions for MFN status. He declared that if China did not improve its human rights record, he would not support normal trade relations.

Clinton's electoral victory in November 1992 boosted the confidence of the human rights lobby, which believed that the new President would take a tougher line. Clinton nominated Winston Lord, who had served as Ambassador to Beijing from 1985 to 1989 but had become increasingly critical of Bush's China policies after the Tiananmen crackdown, as Assistant Secretary of State for East Asia and Pacific affairs. However, in the hearings for his nomination Lord argued that the US should not be hasty. He favoured conditional MFN but cautioned

Congress about the overall importance of maintaining a continued relationship with the Beijing regime. He cited China's influence over North Korean policy on nuclear weapons as just one area where the United States could not afford to alienate the Chinese government. He was also aware that Chinese politicians and businessmen find themselves being wooed by so many major European and Japanese companies that they could dispense with the Americans. On 28 May 1993 Clinton informed Congress that he intended to renew China's MFN status for the year beginning July 1993, but at the same time signed an executive order directing the Secretary of State to certify that China had complied with stipulations that proscribed the use of prison labour on goods exported to the US and that China was not erecting barriers to free emigration of its citizens. However, Clinton did not tie MFN renewal to changes in China's policies on the export of weapons technology to Third World countries. Clinton had been persuaded – possibly as a result of a forceful representation from Chris Patten, Governor of Hong Kong, who warned Clinton against undermining Hong Kong's economy – that China's offending policies should be dealt with separately, outside the MFN framework.[25]

Clinton still hoped that increased trade and the ending of China's own commercial barriers would serve to assimilate the PRC into the world community. In March 1993 talks on China's reentry to GATT were opened up again – they had been suspended after the Tiananmen crackdown. Proponents of Chinese membership want to blunt China's competitive edge by binding it to international trading regulations. The United States has contended that China should only be admitted to membership of GATT on certain conditions. It must agree, say the Americans, to adopt a uniform system of trading practices throughout the country, eliminate quantitative import controls, and pledge itself generally to move towards a full market economy. It has also insisted that GATT membership would not lay to rest the question of MFN status for China. The issue of China's huge trade surplus with the United States (estimated at $23 billion by the Americans) and its record on human rights and arms sales would still be obstacles to the full normalization of trade.[26]

China's poor record on human rights and its practice of selling weapons to the Third World were also used by China's critics to thwart its bid to host the millennial Olympic Games in Beijing in 2000. City officials went to great lengths to clean up the city for the visits of

Olympic inspectors. Beijing residents were banned from burning coal in order to reduce pollution during a visitation from the International Olympic Committee (IOC). The security ministry stopped shadowing foreign journalists. When the IOC asked each bidding country to lend a national treasure to the Olympic Museum in Lausanne, the Chinese outstripped their competitiors by lending a Qin terracotta warrior. Just before the IOC announced its decision in September 1993, Wei Jingsheng, a Chinese dissident, was released from prison after fourteen years' custody. China seemed intent on demonstrating that change was in the air and that the West's judgements after Tiananmen were hasty and ill-founded. It continued to argue that America's posture on human rights was arrogant. One Chinese official pointed to the five rings on the Olympic flag and said 'China has 1.27 billion people, more than one-fifth of the world's population. Therefore one of those rings on the flag represents us.' The argument failed to impress. China's gestures did not change the minds of its critics in the US. The House of Representatives' Foreign Affairs Subcommittee passed a resolution opposing Beijing's Olympic bid on the grounds that China's continuing gross violations of human rights were incompatible with the Olympic spirit. Most Americans agreed. It is conceivable that the campaign tipped the balance. Beijing narrowly failed in its bid and was pipped by Sydney.[27]

It was not just differences over human rights that continued to drive a wedge between China and the United States. China's flourishing arms trade was a rich source of foreign revenue, and also served to extend its influence in several of the world's flashpoints. The United States, itself a large arms exporter as Beijing has repeatedly pointed out, is concerned that weapons in the hands of powers outside the nuclear club are an inherent threat to world peace. Although China agreed to abide by the guidelines of the Missile Technology Control Regime, it had long been suspected of supplying advanced missile technology to the Middle East and Pakistan. In the 1992 election campaign Clinton promised a full review of America's tolerance of China's arms policy. The first test of Clinton's resolve came in August 1993, when he learned that China had sold M-11 surface-to-surface missile technology to Pakistan. In retaliation against the sale the State Department announced that American companies would be banned from supplying China with satellite and high technology products. China objected to the ban and insisted that the specifications of the M-11 items sold did not fall under the aegis of the Missile Technology Control Regime. In the same week

China revoked the passport of a dissident labour activist, Han Donfang, who had just returned from a spell in the United States, and expelled him from the country. A former ambassador to China, James Lilley, commented that 'The Chinese are testing the new administration ... By now they've gotten the message that MFN is a bullet which we put in the gun and never fire. So they're playing hardball on human rights.'[28]

China did not want the matter to spiral, particularly as the IOC had not yet made its decision on the siting of the 2000 Olympic Games. Both nations faced parallel dilemmas. They were trying to strike a difficult and delicate balance. They both saw the desirability of closer economic and cultural ties with one another, but they did not intend to bow to pressure and surrender their sovereign right to make alliances and establish their own legal rules. Neither side wanted to see their differences escalate. China, in particular, wished to demonstrate that it would not be coerced in matters that it considered to be entirely within the domestic domain. Thus its resumption of nuclear testing on 5 October 1993 in Xinjiang province was a demonstration of its independence and, less probably, the possible start of a new campaign against pressure from the United States. Clinton reacted by ordering the Energy Department to prepare for a resumption of testing, but later he let it be known that the US would not end its moratorium on testing as a result of one single test. Clinton's strategy after one year in office was to send mixed messages. In early January 1994 US Trade Representative Mickey Kantor threatened to slash China's textile quotas by 25 to 35 per cent. In the same week the US government approved the sale of three US satellites for launch on Chinese rockets and welcomed China's apparent readinesss to open talks on missile sales. The Sino–American relationship had not lost any of its unpredictable contrariness.[29]

The Clinton administration recognized that while China was an unlikely and unacceptable candidate for close partnership with the United States, it was still a country with which it needed to work. Most of Clinton's advisers argued that Washington was more likely to influence Chinese development if trade and contacts continued to flourish. Clinton realized that his decision in 1993 to put China on probation for a year simply postponed the day of judgement on MFN status and did not solve any dilemmas. China was not likely to abandon its political and penal system to satisfy the human rights lobby in the United States. The administration faced huge pressure from business and the Treasury and Commerce Departments not to crush the hopes of American business in the world's largest market and to yield trade opportunities to America's competitors. The United States could not pretend that the threat of trade sanctions would cause the Chinese government to change track. There were other investors and producers waiting to jump at the prospect of Chinese custom.

Clinton knew that he would have to find a way of climbing down from the high moral tone he had adopted in the 1993 talks on MFN status. His critics were harping on Clinton's tendency to muddle through and his lack of spine in foreign policy. The President came to the conclusion that he would have to knock the MFN issue off the agenda. He had fought hard to get the North American Free Trade Agreement (NAFTA) through Congress and still has to persuade Congress to ratify the Uruguay-round GATT agreement. He could hardly argue for the reduction of trade barriers with one breath and for their erection against China in the next. He had billed himself as a leader who would give top priority to economic affairs. He understood that lessening trade with China would take its toll in American jobs. Officials in the economic departments had undermined the human rights stand of Warren Christopher at the State Department and applied intense pressure on the President not only to renew MFN discussions again in 1994, but also to abandon the annual ritual of review. In their view the threat was short-sighted, particularly as the Chinese did not seem to take it seriously any longer. In May, Jiang Zemin provocatively defended the crackdown of 1989 and said that it had created the stable conditions in which economic reforms could develop.[30]

Clinton decided to end the annual saga and announced on 26 May that he would renew MFN status for China without provision for further review. He incurred the wrath of human rights groups by refusing to tackle China's failure to make significant progress on human rights. Supporters of trade sanctions accused the President of turning his back on millions of oppressed Chinese and of ignoring recent reports of a string of political prisons throughout the country. Li Lu, one of the leaders of the 1989 pro-democracy movement, said he was 'discouraged, disappointed and frustrated'. But many Americans were glad to see the back of this annual tangle. The *New York Times* remarked that Clinton's announcement was 'surely the most eloquent defense of the Bush Administration's China policy ever uttered in the White House.'[31] Clinton recognized that Americans' fragile sense of economic welfare featured larger than the belief that the United States could change China's practices on human rights. He had declared that the trade weapon had reached the end of its useful life. The United States needed China's custom and its support in the confrontation with North Korea over that country's refusal to admit international inspectors to its nuclear installations. The United States could simply not afford to drive China away.

The United States had come to realize that there was little to be gained in putting a gun to China's head. It is convinced that China's energetic quest for investment and modernization is a continuing sign of its disguised conversion to a capitalist economy. It believes, as it has always done, that the march to capitalism is also a march towards political freedoms. The Chinese leadership continues to deny that they are inherently connected. In many parts of China economic management is passing from central government to the provinces and from unwieldy state institutions to individual enterprises. Most Western commentators believe that the more decision-making moves away from the centre, the more the role of the ruling Communist Party will fade. Successive administrations have striven to put the United States in the driving seat of China's road to capitalism. They have argued that if they impose trade sanctions, America's ability to guide China will be hindered. While the United States is mindful of the fact that capitalism and economic growth do not necessarily guarantee liberty, it does believe that the market-place makes the abuse of liberty more difficult to effect.

America's relations with the People's Republic of China are also part of the larger mosaic of the world order that has emerged since the demise of the Soviet Union. The end of the Cold War has provided the United States with an opportunity to reduce military spending and reconsider its commitments. Americans no longer have the political will to act as the world's policemen. They think it neither necessary nor fruitful. International involvement in Somalia and Bosnia only confirmed the belief that America's leverage on events is limited. The beleaguered population of Rwanda is but the latest victim of the growing recognition worldwide that the ability to change events is limited. There are still fault lines left by the Cold War, particularly in the Korean peninsula. The country's domestic problems, with inner city disintegration, the growth of a seemingly permanent underclass and its $300 billion budget deficit, have persuaded many Americans that foreign policy should be based more narrowly on immediate conceptions of the national interest. If they are going to spend the 'peace dividend', they want it to go on domestic projects. The United States will choose its battle grounds more judiciously and will be reluctant to become entangled in commitments from which there are no clear exits. The United States will not be able to sustain its role if its economic problems remain unsolved.

However, a nation does not just shrug off its political culture and the international traditions of over half a century. Because the United States is still a military power without serious rival, it clings, albeit more tenuously, to that sense of moral obligation that guided it in the Cold War era. It knows it cannot make the world right. But it will still seize opportunities for demonstrating its belief that conviction must play a role in international affairs. Its relations with the People's Republic of China provide such an opportunity. Its short-term interest in promoting trade and investment without incurring large deficits can be combined with its sense that there is still a place for principle in its foreign policy. The collapse of the Soviet Union taught one major lesson: political systems cannot be separated from economic systems. The United States remains convinced as ever that in China, as elsewhere, a free market in goods will inevitably be followed by the market of ideas.

NOTES

1. Michael Duffy and Dan Goodgame, *Marching in Place: The Status Quo Presidency of George Bush* (New York, 1992), pp. 182–3; *New York Times*, 5 June 1989.

2. *New York Times*, 6 June 1989; Orville Schell, 'Deng's Ploy, Bush's Test,' *New York Times*, 15 June 1989; Allen S. Whiting,' China's Foreign Relations after 40 Years' in Anthony J. Kane, *China Briefing*, 1990 (Boulder, CO, 1990), pp. 72–5.

3. Allen S. Whiting, 'China's Foreign Relations after 40 Years'; Leo Ou-fan Lee, 'The Crisis of Culture,' both in Anthony J. Kane, *China Briefing, 1990* (Boulder, CO, 1990), pp. 65–82, 102–5.

4. Hearings before the Subcommittee on Trade of the House Committee on Ways and Means, 101 Cong 2 Sess, *United States–People's Republic of China (PRC) Trade Relations, Including Most-Favored-Nation Status for the PRC* (Washington, DC, 1990); statement by President, Secretary Fitzwater on Renewal of MFN Status for China, 24 May 1990, *Public Papers of the Presidents: George Bush, 1990, I* (Washington, DC, 1991), pp. 715–16.

5. 'Efforts at Hard Line on China Thwarted,' *Congressional Quarterly Almanac, 1990* (Washington, DC, 1991), pp. 764–8.

6. News conferences, 24, 25 January 1990, *Public Papers: Bush, 1990, I*, pp. 79–80, 102–3.

7. On the Gulf War see John Bulloch, *Saddam's War: The Origins of the Kuwait Conflict and the International Response* (London, 1991); Dilip Hiro, *Desert Shield to Desert Storm: the Second Gulf War* (New York, 1992).

8. Hwei-ling Huo, 'Patterns of Behavior in China's Foreign Policy: The Gulf Crisis and Beyond,' *Asian Survey*, 33 (March 1992), pp. 266–72.

9. *Beijing Review*, 8 and 15 January 1990.

10. Excerpt, *People's Daily*, 25 February 1990; 'Jiang Zemin Replies to American Students,' *Beijing Review*, 12 March and 25 June 1990.

11. Harry Harding, *A Fragile Relationship: The United States and China since 1972* (Washington, DC, 1992), pp. 272–3; Harry Harding, 'China's American Dilemma,' *The Annals of the American Academy of Political and Social Science*, 519, January 1992, pp. 13–26; Harrison Salisbury, *The New Emperors: China in the Era of Mao and Deng* (New York, 1992), p. 460; *The Economist*, 26 January 1991, p. 53; Alan D. Romberg and Marshall M. Bouton, 'The U.S. and Asia in 1991,' *Asian Survey*, 32, January 1992, p. 4.

12. Address before a Joint Session of Congress, *Public Papers of the Presidents of the United States: George Bush, 1990, II* (Washington, DC, 1991), pp. 1218–22; 'New World Order: What's New? Which World? Whose Orders?' *The Economist*, 23 February 1991.

13. Speech, Qian Qichen, 'Establishing a Just and Equitable New International Order'; Pan Tongwen, 'New World Order – According to Mr. Bush,' *Beijing Review*, 7 and 28 October 1991.

14. 'The South China Miracle,' *The Economist*, 5 October 1991; Nicholas Lardy, *Foreign Trade and Economic Reform in China, 1978–1990* (Cambridge, 1992), passim; John C. Hsu, *China's Foreign Trade Reforms: Impact on Growth and Stability* (Cambridge, 1989), pp. 76–91; George T. Crane, 'China and Taiwan: not yet "Greater China",' *International Affairs*, 69 (October 1993), pp. 705–23; Gerald Segal, 'China and the Disintegration of the Soviet Union,' *Asian Survey*, 32, September 1992, pp. 848–55.

15. Segal, 'China and the Disintegration of the Soviet Union,' pp. 855–68; 'Running Out of Time,' *Far Eastern Economic Review*, 8 July 1993; Jianwei Wang and Zhimin Lin, 'Chinese Perceptions in the Post-Cold War Era: Three Images of the United States,' *Asian Survey*, 32, October 1992, pp. 902–917.

16. Elizabeth J. Perry, 'China in 1992: An Experiment in neo-Authoritarianism,' *Asian Survey*, 33, January 1993, pp. 12–21; *Beijing Review*, 12 October 1992.

17. Segal, 'China and the Disintegration of the Soviet Union,' pp. 850–51; Richard Baum, 'Political Stability in Post-Deng China: Problems and Prospects,' *Asian Survey*, 32, June 1992, pp. 491–7.

18. *Congressional Quarterly Almanac, 1991*, pp. 120–25; Harding, *A Fragile Relationship*, pp. 275–80; *The Economist*, 7 March 1992.

19. Remarks at the Yale University Commencement Ceremony, New Haven, 27 May 1991, *Public Papers of the Presidents: George Bush, 1991, I* (Washington, DC, 1992), pp. 565–8; *Congressional Quarterly Almanac, 1991*, pp. 120–25; Harding, *A Fragile Relationship*, pp. 280–83; *China–Britain Trade Review*, January 1992.

20. *Congressional Quarterly*, 6 June and 8 August 1992, pp. 1594–5, 2336; *Congressional Quarterly Almanac, 1992*, pp. 157–61.

21. Gary H. Jefferson, 'The Chinese Economy: Moving Forward,' in William A. Joseph, *China Briefing, 1992* (Boulder, CO, 1993), pp. 43–5; Perry, 'China in 1992,' pp. 12–21; Crane, 'China and Taiwan,' pp. 705–23; 'China Feels the Heat,' *The Economist*, 23–29 January 1993.

22. Michael Yahuda, 'Hong Kong's Future: Sino-British Negotiations, Perceptions, Organization and Political Culture,' *International Affairs*, 69, 1993, pp. 245–66; Kenneth Lieberthal, 'The Future of Hong Kong,' *Asian Survey*, 32, July 1992, pp. 665–82.

23. Segal, *The Fate of Hong Kong*, pp. 112–27; *Far Eastern Economic Review*, 22 October 1992; Sheldon W. Simon, 'U.S. Interests in Southeast Asia: The Future Military Presence,' *Asian Survey*, 31, July 1991, pp. 662–75; Zhang Xiaodong, 'Trade War Averted,' *Beijing Review*, 1 November 1992.

24. 'Visitors to the Middle Kingdom,' *The Economist*, 3–9 October 1992.

25. 'Lord Seeks China Consensus'; 'Clinton Ties MFN for China to Human Rights Gains,' both in *Congressional Quarterly*, 3 April and 29 May 1993, pp. 855, 1346; 'Mr. Patten's Message,' *The Economist*, 8–14 May 1993, p. 54.

26. 'Snail's Pace,' *The Economist*, 6–12 March 1993; 'Head for Heights,' *Far Eastern Economic Review*, 23 December 1993.

27. The Beijing Olympics?' *The Economist*, 21 August 1993; 'Doubts Arise over Peking Olympic Bid,' 'China Stage-Manages Mass Rally for its Olympic Hopes,' *The Times*, 21 and 22 September 1993.

28. 'US Could Widen Penalties on China,' *International Herald Tribune*, 27 August 1993; 'Han Linked to Games Bid, MFN,' 'Beijing Condemns US Move to Impose Hi-tech Sanctions,' *South China Morning Post*, 25, 27 August 1993.

29. 'China's Bomb Test Risks Accelerating Nuclear Arms Race,' *The Times*, 6 October 1993; 'Trading Troubles,' *Far Eastern Economic Review*, 25 November 1993; 'Hong Kong Suffers Most from US–China Trade Arguments,' *Financial Times*, 8–9 January 1994.

30. 'Clinton's Chinese Lessons,' *The Economist*, 21 May 1994.

31. Quoted in *The Times*, 28 May 1994.

BIBLIOGRAPHY

Books

Acheson, Dean, *Present at the Creation: My Years in the State Department* (London, 1970).

Adams, Sherman, *Firsthand Report: The Story of the Eisenhower Administration* (New York, 1961).

Ambrose, Stephen E., *Eisenhower, The President: II, 1952–1969* (London, 1984).

Ambrose, Stephen E., *Nixon: II, The Triumph of a Politician, 1962–1972* (New York, 1989).

Ambrose, Stephen E., *Nixon: III, Ruin and Recovery, 1973–1990* (New York, 1991).

Anderson, David L., *Trapped by Success: The Eisenhower Administration and Vietnam, 1953–61* (New York, 1991).

Bachrack, Stanley D., *The Committee of One Million: China Lobby Politics, 1953–1971* (New York, 1976).

Barnett, A. Doak, *China on the Eve of Communist Takeover* (New York, 1963).

Barnett, A. Doak, *Communist China: The Early Years, 1949–1955* (New York, 1955).

Barnett, A. Doak, *The Making of Foreign Policy in China: Structure and Process* (London, 1985).

Barnett, A. Doak and Reischauer, Edwin O., eds, *The United States and China: The Next Decade* (London, 1970).

Barrett, David D., *Dixie Mission: The United States Army Group in Yenan, 1944* (Berkeley, CA, 1970).

Baum, Richard, ed., *Reform and Reaction in Post-Mao China: The Road to Tiananmen* (New York and London, 1991).

Berman, Larry, *Planning a Tragedy: The Americanization of the War in Vietnam* (New York, 1982).

Bernstein, Barton J., ed,. *Politics and Policies of the Truman Administration* (Chicago, IL, 1972).

Beschloss, Michael R., *Kennedy v. Khrushchev: The Crisis Years, 1960–63* (London, 1991).

Billings-Yun, Melanie, *Decision Against War: Eisenhower and Dien Bien Phu* (New York, 1988).

Blum, Robert, *The United States and China in World Affairs* (New York and London, 1966).

Blum, Robert M., *Drawing the Line: The Origin of the American Containment Policy in East Asia* (New York, 1982).

Borg, Dorothy, *The United States and the Far Eastern Crisis* (Cambridge, MA, 1964).

Borg, Dorothy and Heinrichs, Waldo, *Uncertain Years: Chinese–American Relations, 1947–1950* (New York, 1980).

Broadwater, Jeff, *Eisenhower and the Anti-Communist Crusade* (Chapel Hill, NC, 1992).

Brown, Thomas, *JFK: History of an Image* (Bloomington, IN, 1988)

Brown, William Adam and Opie, Redvers, *American Foreign Assistance* (Washington, DC, 1953).

Brown, T. Louise, *War and Aftermath in Vietnam* (London, 1991).

Brugger, Bill, *China: Radicalism to Revisionism, 1962–1979* (London, 1981).

Brzezinski, Zbigniew, *Power and Principle: Memoirs of the National Security Adviser* (New York, 1983).

Buchanan, A. Russell, *The United States and World War II* (2 vols, New York, 1964).

Buhite, Russell D, *Patrick J. Hurley and American Foreign Policy* (Ithaca, NY, 1973).

Buhite, Russell D, *Soviet–American Relations in Asia, 1945–1954* (Norman, OK, 1981).

Bulloch, John, *Saddam's War: The Origins of the Kuwait Conflict and the International Response* (London, 1991).

Burner, David, *John F. Kennedy and a New Generation* (Boston, MA, 1980).

Cable, James, *The Geneva Conference of 1954 on Indochina* (London, 1986)

Cable, Larry, *Unholy Grail: The US and the Wars in Vietnam, 1965–8* (London and New York, 1991).

Califano, Jr., Joseph A., *The Triumph and Tragedy of Lyndon Johnson* (New York, 1991).

Carter, Jimmy, *Keeping Faith: Memoirs of a President* (New York, 1982).

Caute, David, *The Great Fear: The Anti-Communist Purge under Truman and Eisenhower* (New York, 1978).

Chang, Gordon H., *Friends and Enemies: The United States, China, and the Soviet Union, 1948–1972* (Stanford, CA, 1990).

Chang, Parris H., *Power and Policy in China* (University Park, PA, 1978).

Chay, John, ed., *The Problems and Prospects of American–East Asian Relations* (Boulder, CO, 1977).

Cheng, Chu-Yuan, *Communist China's Economy, 1949–1962* (South Orange, NJ, 1963).

Cheng, Chu-Yuan, *Behind the Tiananmen Massacre: Social, Political, and Economic Ferment in China* (Boulder, CO, 1990).

China Year Book, 1975 (Taipei, 1975).

Chomsky, Noam, *At War with Asia* (London edn, 1971).

Churchill, Winston, *The Second World War, IV: The Hinge of Fate* (London, 1951).

Clemens, Diane S., *Yalta* (New York, 1970).

Clifford, Clark (with Richard Holbrooke), *Counsel to the President: A Memoir* (New York, 1991).

Cohen, Warren I. and Iriye, Akira (eds), *The Great Powers in East Asia, 1953–1960* (New York, 1990).

Collected Documents of Sino-American Relations (Beijing, 1960).

Cumings, Bruce, *The Origins of the Korean War, II: The Roaring of the Cataract, 1947–1950* (Princeton, NJ, 1990).

Dallek, Robert, *Ronald Reagan: The Politics of Symbolism* (Cambridge, MA, 1984).

Davis, Deborah and Vogel, Ezra F., *Chinese Society on the Eve of Tiananmen* (Cambridge, MA, and London, 1990).

Dittmer, Lowell, *Liu Shao-ch'i and the Chinese Cultural Revolution: The Politics of Mass Criticism* (Berkeley and Los Angeles, CA, 1974).

Domes, Jürgen with Näth, Marie Luise, *China After the Cultural Revolution: Politics between Two Party Congresses* (London, 1975).

Domes, Jürgen et al,, *After Tiananmen Square: Challenges for the Chinese–American Relationship* (Washington, DC, 1990).

Donovan, Robert J., *Tumultuous Years: The Presidency of Harry S. Truman, 1949–1953* (New York, 1982).

Duffy, Michael and Goodgame, Dan, *Marching in Place: The Status Quo Presidency of George Bush* (New York, 1992).

Dumbrell, John, ed., *Vietnam and the Antiwar Movement* (Aldershot, 1989).

Dumbrell, John, *Vietnam: American Involvement at Home and Abroad* (Halifax, NS, 1992).

Eckstein, Alexander, *China's Economic Revolution* (New York, 1977).

Eisenhower, Dwight D., *Mandate for Change* (Garden City, NY, 1963).

Ellison, Herbert J., ed., *The Sino-Soviet Conflict: A Global Perspective* (Seattle, WA, 1982).

Fathers, Michael and Higgins, Andrew, *Tiananmen: The Rape of Peking* (London, 1989).

Feis, Herbert, *The Road to Pearl Harbor: The Coming of the War between the United States and Japan* (Princeton, NJ, 1950).

Feis, Herbert, *The China Tangle: the American Effort in China from Pearl Harbor to the Marshall Mission* (Princeton, NJ, 1953).

Fingar, Thomas and the Stanford Journal of International Studies, eds, *China's Quest for Independence: Policy Evolution in the 1970s* (Boulder, CO, 1980).

Fitzgerald, Frances, *Fire in the Lake: The Vietnamese and the Americans in Vietnam* (New York, 1972), pp. 518–34.

Foot, Rosemary, *A Substitute for Victory: The Politics of Peacemaking at the Korean Armistice Talks* (Ithaca NY, and London, 1990)

Foot, Rosemary, *The Wrong War: American Policy and the Dimensions of the Korean Conflict, 1950–53* (Ithaca, NY, 1985).

Ford, Gerald R., *A Time to Heal: The Autobiography of Gerald R. Ford* (New York, 1979).

Freeland, Richard M., *The Truman Doctrine and the Origins of McCarthyism: Foreign Policy, Domestic Politics and Internal Security, 1946–1948* (New York, 1972).

Fugh, Philip, ed., *John Leighton Stuart's Diary (Mainly of the Critical Year 1949)* (Palo Alto, CA, 1980).

Gaddis, John Lewis, *The United States and the End of the Cold War: Implications, Reconsiderations, Provocations* (New York and Oxford, 1992).

Gaddis, John Lewis, *The United States and the Origins of the Cold War, 1941–1947* (New York, 1972).

Gallicchio, Marc S., *The Cold War begins in Asia: American East Asian Policy and the Fall of the Japanese Empire* (New York, 1988).

Garner, John W.. *China's Decision for Rapprochement with the United States, 1968–1971* (Boulder, CO, 1982).

Garthoff, Raymond L., *Détente and Confrontation: American–Soviet Relations from Nixon to Reagan* (Washington, DC, 1985).

Gelb, Leslie H. and Betts, Richard K., *The Irony of Vietnam: The System Worked* (Washington, DC, 1979).

Gibbons, William Conrad, *The US Government and the Vietnam War: Executive and Legislative Relationships: II, 1961–1964* (Princeton, NJ, 1986).

Gilbert, Stephen B., *Northeast Asia in US Foreign Policy* (Washington, DC, 1979).

Gillin, Donald and Myers, Ramon, eds, *Last Chance in China: The Diary of Chang Kia-ngau* (Stanford, CA, 1989).

Ginneken, Jaap van, *The Rise and Fall of Lin Piao* (Harmondsworth, 1976).

Gittings, John, *China Changes Face: The Road from Revolution, 1949–1989* (Oxford, 1989).

Goldstein, Avery, *From Bandwagon to Balance-of-Power Politics: Structural Constraints and Politics, 1949–1978* (Stanford, CA, 1991).

Goodman, Allan E., *The Lost Peace: America's Search for a Negotiated Settlement of the Vietnam War* (Stanford, CA, 1978).

Goulden, Joseph C., *Korea: The Untold Story of the War* (New York, 1982).

Gravel (Senator) Edition, *The Pentagon Papers: The Defense Department History of United States Decisionmaking on Vietnam*, 4 vols. (Boston, MA, n.d.).

Grayson, Benson L., *The American Image of China* (New York, 1979).

Greenstein, Fred I., ed., *The Reagan Presidency: An Early Assessment* (Baltimore, MD, and London, 1983).

Gregor, A. James, *The China Connection: U.S. Policy and the People's Republic of China* (Stanford, CA, 1986).

Gregor, A. James, *Arming the Dragon: U.S. Security Ties with the People's Republic of China* (Washington, DC, 1987).

Griffith, William E., *Peking, Moscow and Beyond* (Washington, DC, 1973).

Guhin, Michael A., *John Foster Dulles: A Statesman and his Times* (New York, 1972).

Gurtov, Melvin and Hwang Byong-Moo, *China under Threat: The Politics of Strategy and Diplomacy* (Baltimore, MD, and London, 1980).

Guthman, Edwin O. and Shulman, Jeffrey, *Robert Kennedy: In His Own Words: The Unpublished Recollections of the Kennedy Years* (New York, 1988).

Haig, Alexander M., Jr., *Caveat: Realism, Reagan, and Foreign Policy* (London, 1984).

Halberstam, David, *The Best and the Brightest* (New York, 1972).

Haldeman, H.R. and DiMona, Joseph, *The Ends of Power* (New York, 1978).

Halliday, Jon and Cumings Bruce, *Korea: The Unknown War* (London, 1988).

Harding, Harry, ed *China's Foreign Relations in the 1980s* (New Haven, CT, 1980).

Harding, Harry, *China's Second Revolution: Reform after Mao* (Washington, DC, 1987).

Harding, Harry and Gurtov, Melvin, *The Purge of Lo Jui-ch'ing: The Politics of Chinese Strategic Planning* (Santa Monica, CA, 1971).

Harding, Harry, *A Fragile Relationship: the United States and China Since 1972* (Washington, DC, 1992).

Harding, Harry and Yuan Ming, *Sino-American Relations, 1945–1955: A Joint Reassessment of a Critical Decade* (Wilmington, DE, 1989).

Herring, George C., *America's Longest War: The United States and Vietnam, 1950–75* (New York, 1979).

Hersh, Seymour M., *The Price of Power: Kissinger in the Nixon White House* (New York, 1983).

Hess, Gary R., *Vietnam and the United States: Origins and Legacy of a War* (Boston, MA, 1990).

Hilsman, Roger, *To Move a Nation: The Politics of Foreign Policy in the Administration of John F. Kennedy* (New York, 1967).

Hinton, Harold C., ed., *The People's Republic of China, 1949–1979: A Documentary Survey, II, 1957–1965: The Great Leap Forward and its Aftermath* (Wilmington, DE, 1980).

Hinton, Harold C., ed., *The People's Republic of China, 1949–1979, A Documentary Survey, V: 1971–1979, After the Cultural Revolution* (Wilmington, DE, 1980).

Hinton, Harold C., ed., *The People's Republic of China, 1949–1979: A Documentary Survey, IV: 1967–1970, The Cultural Revolution* (Wilmington, DE, 1980).

Hinton, Harold C., *Peking–Washington: Chinese Foreign Policy and the United States* (Washington, DC, 1976).

Hinton, William, *Hundred Day War* (New York, 1972).

Hiro, Dilip, *Desert Shield to Desert Storm: the Second Gulf War* (New York, 1992).

Hollingworth, Clare, *Mao and the Men Against Him* (London, 1985).

Hong Yung Lee, *The Politics of the Cultural Revolution: A Case Study* (Berkeley and Los Angeles, CA, 1978).

Hooper, Beverley, *China Stands Up: Ending the Western Presence, 1948–1950* (Sydney, 1986).

Hoopes, Townsend, *The Limits of Intervention (an inside account of how the Johnson policy of escalation in Vietnam was reversed)* (New York and London, 1987 edn).

Hoopes, Townsend, *The Devil and John Foster Dulles* (Boston, MA, 1973).

Hsiao, Gene T., *Sino-American Detente and its Policy Implications* (New York and London, 1974).

Hsieh, Chiao Chiao, *Strategy for Survival: The Foreign Policy and External Relations of the Republic of China on Taiwan, 1949–79* (London, 1985).

Hsu, John C., *China's Foreign Trade Reforms: Impact on Growth and Stability* (Cambridge, 1989).

Hsu, Immanuel C.Y., *China Without Mao: The Search for a New Order* (New York and Oxford, 1990).

Human Rights Watch and Lawyers Committee for Human Rights, *The Reagan Administration's Record on Human Rights* (New York, 1987).

Iriye, Akira, *The Origins of the Second World War in Asia and the Pacific* (London and New York, 1987).

Iriye, Akira, *Power and Culture: The Japanese–American War, 1941–1945* (Cambridge, MA, 1981).

Isaacs, Arnold R., *Without Honor: Defeat in Vietnam and Cambodia* (Baltimore, MD, 1983).

Isaacs, Harold R., *Images of Asia: American Views of China and India* (New York, 1962).

Isaacson, Walter and Thomas, Evan, *The Wise Men: Six Friends and the World They Made* (New York, 1986).

Isaacson, Walter, *Kissinger: A Biography* (New York and London, 1992).

Jain, B.M., *India and the United States, 1961–1963* (New Delhi, 1987).

Johnson, U. Alexis (with Jef Olivarius McAllister), *The Right Hand of Power* (Englewood Cliffs, NJ, 1984).

Johnson, Lyndon B., *The Vantage Point: Perspectives of the Presidency* (New York, 1971).

Jones, Joseph M., *The Fifteen Weeks* (New York, 1955).

Joseph, William A., *China Briefing, 1992* (Boulder, CO, 1993).

Joseph, William A., Wong, Christine P.W. and Zweig, David, eds, *New Perspectives on the Cultural Revolution* (Cambridge, MA and London, 1991).

Jung Chang, *Wild Swans: Three Daughters of China* (London, 1991).

Kahn Jr., E.J., *The China Hands: America's Foreign Service Officers and What Befell Them* (New York, 1975).

Kalb, Marvin and Bernard, *Kissinger* (Boston, MA, 1974).

Kalicki, J.H., *The Pattern of Sino-American Crises: Political–Military Interactions in the 1950s* (Cambridge, 1975).

Kane, Anthony J., *China Briefing, 1990* (Boulder, CO, 1990).

Kane, Anthony J., *China Briefing, 1989* (Boulder, CO, 1989).

Karnow, Stanley, *Mao and China: Inside China's Cultural Revolution* (Harmondsworth, 1984 edn).

Karnow, Stanley, *Vietnam: A History* (New York, 1986).

Keeley, Joseph C., *The China Lobby Man: The Story of Alfred Kohlberg* (New York, 1969).

Keith, Ronald C., *The Diplomacy of Zhou Enlai* (London, 1989).

Kien-hong Yu, Peter, *A Strategic Model of Chinese Checkers: Power and Exchange in Beijing's Interactions with Washington and Moscow* (New York, 1984).

Kim, Samuel S., ed., *China and the World: New Directions in Chinese Foreign Relations* (Boulder, CO, 1989).

Kirby, S. Woodburn, *The War Against Japan* (5 vols, London, 1958–69).

Kissinger, Henry, *White House Years* (Boston, MA, 1970).

Kissinger, Henry, *Years of Upheaval* (Boston, MA, 1982).

Kissinger, Henry, *American Foreign Policy: Three Essays* (New York, 1969).

Kleinberg, Robert, *China's 'Opening' to the Outside World: The Experiment with Foreign Capitalism* (Boulder, CO, 1990).

Koen, Ross Y., *The China Lobby in American Politics* (New York, 1975).

Koenig, Louis W., Hsiung, James C. and King-yuh Chang, eds, *Congress, the Presidency, and the Taiwan Relations Act* (New York, 1985).

Kolko, Joyce and Gabriel, *The Limits of Power: The World and US Foreign Policy, 1945–1954* (New York, 1972).

Kolko, Gabriel, *Vietnam: Anatomy of a War, 1940–1975* (London, 1985).

Kuniholm, Bruce R., *The Origins of the Cold War in the Near East: Great Power Conflict and Diplomacy in Iran, Turkey, and Greece* (Princeton, NJ, 1980).

Kusnitz, Leonard A., *Public Opinion and Foreign Policy: America's China Policy, 1949–1979* (Westport, CT, 1984).

Kutler, Stanley I., *The Wars of Watergate: The Last Crisis of Richard Nixon* (New York, 1990).

Kyvig, David E., *Reagan and the World* (New York and London, 1990).

LaFeber, Walter, *America, Russia and the Cold War, 1945–1966* (New York, 1980).

Lang, Gladys Engle and Lang, Kurt, *The Battle for Public Opinion: The President, the Press and the Polls During Watergate* (New York, 1983).

Lardy, Nicholas, *Foreign Trade and Economic Reform in China, 1978–1990* (Cambridge, 1992).

Larson, Deborah Welch, *Origins of Containment: A Psychological Explanation* (Princeton, NJ, 1985).

Lasater, Martin, *The Taiwan Issue in Sino-American Strategic Relations* (Boulder, CO, 1984).

Lauren, Paul Gordon, *The China Hands' Legacy: Ethics and Diplomacy* (Boulder, CO, and London, 1987).

Leffler, Melvyn P., *A Preponderance of Power: National Security, the Truman Administration, and the Cold War* (Stanford, CA, 1992).

Levine, Steven I., *Anvil of Victory: The Communist Revolution in Manchuria, 1945–1948* (New York, 1987).

Lewis, John Wilson and Xue, Litai, *China Builds the Bomb* (Stanford, CA, 1988).

Lewy, Guenther, *America in Vietnam* (New York, 1978).

Li, Peter, Mark, Steven and Li, Marjorie H., *Culture and Politics in China: An Anatomy of Tiananmen Square* (New Brunswick, NJ, 1990).

Liao, Kuang-Sheng, *Antiforeignism and Modernization in China,* (Hong Kong, 1990).

Lieberthal, Kenneth, *Revolution and Tradition in Tientsin, 1949–1952* (Stanford, CA, 1980).

Lin Biao, *Long Live the Victory of People's War!* (Beijing, 1965).

Litwak, Robert S., *Detente and the Nixon Doctrine: American Foreign Policy and the Pursuit of Stability, 1969–1976* (Cambridge, 1984).

Liu Binyan, *China's Crisis, China's Hope* (Cambridge, MA and London, 1990).

Louis, William Roger, *Imperialism at Bay: The United States and the Decolonization of the British Empire, 1941–1945* (New York, 1978).

Lowe, Peter, *The Origins of the Korean War* (London, 1986).

MacDonald, Callum A., *Korea: The War before Vietnam* (London, 1986).

MacFarquhar, Roderick, Cheek, Timothy and Wu, Eugene, *The Secret Speeches of Chairman Mao: From the Hundred Flowers to the Great Leap Forward* (Cambridge, MA, 1989).

MacFarquhar, Roderick, *The Origins of the Cultural Revolution, I: Contradictions among the People, 1956–1957* (New York, 1974).

MacKinnon, Stephen R. and Friesen, Oris, *China Reporting: An Oral History of American Journalism in the 1930s and 1940s.* (Berkeley, CA, and London, 1987).

Mao Tse-tung, *Quotations from Chairman Mao Tse-tung* (Beijing, 1967).

Mao Tse-tung, *Selected Works* (Peking, 1961).

Marolda, Edward J. and Fitzgerald, Oscar P., *The US Navy and the Vietnam Conflict: II, From Military Assistance to Combat, 1959–1965* (Washington, DC, 1986).

Martin, Edwin W., *Southeast Asia and China: the End of Containment* (Boulder, CO, 1977).

Matloff, Maurice and Snell, Edwin, *Strategic Planning for Coalition Warfare, 1941–42* (Washington, DC, 1953).

Matray, James, *The Reluctant Crusade: American Foreign Policy in Korea, 1941–1950* (Honolulu, 1985).

Matthews, Lloyd J. and Brown, Dale E., *Assessing the Vietnam War: A Collection from the Journal of the U.S. Army War College* (Washington, DC and London, 1987).

May, Gary, *China Scapegoat: The Diplomatic Ordeal of John Carter Vincent* (Prospect Heights, IL, 1979).

Mayers, David Allan, *Cracking the Monolith: US Policy Against the Sino-Soviet Alliance, 1949–1955* (Baton Rouge, LA, and London, 1986).

McPherson, Harry, *A Political Education* (Boston, MA, 1972).

Johnson, Lyndon B., *The Vantage Point: Perspectives of the Presidency* (New York, 1971).

Martin, Edwin, *Divided Counsel: The Anglo-American Response to Communist Victory in China* (Lexington, KY, 1986).

Medvedev, Roy, *China and the Superpowers* (Oxford, 1986).

Meisner, Maurice, *Mao's China and After: A History of the People's Republic* (rev. edn, New York and London, 1986).

Messer, Robert, *The End of an Alliance: James F. Byrnes, Roosevelt, Truman, and the Origins of the Cold War* (Chapel Hill, NC, 1982).

Miles, Milton E., *A Different Kind of War* (Garden City, NY, 1967).

Mosher, Steven, *China Misperceived: American Illusions and Chinese Reality* (New York, 1990).

Mozingo, David, *China's Foreign Policy and the Cultural Revolution* (Ithaca, NY, 1970).

Muravchik, Joshua, *The Uncertain Crusade: Jimmy Carter and the Dilemmas of Human Rights Policy* (Washington, DC, 1988)

Nathan, Andrew J., *China's Crisis: Dilemmas of Reform and Prospects for Democracy* (New York, 1990)

Newman, John M., *JFK and Vietnam: Deception, Intrigue, and the Struggle for Power* (New York, 1992).

Nixon, Richard, *The Memoirs of Richard Nixon* (London, 1979).

Olson, James S. and Roberts, Randy, *Where the Domino Fell: America and Vietnam 1945 to 1990* (New York, 1991).

Paige, Glenn D., *The Korean Decision [June 24–30,1950]* (New York and London, 1968).

Parker IV, F. Charles, *Vietnam: Strategy for a Stalemate* (New York, 1989).

Parmet, Herbert S., *JFK: The Presidency of John F. Kennedy* (Harmondsworth, 1984).

Paterson, Thomas G., *Soviet–American Confrontation: Postwar Reconstruction and the Origins of the Cold War* (Baltimore, MD, 1973).

Paterson, Thomas G., ed., *Kennedy's Quest for Victory: American Foreign Policy, 1961– 1963* (New York and Oxford, 1989).

Pelz, Stephen, *The Road to Pearl Harbor* (Cambridge, MA, 1974).

Pepper, Suzanne, *Civil War in China: The Political Struggle, 1945 1949* (Berkeley, CA, 1978).

Pike, Douglas, ed., *The Bunker Papers: Reports to the President from Vietnam, 1967–1973* (3 vols, Berkeley, CA, 1990).

Pollard, Robert A., *Economic Security and the Origins of the Cold War, 1945–1950* (New York, 1985).

Porter, Gareth ed., *Vietnam: The Definitive Documentation of Human Decisions, II* (Philadelphia PA, and London, 1979).

Prange, Gordon, *Pearl Harbor: The Verdict of History* (New York, 1985).

Public Papers of the Presidents: George Bush, 1990, 2 vols (Washington, DC, 1991).

Public Papers of the Presidents: George Bush, 1991, 2 vols (Washington, DC, 1992).

Public Papers of the Presidents: Lyndon B. Johnson, 1967, 2 vols (Washington, DC, 1968).

Public Papers: Reagan, 1982 (Washington, DC, 1982).

Purifoy, Lewis, *Harry Truman's China Policy: McCarthyism and the Diplomacy of Hysteria, 1947–1951* (New York, 1976).

Rankin, Karl Lott, *China Assignment* (Seattle, WA, 1964).

Rannry, Austin, ed., *The American Elections of 1980* (Washington, DC 1981).

Rea, Kenneth W. and Brewer, John C., eds, *The Forgotten Ambassador: The Reports of John Leighton Stuart, 1946–1949* (Boulder, CO, 1981).

Reagan, Ronald, *An American Life* (London, 1990).

Reardon-Anderson, James, *Yenan and the Great Powers: the Origins of Chinese Communist Foreign Policy, 1944–1946* (New York, 1980).

Rees, David, *Korea: The Limited War* (London and New York, 1964).

Reeves, Thomas, *A Question of Character: A Life of John F. Kennedy* (London, 1991).

Roberts, Priscilla, ed., *Sino-American Relations Since 1900* (Hong Kong, 1991).

Robinson, Thomas W., ed., *The Cultural Revolution in China* (Berkeley and Los Angeles, CA, 1971).

Romanus, Charles and Sunderland, Riley, *The China–Burma–India Theater* (3 vols, Washington, DC, 1953–59).

Romanus, Charles F. and Sunderland, Riley, *Stilwell's Mission to China* (Washington, DC, 1953).

Roosevelt, Elliott and Brough, James, *A Rendezvous with Destiny: The Roosevelt of the White House* (New York, 1975).

Rose, Lisle, *Roots of Tragedy: The United States and the Struggle for Asia, 1945–1953* (Westport, CT, 1976).

Rosen, Stanley. *Red Guard Factionalism and the Cultural Revolution in Guangzhou (Canton)* (Boulder, CO, 1982)

Ross, Robert S, *The Indochina Tangle: China's Vietnam Policy, 1975–1979* (New York, 1988).

Saburo, Ienaga, *The Pacific War: World War II and the Japanese, 1931–1945* (New York, 1978).

Safire, William, *Before the Fall* (New York, 1975).

Saich, Tony, ed., *The Chinese People's Movement: Perspectives on Spring 1989* (Armonk, NY, and London 1990).

Salinger, Pierre, *With Kennedy* (London, 1967).

Salisbury, Harrison, *The New Emperors: China in the Era of Mao and Deng* (New York, 1992).

Schaller, Michael, *Douglas MacArthur: The Far Eastern General* (New York, 1989).

Schaller, Michael, *Reckoning With Reagan: America and its President in the 1980s* (New York and Oxford, 1992).

Schaller, Michael, *The U.S. Crusade in China, 1938–1945* (New York, 1979).

Schandler, Herbert Y., *The Unmaking of a President: Lyndon Johnson and Vietnam* (Princeton, NJ, 1977).

Schlesinger Jr., Arthur, *A Thousand Days: John F. Kennedy in the White House* (London, 1965).

Schnabel, James E. and Watson, Robert J., *The History of the Joint Chiefs of Staff: The Joint Chiefs and National Policy, 1945–1953, III: The Korean War, part I* (Wilmington, DE, 1979).

Schoenbaum, Thomas J., *Waging Peace and War: Dean Rusk in the Truman, Kennedy and Johnson Years* (New York and London, 1988).

Schurmann, Franz, *Ideology and Organization in Communist China* (Berkeley and Los Angeles, CA, 1966).

Seaborg, Glenn T. and Loeb, Benjamin S., *Kennedy, Khrushchev, and the Test Ban* (Berkeley, CA, 1981).

Segal, Gerald, *Defending China* (Oxford, 1985).

Segal, Gerald, *The Soviet Union and the Pacific* (London, 1990).

Segal, Gerald, *The Fate of Hong Kong* (London, 1993).

Shabad, Theodore, *China's Changing Map: National and Regional Development, 1949–1971* (New York, 1972).

Shambaugh, David, *Beautiful Imperialist: China Perceives America, 1972–1990* (Princeton, NJ, 1991).

Shaplen, Robert, *The Lost Revolution: The US in Vietnam, 1946–1966* (New York, 1966).

Shaw, Yu-ming, *Mainland China: Politics, Economics and Reform* (Boulder, CO, 1986).

Shawcross, William, *Sideshow: Kissinger, Nixon, and the Destruction of Cambodia* (London, 1979).

Shewmaker, Kenneth, *Americans and Chinese Communists, 1927–1945: A Persuasive Encounter* (New York, 1971).

Short, Anthony, *The Origins of the Vietnam War* (London and New York, 1989).

Shultz, George P., *Turmoil and Triumph: My Years as Secretary of State* (New York and Toronto, 1993).

Sloan, John W., *Eisenhower and the Management of Prosperity* (Lawrence, KS, 1991).

Smith, Gaddis, *Dean Acheson* (New York, 1972).

Smith, R.B., *An International History of the Vietnam War: II, The Struggle for Southeast Asia, 1961–65* (London, 1985).

Snepp, Frank, *Decent Interval: The American Debacle in Vietnam and the Fall of Saigon* (Harmondsworth, 1980).

Sorensen, Theodore C., *Kennedy* (New York, 1965).

Spanier, John W., *The Truman-MacArthur Controversy and the Korean War* (New York, 1965).

Spence, Jonathan D., *The Search for Modern China* (New York, 1990).

Spencer, Donald S., *The Carter Implosion: Jimmy Carter and the Amateur Style of Diplomacy* (New York, 1988).

Spurr, Russell, *Enter the Dragon: China's Undeclared War against the U.S. in Korea, 1950–51* (New York, 1988).

Steele, A.T., *The American People and China* (New York and London, 1966).

Stolper, Thomas E., *China, Taiwan, and the Offshore Islands: Together with an Implication for Outer Mongolia and Sino-Soviet Relations* (Armonk, NY, 1985).

Stueck, William Whitney, *The Road to Confrontation: American Policy toward China and Korea, 1947–1950* (Chapel Hill, NC, 1981).

Stueck, William, *The Wedemeyer Mission: American Politics and Foreign Policy during the Cold War* (Athens, GA, 1984).

Sutter, Robert G., *The China Quandary: Domestic Determinants of US China Policy, 1972–1982* (Boulder, CO, 1982).

Sutter, Robert G., *China-Watch: Toward Sino-American Reconciliation* (Baltimore, MD, 1978).

Szulc, Tad, *The Illusion of Peace: Foreign Policy in the Nixon Years* (New York, 1978).

Tang Tsou, *The Cultural Revolution and the Post-Mao Reforms: A Historical Perspective* (Chicago, 1986).

Tang Tsou, *America's Failure in China, 1941–50* (Chicago, IL and London, 1963).

Tang Tsou, ed., *China in Crisis, II: China's Policies in Asia and America's Alternatives* (Chicago, IL, 1968).

Tanzer, Lester, *The Kennedy Circle* (New York, 1961).

Thayer, Carlyle A., *War By Other Means: National Liberation and Revolution in Vietnam, 1954–60* (Sydney and London, 1989).

Thorne, Christopher, *Allies of a Kind: The United States, Britain and the War Against Japan, 1941–1945* (London, 1978).

Thurston, Anne F., *Enemies of the People: The Ordeal of the Intellectuals in China's Great Cultural Revolution* (New York, 1987).

Tow, William T. and Feeney, William R., *US Foreign Policy and Asian–Pacific Security: A Transregional Approach* (Boulder, CO, 1982).

Treadgold, Donald, ed., *Soviet and Chinese Communism: Similarities and Differences* (Seattle, WA, 1967).

Truman, Harry S., *Memoirs, II: Years of Trial and Hope, 1946–52* (Garden City, NY, 1956).

Tuchman, Barbara W., *Stilwell and the American Experience in China, 1911–45* (New York, 1972 edn).

Tucker, Nancy Bernkopf, *Patterns in the Dust: Chinese–American Relations and the Recognition Controversy, 1949–1950* (New York, 1983).

Turley, William S., *The Second Indochina War* (Boulder, CO, 1986).

U.S. Department of State, *American Foreign Policy: Current Documents, 1961–1966* (Washington, DC, 1965–69).

U.S. Department of State, *American Foreign Policy: Current Documents, 1981* (Washington, DC, 1984).

U.S. Department of State, *Foreign Relations of the United States, 1942: China* (Washington, DC, 1956).

U.S. Department of State, *Foreign Relations of the the United States: The Conferences at Cairo and Tehran, 1943* (Washington, DC, 1961).

U.S. Department of State, *Foreign Relations of the United States, 1945: China* (Washington, DC, 1969).

U.S. Department of State, *Foreign Relations of the United States, 1950, VI: East Asia and the Pacific* (Washington, DC, 1976).

U.S. Department of State, *Foreign Relations of the United States, 1950, VII: Korea* (Washington, DC, 1976).

U.S. Department of State, *Foreign Relations of the United States, 1951, VII: Korea and China* (Washington, DC, 1983).

U.S. Department of State, *Foreign Relations of the United States, 1952–54, XII: East Asia and the Pacific* (Washington, DC, 1984).

U.S. Department of State, *Foreign Relations of the United States, 1952–54, XIV: China and Japan* (Washington, DC, 1985).

U.S. Department of State, *Foreign Relations of the United States, 1952–54, XV: Korea* (Washington, DC, 1984).

U.S. Department of State, *Foreign Relations of the United States, 1955–57, II: China* (Washington, DC, 1986).

U.S. Department of State, *Foreign Relations of the United States 1955–57, III: China* (Washington, DC, 1986).

U.S. Department of State, *Foreign Relations of the United States, 1961–1963, II: Vietnam, 1962* (Washington, DC, 1990).

U.S. Department of State, *Foreign Relations of the United States, 1961–1963, III: Vietnam, 1963* (Washington, DC, 1991).

U.S.Department of State, *United States Relations with China: With Special Reference to the Period 1944–1949* (Washington, DC, 1949).

U.S. House of Representatives, Hearings before the Subcommittee on Trade of the House Committee on Ways and Means, *United States–People's Republic of China (PRC) Trade Relations, Including Most-Favored-Nation Status for the PRC* (Washington, DC, 1990).

U.S. House of Representatives, Hearings before the Subcommittee on Asian and Pacific Affairs of the Committee on Foreign Affairs (Washington, DC, 1972).

U.S. House of Representatives, Hearings before the Special Subcommittee on Investigations of the Committee on International Relations, *United States–China Relations: The Process of Normalization of Relations* (Washington, DC, 1976).

U.S. Senate, Committee on Foreign Relations, Hearings Held in Executive Session, *Reviews of the World Situation: 1949–1950* (Washington, DC, 1974).

U.S. Senate, Committee on the Judiciary, *The Amerasia Papers: A Clue to the Catastrophe of China* (Washington, DC, 1970).

U.S. Senate, Committee on the Judiciary, *Morgenthau Diary (China), I* (Washington, DC, 1965).

U.S. Senate, Hearings before the Committee on Foreign Relations, *China and the United States: Today and Yesterday* (Washington, DC, 1972).

U.S. Senate, Hearings before the Committee on Foreign Relations, *United States Relations with the People's Republic of China* (Washington, DC, 1972).

U.S. Senate, Highlights of the Hearings of the Senate Foreign Relations Committee, *China, Vietnam, and the United States* (Washington, DC, 1966).

Van Ginneken, Jaap, *The Rise and Fall of Lin Piao* (Harmondsworth, 1976).

Vance, Cyrus, *Hard Choices: Critical Years in American Foreign Policy* (New York, 1983).

Varg, Paul, *The Closing of the Door: Sino-American Relations, 1936–1946* (East Lansing, MI, 1973).

Vatcher, William H., *Panmunjom: The Story of the Korean Military Armistice Negotiations* (New York, 1958).

Vogel, Ezra F., *One Step Ahead in China: Guangdong under Reform* (Cambridge, MA, 1989).

Walton, Richard J., *Cold War and Counterrevolution* (New York, 1972).

Wedeman, Andrew Hall, *The East Wind Subsides: Chinese Foreign Policy and the Origins of the Cultural Revolution* (Washington, DC, 1987).

Weinberger, Caspar, *Fighting for Peace: Seven Critical Years at the Pentagon* (London, 1990).

Welles, Sumner, *Seven Decisions that Shaped History* (New York, 1951).

West, Philip and von Gesau, Frans A.M. Alting, eds, *The Pacific Rim and the Western World* (Boulder, CO, 1987).

Whelan, Richard, *Drawing the Line: The Korean War, 1950–1953* (London, 1990).

White III, Lynn T., *Policies of Chaos: The Organizational Causes of Violence in China's Cultural Revolution* (Princeton, NJ, 1989).

Whiting, Allen, *China Crosses the Yalu: The Decision to Enter the Korean War* (New York, 1960).

Wich, Richard, *Sino-Soviet Crisis Politics: A Study of Political Change and Communication* (Cambridge, MA, 1980).

Wolff, Lester L. and Simon, David L., eds, *A Legislative History of the Taiwan Relations Act* (New York, 1982).
Woodward, Bob and Bernstein, Carl, *The Final Days* (New York, 1976).
Yahuda, Michael B., *China's Role in World Affairs* (London, 1978).
Yahuda, Michael, *Towards the End of Isolationism: China's Foreign Policy After Mao* (London, 1983).
Yergin, Daniel, *Shattered Peace: The Origins of the Cold War and the National Security State* (Boston, MA, 1977).
Young, Kenneth T., *Negotiating with the Chinese Communists: The United States Experience, 1953–1967* (New York and London, 1968).
Young, Kenneth T., *Diplomacy and Power in Washington-Peking Dealings:1953–1967* (Chicago, IL, 1967).
Yuan Gao, *Born Red: A Chronicle of the Cultural Revolution* (Stanford, CA, 1987).
Zagoria, Donald, *The Sino-Soviet Conflict, 1956–1961* (Princeton, NJ, 1962).

Journal Articals

Accinelli, Robert, 'Eisenhower, Congress and the 1954–55 Offshore Island Crisis,' *Presidential Studies Quarterly*, 20 (Spring 1990), pp. 329–48.
Baum, Richard, 'Political Stability in Post-Deng China: Problems and Prospects,' *Asian Survey*, 32, (June 1992), pp. 491–505.
Bowles, Chester, 'Is Communist Ideology Becoming Irrelevant?' *Foreign Affairs* 40, (July 1962), pp. 553–65.
Bridgham, Philip, 'Mao's Cultural Revolution in 1967: The Struggle to Seize Power,' *China Quarterly* 34 (April–June 1968), pp. 6–37.
Brzezinski, Zbigniew, 'Threat and Opportunity in the Communist Schism,' *Foreign Affairs*, 41 (January 1963), pp. 513–25.
Brzezinski, Zbigniew, 'Peaceful Engagement in Communist Disunity,' *China Quarterly*, 10 (April–June 1962), pp. 64–71.
Chang, Gordon H. and He Di, 'The Absence of War in the U.S.–China Confrontation over Quemoy and Matsu in 1954–1955: Contingency, Luck, Deterrence?' *American Historical Review*, 98 (December 1993), pp. 1500–24.
Chang, A.S., 'The Proletarian Cultural Revolution,' *China Mainland Review*, 2 (1967), pp. 91–102.
Crane, George T., 'China and Taiwan: not yet "Greater China",' *International Affairs*, 69 (October 1993), pp. 705–23.
Cross, Charles T., 'Taipei's Identity Crisis,' *Foreign Policy*, 51 (Summer 1983), pp. 47–63.
Dewenter, John R., 'China Afloat,' *Foreign Affairs*, 50 (July 1972), pp. 738–751.
Falk, Richard A., 'The Cambodian Operation and International Law,' *American Journal of International Law*, 65 (January 1971), pp. 1–25.
Fincher, John, 'Zhao's Fall, China's Loss,' *Foreign Policy* 76 (Fall 1989), pp. 3–25.
Garson, Robert, 'The Road to Tiananmen Square: The United States and China, 1979–1989,' *Journal of Oriental Studies*, 30 (1992), pp. 119–35.
George W. Ball, 'Nixon's Appointment in Peking: Is This Trip Necessary?' *New York Times Magazine*, 13 February 1972.

Goldman, Merle, 'China's Anti-Confucian Campaign, 1973–76,' *China Quarterly*, 63 (September 1975), pp. 435–62.

Griffith II, Samuel B., 'Communist China's Capacity to Make War,' *Foreign Affairs*, 43 (January 1965), pp. 217–36.

Gupta, Karunker, 'How did the Korean War Begin?' *China Quarterly*, 52 (October–December 1972), pp. 699–716.

Gurtov, Melvin, 'The Foreign Ministry and Foreign Affairs during the Cultural Revolution,' *China Quarterly*, 40 (October–December 1969), pp. 65–102.

Halperin, Morton H., 'China and the Bomb: Chinese Nuclear Strategy,' *China Quarterly*, 21 (January–March 1965), pp. 74–86.

Halpern, A.M., 'Communist China's Foreign Policy: The Recent Phase,' *China Quarterly*, 11 (July–September 1962), pp. 89–104.

Harding, Harry, 'China's American Dilemma,' *The Annals of the American Academy of Political and Social Science*, 519 (January 1992), pp. 13–26.

Harris, William R., 'Chinese Nuclear Doctrine: The Decade Prior to Weapons Development (1945–1955),' *China Quarterly*, 21 (January–March, 1965), pp. 87–95.

Hoffmann, Stanley, 'Requiem,' *Foreign Policy*, 42 (Spring 1981), pp. 3–26.

Holbrooke, Richard, 'East Asia: The Next Challenge,' *Foreign Affairs*, 64 (1986), pp. 732–51.

Hwei-ling Huo, 'Patterns of Behavior in China's Foreign Policy: The Gulf Crisis and Beyond,' *Asian Survey*, 33 (March 1992), pp. 263–75.

Ito, Kikuzo and Shibata, Minoru, 'The Dilemma of Mao Tse-tung,' *China Quarterly*, 35 (July–September 1968), pp. 58–77.

Jacoby, Tamar, 'The Reagan Turnaround on Human Rights,' *Foreign Affairs*, 64 (1986), pp. 1066–86.

Javits, Jacob K., 'Congress and Foreign Relations: The Taiwan Relations Act,' *Foreign Affairs,* 60 (Fall 1981) pp. 54–62.

Jaw-ling Joanne Chang, 'Negotiation of the 17 August 1982 U.S.–PRC Arms Communiqué: Beijing's Negotiating Tactics,' *China Quarterly*, 125 (March 1991), pp. 33–54.

Jianwei Wang and Zhimin Lin, 'Chinese Perceptions in the Post-Cold War Era: Three Images of the United States,' *Asian Survey*, 32 (October 1992), pp. 902–17.

Li Xiaobing, Wang Xi, and Chen Jian, 'Mao's Dispatch of Chinese Troops to Korea: Forty-Six Telegrams, July–October 1950,' *Chinese Historians*, 5 (Spring 1992), pp. 67–8.

Lieberthal, Kenneth, 'The Future of Hong Kong,' *Asian Survey*, 32 (July 1992), pp. 665–82.

Lindsay, Michael, 'A New China Policy: Difficulties and Possibilities,' *China Quarterly*, 10 (April–June 1962), pp. 56–63.

Link, Perry, 'The Limits of Cultural Reform in Deng Xiaoping's China,' *Modern China*, 13 (April 1987), pp. 115–76.

Lord, Winston, 'China and America: Beyond the Big Chill,' *Foreign Affairs*, 68 (Fall 1989), pp. 1–26.

Manning, Robert A., 'China: Reagan's Chance Hit,' *Foreign Policy*, 54 (Spring 1984), pp. 83–101.

Marks III, Frederick W., 'The Real Hawk at Dienbienphu: Dulles or Eisenhower?' *Pacific Historical Review*, LIX (1990), pp. 297–321.

Mirsky, Jonathan, 'Broken China', *Foreign Policy*, 66 (Spring 1987), pp. 57–76.

Morgenthau, Hans, 'The Roots of America's China Policy,' *China Quarterly*, 10 (April–June 1962), pp. 45–50

Nixon, Richard M., 'Asia after Vietnam,' *Foreign Affairs*, 46 (October 1967), pp. 111–25.

Oksenberg, Michel, 'China's Confident Nationalism,' *Foreign Affairs*, 65 (1987), pp. 501–23.

Oksenberg, Michel, 'A Decade of Sino-American Relations,' *Foreign Affairs*, 61 (Fall 1982), pp. 175–95.

Perry, Elizabeth J., 'China in 1992: An Experiment in Neo-Authoritarianism,' *Asian Survey*, 33 (January 1993), pp. 12–21.

Possony, Stefan T., 'The Chinese Communist Cauldron,' *Orbis* 13, (1969), pp. 783–821.

Pye, Lucian, 'China in Context,' *Foreign Affairs*, 45 (January 1967), pp. 229–45.

Ravenal, Earl C., 'Approaching China, Defending Taiwan,' *Foreign Affairs*, 50 (October 1971), pp. 44–58.

Rogers, Frank E., 'Sino-American Relations and the Vietnam War, 1964–66,' *China Quarterly*, 66 (June 1976), pp. 293–314.

Romberg, Alan D. and Bouton, Marshall M., 'The U.S. and Asia in 1991,' *Asian Survey*, 32 (January 1992), pp. 1–10.

Ross, Robert, 'From Lin Biao to Deng Xiaoping: Elite Instability and China's U.S. Policy,' *China Quarterly*, 119 (June 1989), pp. 265–299.

Scalapino, Robert A., 'Moscow, Peking and the Communist Parties of Asia', *Foreign Affairs*, 41 (January 1963), pp. 323–43.

Scalapino, Robert A., 'China and the Balance of Power,' *Foreign Affairs*, 52 (January 1974), pp. 349–85.

Scalapino, Robert A., 'Asia's Future,' *Foreign Affairs*, 66 (Fall 1987), pp. 77–108.

Segal, Gerald, 'China and the Disintegration of the Soviet Union' *Asian Survey*, 32 (September 1992), pp. 848–68.

Shaw, Yu-ming, 'John Leighton Stuart and U.S. Rapprochement in 1949: Was There Another "Lost chance in China"?' *China Quarterly*, 89 (March 1982), pp. 74–96.

Simon, Sheldon W., 'U.S.Interests in Southeast Asia: The Future Military Presence,' *Asian Survey*, 31 (July 1991), pp. 662–75.

Shultz, George P. 'New Realities and New Ways of Thinking,' *Foreign Affairs*, 63 (Spring 1985), pp. 706–21.

Solomon, Richard H., 'East Asia and the Great Power Coalitions,' *Foreign Affairs*, 60 (1982), pp. 686–718.

Thomson, Jr., James C., 'On the Making of U.S. China Policy, 1961–1969: A Study in Bureaucratic Politics,' *China Quarterly*, 50 (April–June 1972), pp. 220–43.

Tucker, Robert W., 'Reagan's Foreign Policy,' *Foreign Affairs*, 68 (1988/89), pp. 1–27.

Weathersby, Kathryn, 'New Findings on the Korean War,' *Cold War International History Project Bulletin*, 3 (Fall 1993), pp. 1, 14–18.

Weathersby, Kathryn, 'Soviet Aims in Korea and the Origins of the Korean War, 1945–1950: New Evidence from Russian Archives,' Working Paper 8, *Cold War International History Project* (November 1993).

Yahuda, Michael, 'Hong Kong's Future: Sino-British Negotiations, Perceptions, Organization and Political Culture,' *International Affairs*, 69 (1993), pp. 245–66.

Yahuda, Michael B., 'Chinese Foreign Policy after 1963: The Maoist Phases,' *China Quarterly*, 36 (October–December 1968), pp. 93–113.

Young, Kenneth T. 'American Dealings with Peking,' *Foreign Affairs*, 45 (October 1966), pp.77–87

Zagoria, Donald S., 'China's Quiet Revolution,' *Foreign Affairs*, 62 (Spring 1984), pp. 879–904.

Zagoria, Donald S., 'China by Daylight,' *Dissent*, 22 (Spring 1975), pp. 135–47.

Zagoria, Donald S., 'Soviet Policy in East Asia: A New Beginning?' *Foreign Affairs*, 68 (1988/89), pp. 120–38.

Newspapers and Magazines

Beijing Review, (*Peking Review* before 1979)
China–Britain Trade Review
China News Analysis
China Report: Political, Sociological and Military Affairs
Congressional Quarterly
Congressional Quarterly Almanac.
The Economist
Far Eastern Economic Review
Financial Times
International Herald Tribune
Joint Publications Research Service Reports
New York Times
News from *Xinhua News Agency*
Peking Review, (*Beijing Review* after 1979)
South China Morning Post
Survey of China Mainland Press (American Consulate-General, Hong Kong)
The Times
U.S. Department of State Bulletin

INDEX